INTERPRETING
REVELATION
AND OTHER APOCALYPTIC LITERATURE

INTERPRETING
REVELATION
AND OTHER APOCALYPTIC LITERATURE

An Exegetical Handbook

C. Marvin Pate

AUTHOR

John D. Harvey

SERIES EDITOR

Kregel
Academic

Interpreting Revelation and Other Apocalyptic Literature
© 2016 by C. Marvin Pate

Published by Kregel Publications, a division of Kregel, Inc., 2450 Oak Industrial Dr. NE, Grand Rapids, MI 49505-6020.

The Greek font GraecaU and the Hebrew font New JerusalemU are both available from www.linguistsoftware.com/lgku.htm, +1-425-775-1130.

ISBN 978-0-8254-4364-0

Printed in the United States of America
16 17 18 19 20 / 5 4 3 2 1

Dedicated to
Mary Margaret Hixon Ratliff,
an overcomer who never gave up because
her faith and family sustained her

A special thanks to Seth Spradlin for the
exquisite photos he took of the Arch of Titus
in Rome for me, which helped me immensely
to get a closer view of the Arch and aided
significantly in the commentary found in chapter 5

Thanks Paul, Dennis, and John!

—C. Marvin Pate

CONTENTS IN BRIEF

CONTENTS

SERIES PREFACE

THE AUTHORS OF THE NEW TESTAMENT communicated their witness to the good news of Jesus Christ using a variety of types of literature (literary genres). Those different types of literature require different principles and methods of interpretation and communication. Those principles and methods are best understood in the context of a series of handbooks that focus on the individual types of literature to which they apply. There are three basic literary genres in the New Testament: narrative, letter, and apocalypse. Other subgenres are present within those basic types of literature (e.g., parable), but narrative, letter, and apocalypse provide the framework for those subgenres.

The four volumes in this series will offer the student of Scripture the basic skills for interpreting and communicating the message of the New Testament in the context of the various literary genres. The four volumes will be

- *Interpreting the Gospels and Acts (Matthew–Acts)*
- *Interpreting the Pauline Letters (Romans–Philemon)*
- *Interpreting the General Letters (Hebrews–Jude)*
- *Interpreting Revelation and Other Apocalyptic Literature*

Each volume is designed to provide an understanding of the different types of literature in the New Testament, and to provide strategies for interpreting and preaching/teaching them. The series is intended primarily to serve as textbooks and resources for seminary and graduate-level students who have completed at least a year of introductory Greek. However, because an English translation is always provided whenever

Greek is used, the series is also accessible to readers who lack a working knowledge of Greek. For that reason, upper-level college students, seminary-trained pastors, and well-motivated lay people should also benefit from the series.

The four volumes will cover the twenty-seven books of the New Testament. Each volume will (a) include a summary of the major themes present in the New Testament books covered by it; (b) set methods of interpretation in the context of the New Testament books to which those methods apply; (c) go beyond exegesis to exposition, by providing strategies for communicating each type of New Testament literature; (d) provide step-by-step examples which put into practice the methods and strategies set out in each volume, in the context of an overall exegetical-homiletical framework.

In order to enhance the usefulness of the series, the length, style, and organization of each volume will be consistent. Each volume will include the following elements:

- *The nature of the literary genre (including important subgenres)*
- *The background of the books (historical setting)*
- *The major themes of the books*
- *Preparing to interpret the books (textual criticism, translation)*
- *Interpreting passages in the context of their genre*
- *Communicating passages in the context of their genre*
- *From exegesis to exposition (two step-by-step examples)*
- *A list of selected resources and a glossary of technical terms*

Authors are given freedom in how they title each chapter and in how best to approach the material in it. Using the same basic organization for each book in the series, however, will make it possible for readers to move easily from volume to volume and to locate specific information within each volume.

The authors in this series represent a variety of theological backgrounds and educational institutions, but each is committed to handling God's Word accurately. That commitment reflects a key element in living the Christian life: the functional authority of Scripture. Whatever theological position we might hold, we submit ourselves to the authority of the Bible and align our understanding of life and doctrine to its teaching. It is the prayer of the authors and the publisher that these handbooks will enable those who read them to study the Bible, practice its teachings, and share its truth with others for the advance of Christ's kingdom purposes.

—JOHN D. HARVEY
Series Editor

PREFACE

INTERPRETING REVELATION AND OTHER APOCALYPTIC LITERATURE: AN EXEGETICAL HANDBOOK, the fourth of a four-volume series, intends to shape the way people think and go about studying and communicating Revelation and other apocalyptic literature to today's world. Even though ancient apocalyptic literature is years removed from contemporary society, nevertheless that material is as relevant as tomorrow morning's headlines. Ultimately, the task of this study will be to reveal how close in thinking the two worlds really are. To state in a nutshell the goal of this book: We can say that it will examine apocalyptic literature as it begins in the Old Testament, develops in Second Temple Judaism, and culminates in the New Testament, especially in the book of Revelation, all the while demonstrating how to communicate the message of that literature to today's audience.

Before examining in detail each of the seven chapters of this handbook, we offer a brief overview of them in advance. Chapter 1 identifies the three components of the genre of apocalyptic literature, both canonical and noncanonical: form, content, and function. As we will see, these three components come together as we locate them in the story of Israel in its eschatological setting. More specifically, this material interprets the culmination of the covenant curses come upon Israel as the messianic woes and the future covenant blessings upon Israel as the kingdom of God, or the restoration of Israel. Chapter 2 uncovers various responses to the eschatological story of Israel in the Old Testament by excavating the historical background of Old Testament apocalyptic literature such as Isaiah, Ezekiel, and Daniel. It then analyzes how the story of Israel impacts key apocalyptic texts in the New Testament.

Chapter 3 expands the examination of the apocalyptic genre by moving outside of the Old Testament into the apocalyptic literature of Second Temple Judaism (ca. 500 B.C.–A.D. 100). Chapters 4–7 focus on communicating the messages of New Testament apocalyptic works to today's audiences (especially Rev. 1:1–3; Rom. 11:25–27; and 2 Thess. 2:6–7) by taking three steps. First, the principles of text criticism are applied to the passage to determine the original reading. Second, then we attempt to grasp the meaning of the biblical authors in their respective texts for the readers of their day. Third, we then bridge the first-century setting of the New Testament passages to today's audience by applying the messages of those texts to the future.

John Donne said that no man is an island; neither is a book an island produced by a sole writer. Rather, the author researches his or her subject to the point where he os she feels somewhat competent to delve into the writing process. But before that work can ultimately see the light of day, many people contribute to its journey. And so here I humbly and gladly thank some of those people who have especially joined me in the adventure of writing this book. First, I am honored that Kregel would invite me to write on Revelation and other apocalyptic literature, a topic that has long-occupied my pastoral and academic attention. Second, I can't thank John Harvey enough, general editor of Kregel's New Testament Handbook Series, for his intellectual acumen, eye for detail, and commitment to Christ and his kingdom, not to mention his patience with me until I actually aligned myself with the expectations of this series. Third, it has once again been a pleasure to work with Shawn Vander Lugt, editor of the manuscript. He, like John, rescued me from a multitude of errors, grammatical and otherwise. Fourth, I especially want to express my deep appreciation to those students at Ouachita Baptist University who helped me with typing, documentation, and stylistic changes in the work: Trenton Cooper, Dylan Watson, and Will Peevy. If these young men who are committed Christians have anything to say about the formidable world that we face, it would be that the church should advance the kingdom of God and thereby change the structures of society for righteousness' sake. Fifth, speaking of Ouachita Baptist University, I continue to be so thankful to work in an institution that fosters the love of God and the love of learning. I conclude this preface with the relevant words of the Apostle John:

"Amen. Come, Lord Jesus" (Rev. 22:21).

—C. MARVIN PATE
Author

ABBREVIATIONS

AB	Anchor Bible
BSA	*Annual of the British School at Athens*
ABD	*Anchor Bible Dictionary*
ANTC	Abington New Testament Commentaries
ASV	American Standard Version
BSac	*Bibliotheca Sacra*
BCE	Before the Common Era (equivalent of B.C.)
BDAG	A Greek-English Lexicon of the New Testament and Other Early Christian Literature
BDF	*A Greek Grammar of the New Testament and Other Early Christian Literature*
BECNT	Baker Exegetical Commentary on the New Testament
CBQ	*Catholic Biblical Quarterly*
CE	Common Era (equivalent to A.D.)
CEB	Common English Bible
CEV	Contemporary English Version
DJD	*Discoveries in the Judean Desert*
DSS	Dead Sea Scrolls
EDNT	*Exegetical Dictionary of the New Testament*
EEC	The Evangelical Exegetical Commentary
EncDSS	*Encyclopedia of the Dead Sea Scrolls*
ESV	English Standard Version
ICC	The International Critical Commentary
ISBE	*International Standard Bible Encyclopedia*
JAOS	*Journal of the American Oriental Society*
JBL	*Journal of Biblical Literature*

JETS	*Journal of the Evangelical Theological Society*
Jos	Josephus
JSNTSup	Journal for the Study of the New Testament Supplemental Series
JSJ	*Journal for the Study of Judaism*
JSOT	*Journal for the Study of the Old Testament*
KJV	King James Version
LXX	Septuagint
NASB	New American Standard Bible
NAV	New American Version
NET	New English Translation
NICNT	New International Commentary on the New Testament
NIGTC	New International Greek Testament Commentary
NIV	New International Version
NKJV	New King James Version
NLT	New Living Translation
NRSV	New Revised Standard Version
OEAGR	*Oxford Encyclopedia of Ancient Greece and Rome*
PNTC	Pelican New Testament Commentaries
RCRD	Rule of the Community and Related Documents
SBLDS	Society of Biblical Literature Dissertation Series
SBLMS	Society of Biblical Literature Monograph Series
SP	Sacra Pagina
RSV	Revised Standard Version
RV	Revised Version
TDNT	*Theological Dictionary of the New Testament*
TDOT	*Theological Dictionary of the Old Testament*
TJ	*Trinity Journal*
TLNT	*Theological Lexicon of the New Testament*
TNIV	Today's New International Version
TynBul	*Tyndale Bulletin*
USQR	*Union Seminary Quarterly Review*
WBC	Word Biblical Commentary
WEB	World English Bible
WUNT	*Wissenschaftliche Untersuchungen zum Neuen Testamente*
ZNW	*Zeitschrift fur die Neutestamentliche Wissenschaft*

APOCRYPHA

1 Esd.	First Esdras
2 Esd.	Second Esdras
1 Macc.	First Maccabees
2 Macc.	Second Maccabees
3 Macc.	Third Maccabees

4 Macc.	Fourth Maccabees
Bel	Bel and the Dragon
Judith	Judith
Sir.	Wisdom of Jesus the Son of Sirach (Ecclesiasticus)
Tobit	Tobit
Wisd. Sol.	*Wisdom of Solomon*

OTHER EXTRABIBLICAL SOURCES

Ant.	Antiquitates Judaicae
Ap.	Contra Apionem
Barn.	*Epistle of Barnabas*
Ep. Arist.	*Epistle of Aristeas*
Jub.	*Jubilees*
Odes Sol.	Odes of Solomon
Poly *Hist.*	Polybius *History*
Pss. Sol.	*Psalms of Solomon*
Sib. Or.	Sibylline Oracles
T. Adam	Testament of Adam
T. Benj.	Testament of Benjamin
T. Dan.	Testament of Dan
T. Levi	Testament of Levi
T. 12 Patr.	Testaments of the Twelve Patriarchs
T. Sol.	Testament of Solomon
War	*Bellum Judaicum*

QUMRAN SOURCES

CD	*Damascus Document*	
1QM	*1QWar Scroll*	
1Q28	1QS	*1QRule of the Community*
1Q28a	1QSa	*1QRule of the Congregation*
1Q28b	1QSb	*1QRule of Blessings*
4Q161	4QpIsa[a]	*4QIsaiah Pesher[a]*
4Q174	4QFlor	*4QFlorilegium*
4Q175	4QTest	*4QTestimonia*
4Q246	4QpsDan ar	*4QAramaic Apocalypse*
4Q252	4QcommGen[a]	*4QCommentary on Genesis A*
4Q266	4QD[a]	*4QDamascus Document[a]*
4Q285	4QSM	*4QSefer ha-Milhamah*
4Q376	4QapocrMoses[b]	*4QApocryphon of Moses[b]*
4Q382	*4QParaphrase of the Kings*	
4Q458	*4QNarrative A*	
4Q521	*4QMessianic Apocalypse*	

1

THE GENRE AND FIGURES OF SPEECH OF APOCALYPTIC LITERATURE

The Chapter at a Glance

This chapter provides a basic introduction to apocalyptism and the genre of literature that it produced.

- The genre of apocalypticism consists of form, content, and function.
- There are three mixed genres in Daniel (court tales, apocalyptic dreams, four-kingdom topos), and three genres that comprise Revelation (letter, prophecy, apocalypticism).
- Revelation also contains numerous subgenres, the: Letter/Covenant Structure of Revelation 2–3; *Merkabah* Mysticism and Revelation 4–5; Revelation 6–7 and The Olivet Discourse; Revelation 21–22 and the Restoration of Paradise; beatitudes and woes, 144,000, woman and the dragon, Caesar cult and the beasts, fall of Rome, temporary messianic kingdom, *urzeit-endzeit*, and *ekphrasis*.
- There are numerous figures of speech in Revelation, including simile, metaphor, personification, and parody.
- Apocalypticism is distinct from *Merkabah* Mysticism and Old Testament Prophecy.

DAVID HELLHOLM WRITES, "Genre criticism is that aspect of comparative literature that attempts to understand a literary work in relation to other similar works, both diachronically and synchronically. A literary genre consists of a group of texts that exhibit a coherent and recurring pattern of features constituted by the interrelated elements of form, content, and function."[1] The last three descriptors will rightly receive the bulk of the attention in this chapter as we seek to define the genre of apocalyptic literature. Moreover, we will also consider the subgenres and figures of speech that comprise that literature.

The first ancient composition to be designated an "apocalypse" by its author was the book of Revelation, which begins with, "the revelation [apocalypse] of Jesus Christ" (Rev. 1:1). Since the publications of *1 Enoch* in the nineteenth century, biblical scholars have noted the similarities with it and Revelation. Consequently, a whole body of literature has come to be included in such a category of apocalyptic literature: Daniel, especially chapters 7–12 (cf. Isa. 24–27; 56–66; Ezek. 38–39; Joel 3–4; Zech. 9–14). Outside of the Old Testament and preceding the New Testament era, the aforementioned *1 Enoch* with its five-fold composition (chapters 1–36—the Book of Watchers [known to modern audiences from the film "Noah"!]; chapters 37–71—the Parables of Enoch; chapters 72–82—the Book of Heavenly Luminaries; chapters 83–90—the Animal Apocalypse; chapters 91–105—the Apocalypse of Weeks) is considered to be apocalyptic material. Other works such as *2 Enoch, 3 Enoch, 4 Ezra, 2 Baruch, Testament of Moses,* and especially the Dead Sea Scrolls, are labeled "apocalyptic literature" by biblical scholars.

Later in this chapter we will analyze some of those writings just mentioned most pertinent to our concerns in terms of the threefold components of genre: form, content, and function. We will look only at those writings that either preceded the New Testament era: the relevant Old Testament writings; *1 Enoch* (while the other sections of *1 Enoch* date to before the first century A.D., the date of the Parables of Enoch is de-

---

1. David Hellholm, "The Problem of Apocalyptic Genre and the Apocalypse of John." *Semeia* 36 (1986), 13–64; 13–14. Earlier, W. G. Doty had wrestled with the problem of genre labeling, "Generic definitions ought not be restricted to any one particular feature (such as form, content, etc.), but they ought to be widely enough constructed to allow one to conceive of a genre as a congeries of [a limited number of] factors. The cluster of traits charted may include: authorial intention, audience expectancy, formal units used, structure, use of sources, characterizations, sequential action, primary motifs, institutional setting, rhetorical patterns, and the like" in "The Concept of Genre in Literary Analysis." In *Society of Biblical Literature 1972 Proceedings,* ed. L. C. McGaughy (Missoula, MT: Scholars Press, 1972), 1:413–48; 1:439–40. For a helpful treatment of apocalyptic literature since the 1979 definition of apocalyptic (see below), Hellholm has edited *Apocalypticism in the Mediterranean World and the Near East* (Tübingen: Mohr-Siebeck, 1983).

bated), and the Dead Sea Scrolls (150 B.C.), or were contemporaries to the New Testament material (*Test. of Mos.*; *4 Ezra* and *2 Baruch*).

This chapter has as its goal to discuss four key aspects of the genre of apocalypse: the definition of apocalypse, using the threefold category of form, content, and function, and in particular, how they relate to the books of Daniel and Revelation (Aune already applied the genre to this book; see below); mixed genres in the two biblical apocalypses— Daniel and Revelation; subgenres in Revelation; figures of speech in Revelation (the mother of all apocalypses); the relationship of the genre of apocalyptic literature to the genres of prophecy and *merkabah* mysticism. Unless I miss my guess, the reader is in for some big surprises as the next few chapters unfold!

THE DEFINITION OF APOCALYPSE

Two stages have presented themselves in defining the genre of apocalypse: before the SBL definition in 1979 and after that seminal description.

Before the SBL Definition

The older way of defining apocalyptic literature before 1979 was to identify common literary features of the genre: pseudonymity, reports of visions, reviews of history presented as prophecies (*ex eventu* prophecy), number speculation, the figure of the *angelus interpres* (the interpreting angel), the tendency to make frequent use of the Old Testament, and the proclivity to incorporate a variety of literary forms (testaments, laments, hymns, woes, visions). The more characteristic theological features of apocalypses include imminent eschatology, pessimism, dualism (spatial, temporal, ethical), determinism, esotericism, bizarre imagery, individual transcendent salvation, and revelation of cosmic secrets.[2]

David E. Aune, however, offers several weaknesses of the preceding description of the genre of apocalypse, rendering it insufficient for accurately treating that material: (1) The essential features of apocalypses are not distinguished from optional elements that are present in some apocalypses but absent from others. (2) Many of the characteristics on such lists are also found in other ancient literary genres. (3) Some of

---

2. This older view of the genre of apocalypticism is represented by D. S. Russell, *Apocalyptic Ancient and Modern* (Philadelphia: Fortress, 1978), which is a popular rendition of his earlier work, *The Method and Message of Jewish Apocalyptic* (Philadelphia: Westminster, 1964); Klaus Koch, *The Rediscovery of Apocalyptic, A Polemical Work on a Neglected Area of Biblical Studies and its Damaging Effects on Theology and Philosophy*. Studies in Biblical Theology, 22 (London: SCM Press, 1972); see also R. M. Kuykendall, *The Literary Genre of the Book of Revelation*, Ann Arbor: University Microfilms, 1986), 72–102, who provides a summary of earlier treatments on the genre of apocalypticism.

the compositions widely considered to be apocalypses do not exhibit many of the proposed traits of apocalypses. (4) The usual lists of traits leave out features that are present in apocalypses, such as the interest in cosmology, astrology, demonology, botany, zoology, and pharmacy.[3]

The 1979 SBL Definition of the Genre of Apocalypse

In light of the above weaknesses of the definition of apocalypticism, J. J. Collins, the chair of the Apocalypse Group of the SBL Genres Project, offered what has by now become the standard definition of the genre of apocalypse: "'Apocalypse' is a genre of revelatory literature with a narrative framework, in which a revelation is mediated by an otherworldly being to a human recipient disclosing a transcendent reality which is both temporal, insofar as it envisages eschatological salvation, and spatial insofar as it involves another, supernatural world."[4]

This definition describing the core elements of the genre is related to a master paradigm Collins has proposed, which contains a lengthy list of the constituent features of ancient apocalypses, dividing into the following major categories, each of which describes an aspect of the form or content of apocalypses:[5]

Component	Constituent Feature

Manner (Form)	1 Medium by which the revelation is communicated:
	   1.1 Visual revelation has two forms:
	      1.1.1 Visions
	      1.1.1 Epiphanies
	   1.2 Auditory revelation often clarifies the visual:
	      1.2.1 Discourse
	      1.2.2 Dialogue
	   1.3 Other worldly journey
	   1.4 Writing (revelation in a heavenly book)
	2 Otherworldly mediator
	3 Human recipient:
	   3.1 Pseudonymity
	   3.2 Disposition of recipient
	   3.3 Reaction of recipient

---

3. David E. Aune, *Revelation 1–5*. Word Biblical Commentary. Vol. 52a (Dallas: Word, 1997), lxxvii–lxxviii.

4. J. J. Collins, "Introduction: Toward the Morphology of a Genre, *Semeia* 14 [1979] 1–20; 9.

5. Ibid., 6–8.

Component	Constituent Feature

Temporal Axis (Content)	4 Protology (matters concerning beginnings):
	    4.1 Cosmogony
	    4.2 Primordial events
	5 History is reviewed as either:
	    5.1 Recollections of past or
	    5.2 *Ex Eventu* prophecy
	6 Present salvation through knowledge (Gnostic)[6]
	7 Eschatological crisis:
	    7.1 Persecution
	    7.2 Other eschatological upheavals
	8 Eschatological judgment or destruction:
	    8.1 The wicked or the ignorant
	    8.2 The world
	    8.3 Otherworldly beings
	9 Eschatological salvation may involve:
	    9.1 Cosmic transformation
	    9.2 Personal salvation may take the form of:
	        9.2.1 Resurrection
	        9.2.2 Other forms of afterlife

Spatial Axis (Content)	10 Otherworldly elements:
	    10.1 Otherworldly regions
	    10.2 Otherworldly beings

Parenesis (Content)	11 Parenesis
Concluding Instructions (Form)	12 Concluding Instructions

Group in Crisis (Function)	13 Exhortation/Consolation:
	    13.1 Covenant curses
	    13.2 Covenant blessings

This definition by Collins and the SBL group has become the standard in ascertaining the definition of the genre of apocalypse, but the one weakness of this definition, as D. Hellholm as pointed out, is that it does

---

6. "Gnostic" is an unfortunate choice of words since it brings unnecessary baggage to the discussion regarding the movement known as "Gnosticism," a second-century development. Collins uses the term "gnostic" in the sense of secret revelation, not the movement of Gnosticism.

not include the element of function. For that author, function notes that the apocalyptic work is, "intended for a group in crisis with the purpose of exhortation and/or consolation by means of divine authority."[7]

The above paradigm based on form and content needs to be supplemented by the function of apocalyptic literature, as D. Hellholm well points out. As I have studied the pertinent literature under investigation, it is my contention that the authors situate their audiences in an eschatological reading of the covenant curses and blessings. Everyone of the previously listed apocalyptic pieces are designed by the respective authors to remind their communities that they are still in exile, that is, under the covenant curses due to Israel's disobedience to God's law. If they will repent, however, and embrace the Torah, God will bring Jews home to Israel to enjoy the covenant blessings in the land. This story is the heart of the book of Deuteronomy and is illustrated in the historical books of the Old Testament as well as enforced by the prophets. As N. T. Wright has conclusively demonstrated, the story of Israel—sin, exile, restoration—was embraced by Second Temple Judaism along with the New Testament as the dominant paradigm of the day, in particular, that Israel though returned to her land was nevertheless still in exile.[8] This paradigm applied to apocalyptic and non-apocalyptic materials.

We would add, however, that apocalyptic literature intensifies its assumption that Israel was still under the covenant curses by relating them to the messianic woes or the eschatological trials of the end-time; that is, the great tribulation. Conversely, when Israel repented of its sin and returned to God He would pour out the covenant blessings upon His people, perhaps through the Messiah, in the form of the kingdom of God or, in some instances, the temporary messianic kingdom. We might illustrate this dynamic in chart form (which we earlier added to the master paradigm):

Covenant Curses	Covenant Blessings
Messianic Woes	Kingdom of God/Temporary Messianic Kingdom

Therefore, in the following chart that applies the SBL matrix of form and content to the book of Daniel, we will add the category of function based on our proposal that such is an eschatological reading of the

---

7. Hellhom, *Semeia* 36 (1986), 26–27.

8. N. T. Wright first developed and defended this theory in his two books, *The New Testament and the People of God* (Minneapolis: Fortress, 1992) and *Jesus and the Victory of God* (Minneapolis: Fortress, 1996). His latest book on Paul takes as the starting place this hypothesis, *Paul and the Faithfulness of God*. 2 Vols. (Minneapolis: Fortress, 2013), 2–13.

covenant curses and blessings, intensifying them into the messianic woes and kingdom of God /temporary messianic kingdom, respectively.[9]

Component	Daniel

Manner (Form)	1 Medium:
	   Visions: 2:1–45: 4:4–27; 7:1–28
	   Epiphanies: 5:5–25; 10:1–12:4; 12:5–13
	   Discourses: 10:1–12:4
	   Dialogues: 2, 5, 7, 8, 9
	   Otherworldly Journeys: 9:20–27; 10:1–12:4; 12:5–13
	   Writing (Revelation in a Heavenly Book); 7:10; 12:4
	2 Otherworldly Mediator: 7:13–28; 10:1–12:1–4; 12:5–13
	3 Human Recipient: Chapters 1–12
	   Pseudonymity/Disposition of Recipient: 2:14–45; 6:1–28; 10:10; 12:13
	   Reaction of Recipient: 2:20–23; 6; 10:8–10

Temporal Axis (Content)	4 Protology: 7:13–14/7:15–28
	   Cosmogony: 2:44/7:13–14
	   Primordial Events: 7:1–28
	5 History:
	   Recollection of past: 7:9–14
	   Ex Eventu Prophecy: 2; 7; 8–12
	6 Present salvation through knowledge: 12:1–3
	7 Eschatological Crises: 12:1
	   Persecution: 2:19–27; 7:21–26; 12:1–3
	   Other eschatological upheavals: 2:19–27; 2:44
	8 Eschatological judgment or destruction: 2:26/7:27; 2:44
	   The wicked or the ignorant: 2:44; 4; 5; 12:1–3
	   The world: 2:44
	   Otherworldly beings:10:1–2
	9 Eschatological salvation:
	   Cosmic transfiguration: 2:44; 7
	   Resurrection: 12:1–3
	   Other forms of afterlife: 2:44–45; 7:26–27

---

9. To my knowledge no one has either applied the form/content matrix to the above literature (except Aune in his application of the taxonomy to his commentary, *Revelation 1–5,* lxxxi–lxxxviii) nor have scholars included the category of function in the above matrix in terms of the covenant curses/messianic woes and covenant blessings/kingdom of God/temporary messianic kingdom that I do for Daniel here. In another study, I have applied this revised SBL matrix to *1 Enoch,* the Dead Sea Scrolls, the *Testament of Moses, 4 Ezra,* and *2 Baruch.*

Component	Daniel
Spatial Axis (Content)	10 Otherworldly elements: 9:20–27 Otherworldly regions: 2:44–45; 7 Otherworldly beings: 3:28; 5:5–25; 7; 8–12
Parenesis (Content)	11 Parenesis: 9/12:3
Concluding Instructions (Form)	12 Concluding Instructions: Instructions to recipient: 12:4 Narrative conclusion: 12:5–13

Group in Crisis (Function)	13 Exhortation/Consolation:
	    13.1 Covenant curses
	        Exhortation (covenant curses/messianic woes):
	        Compare 9:1–26 (covenant curses) with 8:19;
	        12:1, 11–12 (messianic woes)
	    13.2 Covenant blessings
	        Consolation (covenant blessings/kingdom of God
	        or temporary messianic kingdom): Compare
	        9:27–30 (covenant blessings/restoration of
	        Israel with 2:44 [the kingdom of God]; 12:1–3
	        [resurrection of the righteous])

MIXED GENRES IN DANIEL AND REVELATION

In the second point of this chapter on the genre of apocalyptic material, we now must also note that several common literary forms and features combine in that literature. We focus on Daniel and Revelation because they are canonical. Indeed, from here on we pay particular attention to biblical apocalyptic literature. We turn now to Daniel, and after that, Revelation.

Daniel

It is commonly recognized that three main genres contribute to the book of Daniel. Daniel 1–6 are comprised of court tales; Daniel 7–12 consists of apocalyptic visions; Daniel 2 and 7 match an eschatological topos in postexilic Judaism and in the ancient near east, namely, the four kingdoms. We now discuss each of these three genres.[10]

---

10. We will not discuss the three additions to Daniel found in the Catholic Old Testament—The Prayer of Azariah, Bel and the Serpent, and Suzanna. These apocryphal books are rightly

Daniel 1–6: Court Tales[11]

W. Lee Humphreys proposed a distinction between "tales of court conflict" and "tales of court contest" in Daniel.[12] The conflict tales are found in Daniel 3 and 6, while chapters 2, 4, and 5 are designated as tales of contests. The tale of court conflict conveys the notion of the disgrace and rehabilitation of a minister on the king's court. This genre is found in the Joseph story, in Esther, in the Egyptian story of Ahikar, in Daniel 3, 6 and in Bel and the Serpent. Each of these stories exhibit five stages in the narrative. The hero is: in a state of prosperity on the king's court; is endangered, often because of conspiracy; is condemned to prison or death; is released; is restored to their former honor. In the cases of Joseph, Esther, and Daniel, it is God who vindicates his servant. The tale of court contest follows the typical pattern: the king is confronted with a problem he cannot solve; the king's sages fail to resolve the problem; the hero is called in who solves it; the hero is elevated or restored to high position.

Daniel 7–12: Apocalyptic Visions

Daniel 7–12 casts Daniel in the role of an Old Testament prophet, even though the book is not included in the prophets' section of the Hebrew Bible. Yet the predictive aspects of the visions in Daniel 7–12 clearly portray him as a prophet. Indeed, Josephus (*Antiquities of the Jews* 10.11.7//266–68), the Dead Sea Scrolls [4Q Florilegium 2:5], Jesus (Matt. 24:15), and early rabbinic sources (*Mekilta* 1b; *Pesiq.R* 14, 61) considered Daniel as such. One can only speculate why Daniel is left out of the Hebrew canon. Daniel was written in exile and therefore was considered somewhat ritually unclean compared to the prophets; Daniel was written after the time the prophets section was fixed in the Hebrew Bible; Daniel received divine revelations in dreams rather than directly as did the prophets.[13] Either way, in the prophets' section or not, contemporary biblical scholars consider Daniel 7–12 to be apocalyptic literature, as the taxonomy above shows.

Yet here we offer a caveat regarding Daniel 7–12—because only this part of the book is considered apocalyptic and not chapters 1–6, the

---

rejected by Protestants, though these three works are fascinating testimony to Israel's robust faith in Second Temple Judaism in the second century B.C.

11. The literary term "tale" is a neutral term with regard to whether the material is historical. I take these court tales in Daniel as historical.

12. W. Lee Humphreys, "A Life-Style for Diaspora: A Study of the Tales of Esther and Daniel," *Journal of Biblical Literature* 92 (1973) 211–23.

13. See J. J. Collins for a brief discussion of this issue, *Daniel*. Hermeneia (Minneapolis: Fortress, 1993), 52.

label "apocalyptic" is understood not as the main genre of Daniel but something different, for Daniel 7–12. There are two reasons, however, we rather identify Daniel 1–6 as apocalyptic as well. First, it too, like Daniel 7–12, contains predictive prophecy (notably chapter 2). Second, the apocalyptic matrix utilized above required the whole book of Daniel to fill out the details of the genre of apocalyptic. In light of these two points, we rather label the main genre of Daniel as apocalyptic, not just chapters 7–12.

Daniel 2 and 7: Four Kingdoms

While Daniel 2 is a part of the court tales of Daniel 1–6 and Daniel 7 is a part of Daniel's predictive visions, there is a genre that characterizes these two chapters, namely, the genre of the topos[14] of the four kingdoms. The four kingdoms of Daniel 2 and 7 seem to follow a well-known pattern in the ancient near east. Daniel 7 possibly parallels the Babylonian "Dynastic Prophecy," (this text records four successive ancient empires not unlike Daniel 2 and 7: Assyria, Babylonia; Persia, Macedonia).[15] Daniel 2 possibly parallels the Persian *Bahman Yasht*, chapter 1 (Ahura Mazda revealed to Zoroaster a trunk of a tree on which there were four branches: one of gold, one of silver, one of steel, one of mixed iron).[16] We will offer our interpretation of the identity of these four kingdoms in another chapter. For our purposes here, however, Daniel 2 and 7 may participate in a common attempt in the ancient near east to forecast the future in terms of four successive kingdoms. Of course, Daniel's message is that the ultimate kingdom, the kingdom of God and His Messiah/heavenly Son of Man, is to rule all kingdoms of this world (Daniel 2:44–45).

Revelation

Revelation is more complex and includes numerous subgenres that were common in the Bible and outside the Bible. For convenience's sake, we will simply list those subgenres that are present in Revelation and will provide a brief comment on each.

---

14. Topos is a name for a theme(s) that occurs in similar literature. For example, the eschatological signs of the times constitute a topos in apocalyptic literature; see below.

15. A. K. Grayson, *Babylonian Historical-Literary Texts* (Toronto: University of Toronto, 1975), 24–27. Gerhard F. Hasel has also adduced this text as an example of "four-kingdom" prophecy, "The Four World Empires of Daniel 2 against Its Near Eastern Environment, "*Journal for the Study Of The Old Testament* 12 (1979) 17–30.

16. So Collins, *Daniel*, 163.

Letter/Covenant Structure of Revelation 2–3

The following chart demonstrates how the covenant structure of Deuteronomy thoroughly informs the letters to the seven churches in Revelation: [17]

Genre	Ephesus	Smyrna	Pergamum	Thyatira	Sardis	Philadelphia	Laodicea
Introduction / Messenger Formula: A) These are the words of Christ = Thus says the Lord B) John write to church of . . .	2:1	2:8	2:12	2:18	3:1	3:7	3:14
Preamble: Description of Christ	2:1	2:8	2:12	2:18	3:1	3:7	3:14
Prologue: Christ's Relationship with the church	Commendation (salvation) — 2:2, 3, 6/ Condemnation (judgment) — 2:4	Commendation (salvation) only — 2:9	Commendation (salvation) — 2:13/ Condemnation (judgment) — 2:14–15	Commendation (salvation) — 2:19/ Condemnation (judgment) — 2:20–24	Commendation (salvation) — 3:4/ Condemnation (judgment) — 3:1	Commendation (salvation) only — 3:8–9	Condemnation (judgment) only — 3:15–17
Stipulation	2:5	2:10	2:16	2:25	3:2–3	3:10–11	3:18–20
Curses	2:5		2:16	2:22–25	3:2–3		3:16, 18–19
Blessings	2:7	2:11	2:17	2:26–28	3:5	3:10, 12	3:21
Witness	2:7	2:11	2:17	2:28	3:6	3:13	3:22

---

17. See C. Marvin Pate, *The Writings of John: A Survey of the Gospel, Epistles, and Apocalypse* (Grand Rapids: Zondervan, 2011), 368.

We might also mention at this point that the covenant theme integrates three genres of Revelation: prophecy, letter, and apocalyptic. The covenant theme connects to the genre of prophecy (2–3; 22:6–10, 18–20) in that the Old Testament prophets enforced the covenant with Israel, which is now applied to John and the church. The letter genre (1:4–5; 2–3; 22:21) understands Revelation to be the book of the new covenant (see 5:1–5; 6–7). The apocalyptic genre, as we saw in the first half of this chapter, intensifies the covenant blessings into the eschatological kingdom of God and Messiah while intensifying the covenant curses into the messianic woes. The kingdom of God and Messiah, in juxtaposition with the messianic woes, is the heart of Revelation.

Merkabah *Mysticism and Revelation 4–5*[18]

It is clear that Revelation 4–5 reports a transcendental experience of John, as is evident in three symbols comprising his vision: (a) the heavenly court of Yahweh/Christ (see 1 Kings 22:19; Ps. 89:7; Isa. 24:23); (b) mystic experience as the mode for being transported to the divine throne (Ezekiel 1; *1 Enoch* 14; *4 Ezra* 14); (c) the revelation in heaven of the things that will transpire on earth in the end times (Dan. 2:29, 45; *4 Ezra* 7:14, 83; 13:18; *2 Baruch* 21:12; 1QS 11:5–8).

Whether or not such mysticism is of the *merkabah* variety is debatable. Thus I. Gruenwald identifies a number of features in Revelation 4–5 that distinguish John's experience from *merkabah* mysticism. (1) The author knows only one heaven, not the plurality of as many as seven heavens found in Jewish apocalypses and *merkabah* literature. (2) Although the twenty-four elders have some parallels in Jewish literature, they are not part of the *merkabah* tradition and betray the eclecticism of the author. (3) The throne of God has two peculiar features: (a) that the four living creatures are "in the midst of the throne and round about the throne" may reflect the Jewish tradition that the four living creatures bear the firmament over their heads and that the throne is located on the firmament (so they cannot see God), and (b) the four living creatures are listed in a different order from that found in Ezekiel 1, and they have six wings rather than the four wings of the creatures in Ezekiel 1. These peculiarities further indicate the eclectic character of the vision in Revelation 4. (4) Gruenwald then turns to the *Apocalypse of Paul* (a composition dependent in part on Revelation) and points out that the throne of God appears to be located in the heavenly temple, though apart from Isaiah 6 the temple is never mentioned in *merkabah* visions; this suggests that the author

---

18. Here we treat *merkabah* mysticism in terms of its supposed relationship to Revelation 4–5, but we provide a broader discussion below concerning the relationship between *merkabah* and apocalypticism in general.

of the *Apocalypse of Paul*, like the author of Revelation, has produced a blend of literary motifs.[19]

What these features mean for Gruenwald is that Revelation 4–5 does not convey true visionary ecstatic experience but rather is a pastiche of literary features and conventions derived from sundry sources, including *merkabah* traditions.[20]

Revelation 6–7 and The Olivet Discourse

It is commonly recognized that Jesus's predictions regarding the coming signs of the times as recorded in the Olivet Discourse (Matt. 24/Mark 13/Luke 21) are behind the seal judgments in Revelation 6–7. Indeed, the Olivet Discourse has been labeled the "little apocalypse" (see our later discussion).

Revelation 8:1–11:15, Revelation 15:1–16:21, and the Egyptian Plagues

Similarly, commentators have longed observed that the Egyptian plagues inform the trumpet and bowl judgments, as the following chart demonstrates: [21]

Seven Trumpets (Revelation 8–9)	Ten Plagues (Exodus 7–11)	Seven Bowls (Revelation 16)
1. Earth hit with hail, fire, and blood (8:7)	7. Hail (9:13–34) 6. Boils (9:8–11)	1. People with beast's mark afflicted with sores (16:2)
2. 1/3 of sea turned to blood and 1/3 of sea creatures die (8:8–9)	1. Blood (7:14–21)	2. Sea turned to blood and all sea creatures die (16:3)
3. 1/3 of fresh waters embittered by Wormwood (8:11)	1. Blood (7:14–21)	3. Rivers and springs turned to blood (16:4)
4. 1/3 of sun, moon, and stars darkened (8:12)	9. Darkness (10:21–23)	4. Sun scorches people with fire (16:8–9)
5. Locusts released on earth after Abyss is opened (9:1–11)	8. Locusts (10:3–19) 9. Darkness (10:21–23)	5. Darkness on earth and sores break out (16:10–11)

---

19. Itamar Gruenwald, *Apocalyptic and Merkavah Mysticism.* Arbeiten zur Geschichte des antiken Judentums und des Urchristentums, 14 (Leiden: Brill, 1980), 62–72.

20. Ibid.

21. This chart comes from Mark Wilson, *Charts on Revelation* (Grand Rapids: Kregel, 2007), 80.

Seven Trumpets (Revelation 8–9)	Ten Plagues (Exodus 7–11)	Seven Bowls (Revelation 16)
6. 200 million troops at Euphrates River released by 4 angels (9:13–16)	2. Frogs (8:2–14)	6. Kings from east gathered to Euphrates River by 3 unclean spirits resembling frogs (16:12–13)
7. Heavenly temple opens accompanied by lightning, earthquake, and hail (11:15, 19)	7. Hail (9:18–34)	7. Lightning, severe earthquake, and plague of large hail (16:18–21)
	Egyptians wail loudly because of loss of firstborn (12:30)	People curse God because of the plagues (16:9, 21)
Survivors of plagues refuse to repent (9:20–21)	Pharaoh hardens heart (7:22; 8:15, 19, 32; 9:7, 12, 34–35; 10:20, 27; 11:10)	Survivors of plagues refuse to repent (16:9, 11)

Revelation 21–22 and the Restoration of Paradise

Commentators often note the beautiful themes in Revelation 21–22 that envision the New Jerusalem as restoring paradise lost as reported in Genesis 1–3. This typology is called "Urzeit/Endzeit," with reference to the conviction that the end of time will restore the beginning of time. The following chart makes these themes apparent: [22]

Genesis 1–3	Revelation 21–22 (cf. Rev. 19)	
Sinful people scattered	God's people unite to sing his praises	19:6–7
"Marriage" of Adam and Eve	Marriage of Last Adam and his bride, the church	19:7; 21:2, 9
God abandoned by sinful people	God's people (New Jerusalem, bride of Christ) made ready for God; marriage of Lamb	19:7–8; 21:2, 9–21

22. The chart comes from J. Scott Duvall, J. Daniel Hays, C. Marvin Pate, E. Randolph Richards, W. Dennis Tucker, and Preben Vang, *The Story of Israel: A Biblical Theology*, ed. C. Marvin Pate (Downers Grove, IL: Intervarsity Press, 2004), 271–72.

Genesis 1–3	Revelation 21–22 (cf. Rev. 19)	
Exclusion from bounty of Eden	Invitation to marriage supper of Lamb	19:9
Satan introduces sin into world	Satan and sin are judged	19:11–21; 20:7–10
The serpent deceives humanity	The ancient serpent is bound "to keep him from deceiving the nations"	20:2–3
God gives humans dominion over the earth	God's people will reign with Him forever	20:4, 6; 22:5
People rebel against the true God resulting in physical and spiritual death	God's people risk death to worship the true God and thus experience life	20:4–6
Sinful people sent away from life	God's people have their names written in the book of life	20:4–6, 15; 21:6, 27
Death enters the world	Death is put to death	20:14; 21:4
God creates first heaven and earth, eventually cursed by sin	God creates a new heaven and earth where sin is nowhere to be found	21:1
Water symbolizes unordered chaos	There is no longer any sea	21:1
Sin brings pain and tears	God comforts his people and removes crying and pain	21:4
Sinful humanity cursed with wandering (exile)	God's people given a permanent home	21:3
Community forfeited	Genuine community experienced	21:3, 7
Sinful people are banished from presence of God	God lives among his people	21:3, 7, 22; 22:4
Creation begins to grow old and die	All things are made new	21:5
Water used to destroy wicked humanity	God quenches thirst with water from spring of life	21:6; 22:1
"In the beginning, God . . ."	"I am the Alpha and the Omega, the beginning and the end."	21:6

Genesis 1–3	Revelation 21–22 (cf. Rev. 19)	
Sinful humanity suffers a wandering exile in the land	God gives his children an inheritance	21:7
Sin enters the world	Sin banished from God's city	21:8, 27; 22:15
Sinful humanity separated from presence of holy God	God's people experience God's holiness (cubed city = holy of holies)	21:15–21
God creates light and separates it from darkness	No more night or natural light; God himself is the source of light	21:23; 22:5
Languages of sinful humanity confused	God's people is a multicultural people	21:24, 26; 22:2
Sinful people sent away from garden	New heaven/earth includes a garden	22:2
Sinful people forbidden to eat from tree of life	God's people may eat freely from the tree of life	22:2, 14
Sin results in spiritual sickness	God heals the nations	22:2
Sinful people cursed	The curse removed from redeemed humanity and they become a blessing	22:3
Sinful people refuse to serve/obey God	God's people serve him	22:3
Sinful people ashamed in God's presence	God's people will "see his face"	22:4

Beatitudes and Woes

The seven beatitudes are best explained by the covenant background of Revelation. Covenant blessings (1:3; 14:13; 16:15; 19:9; 20:6) are pronounced by those associated with heaven upon those who in obeying Jesus obey the commandments of God. Laments (for example, 6:11) and woes (9:12–13; 11:14, 18; 14:10; chapter 18) correspond with the covenant curses pronounced upon those on earth who follow the Beast.

Revelation 7 and 14, and the 144,000

The 144,000 are no doubt portrayed as the saints of God who are divinely protected during the messianic woes on earth (cf. Dan. 12:12; Mark 13:13; 1 Thess. 4:15–17; *2 Baruch* 29:1–2; 40:2; 7:11; *4 Ezra* 9:7–8;

12:34: 13:26, 48–49; 1QH 3) just as God protected Jews during the Egyptian plagues. At the appearance of the Messiah, these sealed saints will join the end-time holy war against the enemies of God (cf. Rev. 19; 1QM). Whether these saints are Jews or the church is a matter of debate.

Revelation 12, the Woman and the Dragon

Related to the last point, the mother and her seed that endure persecution from the Dragon is a well-known feature in Egyptian and Greco-Roman literature. Craig Keener writes,

> In Egyptian mythology, Isis (Hathor), portrayed with the sun on her head, birthed Horus, and the red dragon Typhon sought to slay her, but she escaped to an island and her son Horus overthrew the dragon. In the Greek version of the story, the great dragon Python, warned that he would be killed by Leto's son, pursued the pregnant Leto, who was hidden by Poseidon on an island, which he then temporarily submerged. After Python had left, Leto birthed the god Apollo, who in four days was strong enough to slay the dragon. . . . Compare this to Roman propaganda in Asia Minor that the goddess Roma was the new mother goddess and the Roman emperor her child, the world's savior.[23]

All of these features are subsumed under the biblical account of Herod's foiled attempt to kill baby Jesus (Matthew 2:1–18).

Revelation 13 and 16 and the Beast

Revelation 13 and 16 draw on the pervasive practice in John's Asia Minor of the enforcement of the imperial cult upon the masses. Thus the Roman proconsul was charged with requiring his town to bow before the statue to Caesar (Domitian in John's day) in worship.[24] In my estimation, the Emperor cult is the key background to interpreting the entire book of Revelation; but more on that in a later chapter.

Revelation 18 and the Fall of Rome

Revelation 18 joined the chorus of a number of ancient texts that predicted the fall of Rome due to its immoral and luxurious lifestyle. These include Aelius Aristides, *Oratio* 26, A.D. 155 and the *Sibylline Oracles* 8:113–19, A.D. 175.

---

23. Craig S. Keener, *Revelation,* NIV Application Commentary (Grand Rapids: Zondervan, 2000), 316–17.

24. For documentation see Pate, *The Writings of John,* 456–462.

Revelation 21–22 and the New Jerusalem

We have also mentioned the hope of the New Jerusalem mentioned in the prophets and in Second Temple Judaism.

Ekphrasis

We turn now to the subgenre of *ekphrasis*, which I hope to show in a later chapter is the dominant subgenre in Revelation. *Ekphrasis* today is understood to be a rhetorical description of a work of art, but in antiquity *ekphrasis* included descriptions of everything from animals to novels to war. Indeed, so pervasive was this subgenre that it was included in numerous rhetorical Greco-Roman handbooks.[25] David Aune has argued that Revelation 17 is an *ekphrasis* of the *Dea Roma Coin* and later I intend to show that the whole of Revelation 4–19 is an *ekphrasis* of the Arch of Titus. I will develop these two topics in a later chapter.

FIGURES OF SPEECH IN REVELATION

Revelation outshines all other apocalyptic writings in its usage of figures of speech. Here we can do no better than to list figures of speech in Revelation based on Mark Wilson's findings.[26] Space concerns permits us to only provide a sampling of such.

Figure of speech:	Description:
Simile:	Loud voice like a trumpet (1:10); someone like a Son of Man (1:13); eyes like blazing fire (2:18); come like a thief (3:3); the first creature was like a lion, the second like an ox, the third as with the face like a man, the fourth like a flying eagle (4:7); torment like a scorpion's sting (9:5); three unclean spirits like frogs (16:13); pure gold like clear glass (21:18).
Metaphor:	Priest (1:6; 5:10; 20:6); sharp double-edged sword out of the mouth (1:16; 2:12, 16; 19:15, 21); throne of Satan (2:13); lamb (5:6, plus 28 more times!); 144,000 (7:4; 14:1, 3); Sodom; Egypt (11:8); seven heads, ten horns (12:3; 13:1; 17:3, 7, 9); Babylon (14:8; 16:19; 17:5; 18:2, 10, 21); white horse (6:3–4; 19:11); Gog and Magog (20:8); Great White Throne (20:11).

---

25. For details of *ekphrasis* in antiquity, see the definitive treatment by Shadi Bartsch, *Decoding the Ancient Novel: The Reader and the Role of Description in Heliodorus and Achilles Tatius* (Princeton, NJ: Princeton University Press, 1989).

26. Mark Wilson, *Charts on Revelation*, 50–55.

Figure of speech:	Description:
Personification:	"Death" refers to a person; "Hades" to his kingdom (1:18: 6:8; 20:13, 14); every creature singing (5:13); "beast . . . out of the sea" for Roman emperor and his proconsul (13:1); "beast . . . out of the earth" for Asiarch who was priest of imperial cult (13:11); "the woman" (Roma) for Rome (17:3–18); "ten horns" for ten kings (17:12); "holy city, new Jerusalem" for an adorned bride (21:2), the church (22:17).
Apostrophe:	"Woe, woe, the great city…" (18:10, 16, 19); "your merchants . . . your sorcery" (18:23).
Parody:	To kill with a sword parodies Roman *ius gladii* (the right of execution), (6:8); beast's appearance parodies Christ (13:11–16); mark of the Beast parodies seal of the living God (13:6; compare 7:3; 9:4); great supper of God parodies the wedding supper of the Lamb (19:17); the harlot parodies Rome (17); the seal, trumpet, and bowl judgments parody the Arch of Titus (Revelation 4–19).
Metonymy:	"My name" refers to person of exalted Christ (2:3); "palm branches" refers to victory (7:9); "blood of the Lamb" refers to atoning death of Christ (7:14). Merism: Alpha and Omega (1:8; 21:6; 22:13); first and last (1:17; 2:8; 22:13); beginning and end (21:6; 22:13).
Euphemism:	Rest/Wait (6:11); fallen (17:10; compare 14:8; 18:2).
Paradox:	Synagogue of Satan (2:9; 3:9); reputation of being alive but are dead (3:1); claim to be rich but wretched and poor (3:17).
Hyperbole:	Day and night (4:8; 7:15; two hundred million (9:16); blood to the height of the horses' bridles (14:20).
Irony:	Jews to fall down at the feet of Gentile believers (3:9); Lion becomes Lamb (5:5–6).
Gematria	"666" mark of the beast is a numerical riddle alluding to Emperor Nero.

APOCALYPTICISM, OLD TESTAMENT PROPHECY, AND *MERKABAH* MYSTICISM

In the final section of this chapter, we take a brief look at the relationship between apocalypticism and Old Testament prophecy on the one hand, and the relationship between apocalypticism and *merkabah* mysticism on the other hand. We will not provide a lengthy discussion of these two relationships because there has emerged a near-consensus relative to these questions among scholars.

Apocalypticism and Old Testament Prophecy

In the twentieth century, three major theories competed for the claim to be the origin of Jewish apocalypticism[27]: Persian Zoroastrianism,[28] Old Testament wisdom,[29] and Old Testament prophecy.

Regarding the first, perhaps the major component of Zoroastrianism that is thought to have given birth to apocalypticism is the former's teaching on resurrection. Often it was said, for example, that the teaching on the resurrection in Daniel 12 came from the Babylonian and Persian periods. Yet, two rejoinders refute such a claim. First, Daniel 12 is drawing on the oldest apocalyptic piece in the Old Testament—Isaiah 24–27. That passage is pre-exilic and records Israel's early thinking on resurrection, which matches Daniel 12. Second, the distinctive notion in Zoroastrianism concerning a future resurrection is that the individual undergoes a fiery purgation as a stage of the resurrection, yet such an idea is conspicuous by its absence in Zechariah 13:7–9 and Malachi 3:2–3 (both post-exilic), texts that envision an apocalyptic scenario.[30] Therefore, more recent scholarship rejects the claim that Persian influence was the stimulus for Jewish apocalyptic literature.

Concerning the possibility that Old Testament wisdom stimulated the appearance of apocalypticism, it is true that a couple of components of wisdom are present in apocalyptic literature: the mantic wisdom of Daniel's dreams which influences other apocalyptic works like *1 Enoch* and the Dead Sea Scrolls and the catalogues of natural and cosmic phenomena in wisdom texts like Job 28 and 38–39 that appear in apocalyptic works like *1 Enoch, 4 Ezra,* and *2 Baruch.* Yet the first comparison is not compelling,

---

27. See Pate, *Apostle of the Last Days: The Life, Letters, and Theology of Paul* (Grand Rapids: Kregel, 2013).

28. The History of Religions School so popular in the early twentieth century championed the view that Jewish apocalypticism developed out of Persian Zoroastrianism. Stephen L. Cook provides a healthy corrective to this approach in his, "Apocalyptic Prophecy," ed. John J. Collins, *The Oxford Handbook of Apocalyptic Literature* (Oxford: Oxford University Press, 2014), 19–35; 26–27.

29. Gerhard von Rad championed this view in his, *Wisdom in Israel* (London: SCM, 1972).

30. So Cook, "Prophetic-Apocalyptic," 27.

because mantic wisdom itself did not play a significant role in wisdom literature. The second has only an element of truth in it because the two world views of wisdom and apocalypticism are related to two different perspectives: Wisdom is concerned with guiding one in this life, while apocalypticism focuses on the age to come. Indeed, my own examination of wisdom and apocalypticism in Second Temple Judaism demonstrated that the latter reinterprets the former by placing the emphasis on the age to come. That is to say, wisdom is to obey the Torah in this age in order to experience the covenant blessings in the age to come.[31]

In light of these more recent developments, most scholars argue that Old Testament prophecy was the catalyst for the rise of apocalyptic literature. Thus the eschatological concern in apocalypses with human history and the vindication of Israel's hopes echoes prophetic themes in the books of Ezekiel, especially chapters 36–39; 40–48; Isaiah, especially chapters 24–27; 55–56; and Zechariah, especially chapters 9–14. See also Daniel 12. All things considered, then, it is not surprising that biblical scholarship roots apocalypticism in the Old Testament prophets and their prophecies. Moreover, it is understandable that scholars prefer to call this literature "prophetic-apocalyptic."[32] Accordingly, we will use such a label in this work.

Apocalypticism and *Merkabah* Mysticism

Merkabah (chariot [throne]) refers to the divine throne of Yahweh and the attempts of his people to see that throne through mystical experience. Enoch's throne vision in *1 Enoch* 14 seems to represent the oldest example of *merkabah* mysticism. Five comments about this type of mystic experience need to be made at this juncture.

First, the major texts fitting into this category are: *1 Enoch* 14; 2 Corinthians 12:1–7; Colossians 2:1–3:4; *3 Enoch; Hagigah 11b–16a; Helalot Rabbati.* Second, the components of *merkabah* mysticism include: (a) rigorous preparation for the heavenly ascent via prayer and fasting; (b) mystic ascent through the seven "houses" or palaces of heaven; (c) negotiations with the angels assigned to each of the palaces by the use of magical formulae, and seals; (d) danger accompanying the ascent; (e) vision of the glorious, divine throne-chariot.

Third, based on Ezekiel 1:15–21 (cf. other biblical throne visions in Exod. 24:10–11; 1 Kings 22:19; Isa. 6; Ezek. 3:22–24; 8:1–8; 10:9–17; Dan. 7:9–14), one of the purposes of *merkabah* mysticism seems to have

---

31. Pate, *The Reverse of the Curse: Paul, Wisdom, and the Law. Wissenschaftliche Untersuchungen zum Neuen Testament 114* (Tübingen: Mohr/Siebeck, 2000), chapters 3–4.

32. See again Cook's article,"Prophetic-Apocalyptic" as well as his earlier more extensive work on the subject, *Prophecy and Apocalypticism: The Post-Exilic Social Setting* (Minneapolis: Fortress, 1995).

been to legitimate sectarian teaching, as is shown by Rabbinic attempts to monitor it (*Exodus Rabbati* 43:8; *M. Hagigah* 2:1; *Babylonian Hagigah* 14a; 15a; *Hekalot Rabbati* 20:1; *Babylonian Sanhedrin* 38b).

Fourth, although *merkabah* mysticism and apocalypticism are related, three matters distinguish them: (a) *Merkabah* texts concentrate more on the mysteries of heaven and the description of God's throne and less on eschatological themes than does apocalypticism (e.g., last judgment, resurrection of the dead, messianic kingdom, the world to come). This consideration does not deny that *merkabah* does not contain eschatology (e.g., *1 Enoch* 14:8–25). Rather, the difference is one of emphasis. (b) *Merkabah* is less occupied with cosmology than is apocalyptic. (c) *Merkabah* texts stress more the theurgic element than does apocalyptic material.

Fifth, it may be that prior to A.D. 70, *merkabah* mysticism and apocalypticism were intermingled traditions, which would account for similarities between the two, but with the dashed hopes of apocalypticism due to the events between the two Jewish revolts against Rome (A.D. 70–135), *merkabah* emerged as an independent movement.

The conclusion we reach about the relationship between apocalypticism and *merkabah* mysticism is that before A.D. 70 they may have intermingled but between A.D. 70–135, they separated into two traditions. At that time, *merkabah* mysticism became a way to experience the age to come, not on earth as apocalypticism had hoped, but in heaven through mystic ascent to the divine throne.

Chapter in Review

This chapter accomplished four tasks. First, we applied the commonly accepted taxonomy of the genre of apocalyptic literature to Daniel and suggested that the function of apocalyptic writings should be located in the eschatologizing of the covenant curses and blessings. Israel's disobedience concerning the Torah resulted in the intensifying of the covenant curses into the messianic woes at the end of the age. Obedience to God will result in the covenant blessings of the kingdom of God and/or Messiah in the age to come. Second, we examined the presence of mixed genres in Daniel and Revelation. The former contains court tales, apocalyptic visions and the four kingdom typos. The latter contains three main genres—letter, prophecy, and apocalypticism—and numerous subgenres. Third, we summarized the figures of speech that occur in Revelation. Fourth, we argued that Old Testament prophecy gave birth to apocalypticism (hence the label "prophetic-apocalyptic"). Apocalypticism was intimately related to merkabah mysticism before A.D. 70, but the two traditions separated after that date.

2

THE HISTORICAL BACKGROUND OF PROPHETIC-APOCALYPTIC BOOKS

The Chapter at a Glance

This chapter attempts to uncover the historical background of the biblical prophetic-apocalyptic material, which is the story of Israel. We will track four responses to that story, especially concerning the national crises in Israel.

- First, we will examine apocalyptic retellings of the story of Israel in light of the imminent end/actual fall of Jerusalem to the Babylonians in 586 B.C.: Isaiah 24–27; 56–66; Joel 2–3; Ezekiel 38–39.
- Second, we will then examine an apocalyptic retelling of the story of Israel in light of the extension of the Babylonian exile from 70 to 490 years: Daniel 9–12.
- Third, we investigate an apocalyptic retelling of the story of Israel in light of the failure of the restoration of Israel under Cyrus the Persian: Zechariah 9–14.
- Fourth, we consider the Olivet Discourse and Revelation 6 as well as Revelation as a whole to be apocalyptic responses to the fall of Jerusalem to Rome in A.D. 70.

THIS CHAPTER PICKS UP WHERE THE LAST CHAPTER left off, in effect, pursuing the "function" component of the genre of apocalyptic material. This chapter divides into two parts: first, we will analyze Old Testament prophetic-apocalyptic texts like Isaiah 24–27; 56–66; Joel 2–3; Ezekiel 38–39; Daniel 9–12; and Zechariah 9–14 in terms of their historical background. Then, we will situate the New Testament prophetic-apocalyptic texts of Jesus's Olivet Discourse and the book of Revelation in the milieu of the day. These historical considerations are important to the process of interpreting prophetic-apocalyptic literature accurately, for one must understand the significance of the inspired passage in its day before looking to the future for its ultimate fulfillment.[1]

OLD TESTAMENT

In the first part of this chapter, our goal is to examine prophetic-apocalyptic texts in the Old Testament with a view to the historical background that informs them. More particularly, the story of Israel—sin, exile, and restoration—that is the underpinning for all of the Old Testament prophets,[2] is the historical background for Old Testament prophetic-apocalyptic material as well.

There are, however, two crucial differences between the story of Israel in the non-apocalyptic prophets and the story of Israel in the prophetic-apocalyptic material. First, the latter read the story of Israel in apocalyptic fashion such that the covenant curses are intensified into the messianic woes and the covenant blessings are envisioned as the end-time kingdom of God/Messiah. Second, the prophetic-apocalyptic texts are reacting to a national crisis relative to Israel which signals to them the imminent end of history as they knew it. Thus the prophetic-apocalyptic writings cluster into three groups, each with its own reaction to a historical crisis concerning Israel's fortunes. (1) Isaiah 24–27; 56–66; Joel 2–3; Ezekiel 38–39 are apocalyptic reactions to the imminent end or actual fall of Jerusalem and the destruction of the temple at the hands of the Babylonians (586 B.C.). (2) Daniel 9–12, especially 9:1–27 (cf. chapters 1–6), is an apocalyptic reaction to the considerable lengthening of the 70 years of Babylonian exile of Jews to 490 years of exile for Jews (cf. Jer. 25:1–14; 29:10 with Dan. 9:24–27).

---

1. We tip our hand here on how to properly interpret prophetic-apocalyptic literature: for the Old Testament the "near/far" fulfillments should govern one's understanding of these texts while in the New Testament the "already/not" yet hermeneutic should govern one's view of the pertinent passages. These two approaches will unfold in the course of this study.

2. See Hays's discussion of the story of Israel pertaining to Deuteronomy and the Prophets, in ed. C. Marvin Pate, J. Scott Duvall, J. Daniel Hays, E. Randolph Richards, W. Dennis Tucker Jr., and Preben Vang, *The Story of Israel: A Biblical Theology* (Downers Grove, IL: InterVarsity Press, 2004), chapters 3 and 5.

(3) Zechariah 9–14 is an apocalyptic reaction to the failed nature of the hoped-for restoration of Israel under Cyrus (539 B.C.). We will examine each category in turn.

Apocalyptic Retellings of Israel's Story in Light of the Imminent End/Actual Fall of Jerusalem to the Babylonians in 586 B.C.

Isaiah 24–27[3]

Chapters 24–27 of Isaiah are commonly recognized to be an apocalyptic piece, whatever their date. The dominant topic of this unit is the Day of the Lord, which is presented in two aspects: the arrival of that day will mark affliction for Israel, but after that her deliverance. The former is portrayed using standard apocalyptic imagery: distress (26:16), birth pangs (26:17–18), wrath (v. 20), and cosmic disturbances (v. 24). These trials will come upon Israel as the means for atoning for the nation's sin (see 26:21 and especially 27:9).[4] It is clear from all of this apocalyptic imagery that Israel's sin and exile, in effect the Deuteronomic curses, are being equated with the messianic woes. The good news is that after Israel has atoned for her sins by suffering the end-time tribulation, forgiveness, and resurrection await her (25; 26:19; 27:9). Isaiah 27 powerfully concludes chapters 24–26, noting that after Israel has suffered through the exile (vv. 1–8, 9b–11), God will forgive and restore her (vv. 2–9, 12–13). Verse 9b encapsulates such a message: "by this, then, Jacob's guilt will be atoned for, and this will be the full fruitage of the removal of his sin." These promises point to the hoped-for arrival of the kingdom of God. It may also be noted that Isaiah 24–27 envisions both destruction of Israel's enemies (25:11–12; 26:11, 21; 27:1–13) and the opportunity for the nations to be saved if they turn to Israel's God (25:6).

Isaiah 56–66

Critical scholars date Isaiah 56–66 to the post-exilic period, even as late as the Maccabean era. Conservatives attribute these chapters to the eighth-century B.C. prophet Isaiah, even as they date Isaiah chapters 40–55 to

---

3. The classic work on Isaiah 24–27 as apocalyptic literature is that of W. R. Millar, *Isaiah 24–27 and the Origin of Apocalyptic* (Missoula, MT: Scholars Press, 1976). Conservative scholars include this section as a genuine part of the eighth century B.C. prophet Isaiah's work while more liberally inclined scholars view Isaiah 24–27 as an addition by a later author than Isaiah. The difference is significant because if Isaiah is the actual author of chapters 24–27, dating to the eighth century (as I believe), then Isaiah 24–27 constitutes the oldest prophetic-apocalyptic text.

4. N. T. Wright calls attention to the atoning value of suffering in Second Temple Judaism: Isaiah 52–53; *2 Maccabees* 7:36–38; *4 Maccabees* 8:27–29; *Wisdom of Solomon* 2:12–20; 3:1–9; 1QS 8:1–4; *Jesus and the Victory of God* (Minneapolis: Fortress, 1996), 570–84.

the pre-exilic prophet.[5] Like Isaiah 24–27, Isaiah 56–66 connects the covenant curses with the messianic woes and associates the covenant blessings with the kingdom of God/restoration of Israel to her land. Thus the sin of the idolatry of Israel is spelled out in Isaiah 57:14–21; 58:1–7; 59:1–16; 65:1–8; 66:1–6. Such disobedience to the Torah has resulted in the covenant curses falling on Israel in the form of exile, according to Isaiah 56:8–57:13, which is intensified into the messianic woes in Isaiah 66:7–9. This negative consequence is reversed when the prophet looks forward to the day that Israel will repent (57:14–21; 59:20) and then enjoy the covenant blessings (56:1–7; 58:8–59:21; 60:1; 64:12). This renewal of the covenant will be none other than the restoration of Israel to her land of inheritance (58:14; 65:9, 16; 66:10–24), which will be nothing less than a new creation (65:17–25), the kingdom of God.

As we found in Isaiah 24–27, Israel's suffering is the means for her atonement and turning back to the Lord. This collective idea of Israel atoning for her sin by suffering had been narrowed down to the individual suffering servant in Isaiah 42:1–9; 49:1–13; 50:4–11; 52:13–53:12. Such a personage suffers in Israel's place. In Isaiah 56–66, both the individual suffering servant (Isaiah 61:1–4) and a group of servants (65:13–16 speaks of "servants" five times) suffer on behalf of Israel. It may be that the former is vindicated by numerous servant followers. Moreover, similarly to Isaiah 24–27, there is both the promise that Israel's enemies will be destroyed (59:17–18; 60:10–14; 63:1–6; 66:14–16) and yet can be saved if they embrace Israel's God (Isa. 56:3–8; 66:18–21). Indeed, earlier in Isaiah 44:28–45:13 Cyrus the Persian is called "anointed" of God because he will be the pagan instrument through whom God will bring his people out of captivity back to their homeland.

Joel 2–3

Scholars debate the date of Joel. The two main theories are that Joel predicts the coming judgment upon Israel by Assyria (which happened in 721 B.C.) or that the prophet predicts the coming invasion of Judah by the Babylonians (596 B.C.). The latter theory seems closer to the truth. What is clear in Joel is that the story of Israel is patently present.

Thus Joel predicts the coming judgment and exile that will overthrow Israel due to her sin (1:15–2:11). Joel does so pointing to the present crisis of a massive locust invasion of the land (1:1–12) as the foretaste of the coming invasion of Israel by her enemies; these are the covenant curses (1:15–2:11). It is interesting that Joel 1:15–2:11 (cf. Isa. above) reverses the commonly held assumption that the day of the Lord will mean deliverance of Israel to mean the destruction of Israel.

---

5. An assessment with which I agree, though I would not rule out later inspired editing of the text such as one finds in Daniel; see our later discussion.

Joel, however, exhorts Israel to repent (1:2–14; 2:12–17), after which God will restore her to her land and the covenant blessings (2:18–32; 3:17–21). It is clear that such a restoration will occur in the last days of the divine pouring out of the Spirit (2:28–32). Since that is the case, it is reasonable to interpret Israel's suffering for her sin as the intensification of the covenant curses into the messianic woes. Indeed, in the New Testament the "day of the Lord" intimately involves the messianic woes leading to Israel's deliverance. In other words, the day of the Lord can be predicated of both Israel's experience of the covenant curses in the form of the messianic woes and also as the covenant blessings intensified into the eschatological kingdom of God. (For the former, see for example 1 Thess. 4:13–5:11; 2 Thess. 2:1–12; for the latter, see, for example, Acts 2:17–21). We should also note that Joel 3 leaves no room for God's mercy on Israel's enemies; they will all be wiped out when God delivers his people.

Ezekiel 38–39

Before briefly looking at Ezekiel 38–39, the prophetic-apocalyptic section of Ezekiel, we should first note the context of this passage. In Ezekiel 36:26–28 (cf. Jer. 31:33–34), the prophet predicts that God will restore Israel to him by way of the new covenant, while in Ezekiel 37, Israel's future restoration is portrayed as nothing less than a resurrection. Moreover, after Israel has been restored to her land, Ezekiel 40–48 promises a new temple that will surpass the one destroyed by the Babylonians in 586 B.C. In between these chapters of hope comes Ezekiel 38–39 with its prophecy of the defeat of Israel's enemies, Gog and Magog. When Ezekiel made his prophecy in approximately 586 B.C., the reference to these enemies of Israel seemed much clearer to Ezekiel's day than ours. Similarly, there has been much speculation about Ezekiel's temple relative to whether there will be a third temple built in Israel in the eschatological future. Here we simply observe that the destruction of Israel's enemies will occur at the eschatological re-gathering of Israel to her land.[6]

The theme of Israel's sin, exile, and restoration governs the book of Ezekiel. Thus the prophet warns of the coming exile for his people because of Israel's sin (4:1–17; chapters 12–24), he announces judgment against Israel's enemies (chapters 25–32), and yet predicts Israel's restoration from exile (11:15–21; chapters 36–48). It seems clear that the

---

6. I argue elsewhere that Ezekiel 38–39 do not envision an end-time invasion of Israel by Russia, an enormously popular idea among those who interpret biblical prophecy in a sensationalist manner; see my co-authored work, C. Marvin Pate and Calvin B. Haines Jr., *Doomsday Delusions: What's Wrong with Predictions about the End of the World* (Downers Grove, IL: InterVarsity Press, 1995), 61–63.

covenant curses that Israel experiences are understood in Ezekiel as the messianic woes or, as Jeremiah 30:7 calls it, "Jacob's troubles." Included in these messianic woes is the battle of Gog and Magog in Ezekiel, which is portrayed as the end-time battle of the ages, a theme dear to apocalyptic material (see, for example, 1 QM; Rev. 20). Furthermore, it is clear that Ezekiel equates the restoration of Israel/covenant blessings with the arrival of the kingdom of God, which is governed by the Davidic-Messianic king (Ezek. 37:15–28). Ezekiel 36 (new covenant), 37 (resurrection/restoration of Israel), 40–48 (eschatological temple) all reinforce the eschatological interpretation of the covenant blessings here. In Ezekiel 38:25–29, it is unclear, however, whether God will not only destroy Israel's enemies but also save those nations that embrace the one true God.

An Apocalyptic Retelling of Israel's Story in Light of the Extension of the Babylonian Exile from 70 to 490 Years

N. T. Wright well notes of Daniel:

> Whenever the Daniel-traditions reached their present form, it is clear both that they were of critical importance at the time of the Maccabean crisis and that they were read eagerly during the first century [C.E.] as a charter for the revolutionaries who stood within the same Maccabean tradition of holy revolt against the rule of paganist. . . . It is clear that such stories as the three young men in the fiery furnace, and Daniel himself in the lion's den, would have functioned in the Maccabean period and thereafter as an encouragement to Jews under persecution to hold fast to their ancestral laws, even if it meant torture or death.[7]

Apocalypticism and Covenantalism in Daniel 9–12

Two influences significantly shape Daniel's call for purity before the tide of paganism which are intimately related: apocalypticism and Deuteronomistic/covenantal theology. To say that Daniel is apocalyptic in orientation is a truism. The following items attest to that: animal imagery symbolically forecasting the replacement of the kingdoms of this world by the kingdom of God (chapters 2 and 7); end-time mysteries revealed now to the righteous (chapters 1, 2, 4–5, 7, 8–12); via heavenly messengers (chapters 10–12); encouragement for the people of God to stand fast during the great tribulation (11:31–12:10); hope for Israel's

---

7. Wright, *Jesus and the Victory of God*, 584–85

deliverance and the resurrection of the godly (chapter 12); pseudonym-ity[8] and *ex eventu prophecy* are celebrated.

Daniel also breathes the air of Deuteronomistic theology, especially chapter 9: Israel's idolatry is manifest (9:4–5, 8–11) despite the prophets' past denunciations (9:6); thus the reason for the Lord's judgment on Israel (i.e., the Deuteronomic curses [9:7, 12–14]). Alongside of this negative evaluation, there is also the hope for the nation's restoration based on God's mercy (i.e., the Deuteronomic blessings [9:24–27; cf. also the *Prayer of Azariah*, vv. 5–22]). So it is that the story of Israel, namely, sin-exile-restoration, deeply imprints Daniel's exhortations.

The preceding influences—apocalypticism and Deuteronomistic theology—are interrelated, as Daniel 12 makes clear. Consider the following three apocalyptic stage props that take on a Deuteronomistic hue in that chapter. First, the messianic woes are depicted in 12:1, 11–12 (referred to as the time of "distress" in Isa. 33:2; Jer. 14:8; 15:11; 30:7; cf. the phrase in Dan. 8:19, "in the latter time of distress [wrath]"; see also CD 1:5; 1QH 3:28). It is interesting that the same word "distress" (Dan. 8:19) also occurs in Zechariah 1:12, where God is said to have been indignant (distress [wrath]) with Israel for seventy years. According to O. H. Steck, Zechariah 1:12 lays the basis for the reinterpretation of the seventy years in Daniel 9, and provides a nice parallel with CD 1. This observation is in keeping with N. T. Wright's suggestion that the messianic woes Israel experienced were thought to be the culmination of the Deuteronomic curses; compare CD 1:5, where the age of wrath (messianic woes) is probably to be identified with the period of 390 years prophesied by Ezekiel 4:5 for the punishment of Israel.

Second, messianic deliverance is referred to in Daniel 12:1 (cf. Jer. 30:7; 1QM 1:5; 4QDib.Ham) which, in light of the pronouncement of blessedness upon the righteous (v. 12), probably should be understood to be the Deuteronomic blessings. Third, resurrection, 12:3, is obviously apocalyptic in import, connoting in pre-Danielic times the national restoration of Israel in the sense of the return from exile (Ezekiel 37; Hos. 6:2; cf. Isa. 26:19), but developed in the Maccabean period into individual bodily resurrection (cf. e.g., Dan. 12:3 with 1 *Enoch* 22, 27; 90:33; 91:10; 93:2; 104:106; 2 Maccabees 7). The preceding three-stage props are commensurate with the apocalyptic genre of Daniel 10–12.

---

8. I have a problem with labeling Daniel as "pseudonymous," because such a literary device assumes that an unknown author writes his work as an imitation of a famous holy personage in Israel's earlier history. Such a theory, however, does not work for Daniel because the liberal pseudonymous approach assumes that the book was written in the second century B.C. by an anonymous author who created the person of Daniel out of thin air. In other words, they do not believe Daniel was a historical hero in the religion of ancient Israel. In doing so, these interpreters are out of line with the traditional understanding of pseudonymity.

Four Apocalyptic Features

We should also mention that four apocalyptic features emerge for the first time regarding the Old Testament in Daniel. First, there is the abomination of the Jerusalem temple by, second, an antichrist figure (in Daniel's prophecy Antiochus Epiphanes); see Daniel 9–12. Third, there is the anointed one (in Daniel's prophecy Onias III; see Dan. 9:24–27, but note also Daniel 7—the heavenly Son of Man), who, fourth, will in some way initiate the assembling or regathering of Israel during the eschatological restoration (see again Dan. 9:24–27 and chapter 12). We will see that these four apocalyptic features occur again in the prophetic-apocalyptic works in the New Testament, especially in the Olivet Discourse and in Revelation. We will also see in the next chapter that these eschatological personages and happenings are deeply associated with the themes of Second Temple Jewish apocalypticism.

An Apocalyptic Retelling of Israel's Story in Light of the Failure of the Restoration of Israel under Cyrus the Persian

Zechariah 9–14

Many modern scholars divide Zechariah into at least two distinct literary sections (chapters 1–8 and chapters 9–14), based on supposed differences in style, vocabulary, theme, and genre.[9] Chapters 9–14 are customarily dated from the Hellenistic period (ca. 350 B.C. to 160 B.C.), and are often classified as apocalyptic in nature.[10] Such features as: revelation in the form of visions, divine interpreters of those visions, the use of symbolism, the themes of the salvation of Israel and judgment upon the nations, not to mention the hope of an eschatological deliverer, contribute to this impression.[11] The preceding components fall under the governing concept of the day of the Lord (though the phrase itself [which is essentially equivalent to the messianic woes or the great

---

9. See R. Mason, *The Books of Haggai, Zechariah and Malachi.* Cambridge Commentaries on the New English Bible (Cambridge:University Press, 1977), 89.

10. See the discussion by W. Rudolph, *Haggai-Sacharja 1–8-Sacharja 9–14-Maleachi.* KAT XIII, 4 (Gütersloh: Gütershoher Verlagshaus Gerd/Mohr, 1976), 163, 211. Conservative scholars, however, date the totality of Zechariah to the mid-fifth century B.C.. Eric and Carol Meyers' research also argues for such a time period. They appeal to four pieces of data to support their claim: (1) The general impact of the Greco-Egyptian rebellion and its aftermath; (2) the greater control exerted by the Persians on their Levantine holdings, especially Yehud; (3) an awareness that a significant repopulation of Jerusalem and Yehu, and attendant economic prosperity—both of which should have followed upon Temple restoration—had not materialized; and, perhaps, (4) the perception that prophecy in its traditional form was at an end and that the authoritative prophetic works and words of the past needed to be collected for posterity, in *Zechariah 9–14,* AB 25c (New York: Doubleday: 1993), 28.

11. So Andrew E. Hill and John H. Walton, *A Survey of the Old Testament* (Grand Rapids: Zondervan, 1991), 142.

tribulation] does not occur in Zechariah—12:4, 6, 8–11; 13:1–2, 4; 14:4, 6, 8–9, 13, 20–21). N. T. Wright's summary of Zechariah 9–14 along these lines is helpful:

> The writer promises the long-awaited arrival of the true king (9.9–10, the renewed covenant and the real return from exile (9.11–12), the violent defeat of Israel's enemies and the rescue of the true people of YHWH (9.13–17). At the moment, however, Israel is like sheep without a shepherd (10.2); they have shepherds, but they are not doing their job, and will be punished (10.3) as part of the divine plan for the return from exile (10.6–12). The prophet is himself instructed to act as a shepherd but in doing so to symbolize the worthless shepherds who are currently ruling Israel (11.4–17). There will be a great battle between Israel and the nations, in which "the house of David shall be like God, like the angel of YHWH, at the head" of the inhabitants of Jerusalem (12:1–9; quotation from verse 8). There will be great mourning for 'one whom they have pierced (12.10); a "fountain . . . for the house of David and the inhabitants of Jerusalem, to cleanse them from sin and impurity" (13.1); a judgment upon the prophets of Israel (13.2–5); and judgment, too, on the shepherd of Israel, who will be struck down, and the sheep scattered (13.7). . . . The book concludes with the great drama in which all the nations will be together to fight against Jerusalem; YHWH will win a great victory, becoming king indeed, judging the nations and sanctifying Jerusalem (14.1–21).[12]

At center stage in Zechariah 9–14 is the conquering prince of 9:9–10, about whom three comments are in order: First, he is the messianic shepherd king (cf. 9:9–10 and 11:4–14 with 3:8; 6:11).[13] Second, he is a suffering figure behind whom is most likely Isaiah 53. Four correspondences between the two are commonly delineated by the commentators: (1) He is called "my Servant" in Zechariah 3:8, recalling the Servant of Isaiah 53. (2) He is "humble," or "afflicted," alluding to Isaiah 53:4, "yet we accounted him stricken, struck down by God, and afflicted." (3) He is pierced; compare Zechariah 12:10 (see also 11:4–14) with Isaiah 53:5;

---

12. Wright, *Jesus and the Victory of God*, 586–87.

13. See the numerous parallels between Zechariah's prince and notions of the Messiah in Hill and Walton, *A Survey of the Old Testament,* 422.

(4) When the shepherd-king is struck down the flock scatters; compare Zechariah 13:7 with the sheep who go astray of Isaiah 53:6. Third, such suffering of the shepherd-king is extended even to the remnant of Israel, according to Zechariah 13:8–9. Those verses, along with verse 7, read:

> "Awake, O sword, against My Shepherd, and against the man, My Associate," declares the LORD of hosts. "Strike the Shepherd that the sheep may be scattered; and I will turn My hand against the little ones. It will come about in the all the land," declares the LORD, "that two parts in it will be cut off and perish; but the third will be left in it. And I bring the third part through the fire, refine them as silver is refined, and test them as gold is tested. They will call on My name, and I will answer them. I will say, "They are My people," and they will say, "The LORD is my God."

We may summarize this brief look at Zechariah 9–14 by making three comments. First, the messianic shepherd-king, like the suffering servant of Isaiah, atones for the sin and exile of Israel in the last days, end-time suffering that even his followers must also endure; that is, they endure the messianic woes. Second, as a result the messianic king restores the covenant blessings to Israel; that is, the messianic kingdom. Third, Zechariah 9–14 is an apocalyptic reaction to the failed restoration of Israel and its rebuilt temple. Such a failed restoration was the national crisis pertaining to Israel at that time (cf. Haggai). Yet the hope of a final rebuilt temple that will surpass even Solomon's temple and will be constructed by the Messiah at the end of the age burned brightly in Second Temple Judaism (see, for example, the Temple Scroll in the Dead Sea Scrolls).[14] We conclude this summary of Zechariah by observing that while most of the enemies of Israel will be destroyed by the messianic king, there will be a few Gentiles who repent and worship Israel's God (Zech. 14:16–21).

Conclusion to Old Testament Prophetic-Apocalyptic Texts

We conclude the first part of this chapter by summarizing our findings: the Old Testament prophetic-apocalyptic writings distinguish themselves by interpreting the story of Israel along apocalyptic lines to the effect that the covenant curses Israel now suffers for her sin are in-

---

14.   J. Bradley Chance has discussed the expectation in Second Temple Judaism that the Messiah will rebuild the eschatological temple, *Jerusalem, the Temple and the New Age in Luke–Acts* (Macon, GA: Mercer University Press, 1988).

tensified into the messianic woes while the covenant blessings to be restored by Israel's return to God constitute the kingdom of God or His Messiah. Along the way, two secondary issues surfaced in this litera-ture. First, the catalyst for Israel's repentance is the suffering servants' atonement for Israel's sin. In most cases such suffering means that Jews follow in the footsteps of the suffering servant in atoning for their sins before God by enduring their afflictions as they obey Him. Second, the picture varies relative to the fate of the nations: some authors hold out no hope for the enemy nations of Israel while other writers do envision a day when Gentiles will embrace the one true God.

Moreover, we also established that the historical circumstances of the day dictated an apocalyptic interpretation on the part of some Old Testament prophets. Three national crises concerning Israel governed the aforementioned view: Babylonian exile in 586 B.C. (Isaiah 24–27; 56–66; Joel 2–3; Ezekiel 38–39); extension of the Babylonian exile from 70 to 490 years (about 586 to 164 B.C.; Daniel); disappointment at the failure of the supposed restoration of Israel beginning in 539 B.C. (Zechariah 9–14).

NEW TESTAMENT

Ernst Käsemann famously claimed that "apocalyptic is the moth-er of Christian Theology,"[15] and many scholars have agreed with this perspective, including myself. Indeed, since Albert Schweitzer's classic work, *The Quest of the Historical Jesus*,[16] probably the dominant view of New Testament interpreters has been that the main message of Jesus was the imminent arrival of the kingdom of God. Two New Testament texts in particular are understood to be prophetic-apocalyptic: the Olivet Discourse and Revelation. We will see that the story of Israel—sin, exile, restoration—deeply affects the historical background of these writings even as it did for their Old Testament counterparts.

The Olivet Discourse and Revelation 6

We now argue that the Olivet Discourse and the seal judgments in Revelation 6 are affected by the story of Israel. In what follows, we intend

---

15. Ernst Käsemann, "The Beginnings of Christian Theology," in Käsemann, *New Testament Questions of Today* (Philadelphia: Fortress, 1969), 82–107; 102. For the already/not-yet apocalyptic interpretation of the New Testament in its entirety, see the classic work of George Ladd's *A Theology of the New Testament*. 2nd edition with Donald Hagner (Grand Rapids: Eerdmans, 1991). For an attempt to follow Ladd's approach but in a more nuanced way, see C. Marvin Pate and Douglas W. Kennard, *Deliverance Now and Not Yet: The New Testament and the Great Tribulation* (New York: Peter Lang, 2004).

16. Albert Schweitzer, *The Quest of the Historical Jesus: A Critical Study of Its Progress from Reimarus to Wrede,* trans. W. Montgomery (New York: Macmillan, 1910).

to discuss the seal judgments of Revelation 6 vis-à-vis the Olivet Discourse in three points: the connections between Revelation 6 and the Olivet Discourse; the already/not-yet eschatological tension and Revelation 6 (that is, the fall of Jerusalem to Rome in A.D. 70 is the backdrop to the hoped-for future fall of Rome/parousia of Christ); and the Old Testament phenomenon that explains the apostle John's ambiguous feelings concerning the past fall of Jerusalem to Rome. The second point will be our main consideration in this section and therefore will require the most discussion.

We supply here the connections between Revelation 6, the seal judgments in the Apocalypse, and the Olivet Discourse in the Synoptics in chart form:[17]

Matthew 24:6–7, 9a, 29	Mark 13:7–9a, 24–25	Luke 21:9–12a, 25–26	Revelation 6:2–17; 7:1
1. Wars	1. Wars	1. Wars	Seal 1. Wars
2. International strife	2. International strife	2. International strife	Seal 2. International strife
3. Famines	3. Earthquakes	3. Earthquakes	Seal 3. Famine
4. Earthquakes	4. Famines	4. Famines	Seal 4. Pestilence (Death and Hades)
5. Persecutions	5. Persecutions	5. Pestilence	Seal 5. Persecutions
6. Eclipses of the sun and moon; falling of the stars; shaking of the powers of heaven	6. Eclipses of the sun and moon; falling of the stars; shaking of the powers of heaven	6. Persecutions	Seal 6 Earthquakes, eclipse of the sun, ensanguining of the moon

The Reapplication of the Past Fall of Jerusalem Recorded in the Olivet Discourse to a Future Fall of Rome

The title of the second point reflects my thesis for this section and, to my knowledge, has not been argued by other scholars. I begin this discussion by stating my thesis for Revelation 6. Then I proceed to apply that thesis to the seal judgments of the Apocalypse.

Simply put, I understand Revelation 6 to be John's *reapplication* of the fall of Jerusalem recorded in the Olivet Discourse to a future fall of

---

17.   This chart and discussion were first put forth by Louis A. Vos, *The Synoptic Traditions in the Apocalypse* (Kampen: Kok, 1965), 181–92.

Rome. Such an understanding involves two changes to a thesis that I once espoused. Some ten to fifteen years ago, I argued in two separate books that Revelation 6, the seal judgments, were fulfilled at the fall of Jerusalem to Rome in A.D. 70 and that these judgments should be equated with the first half of the Olivet Discourse, while the trumpet and bowl judgments portrayed in Revelation 8–18 should be correlated with the future Second Coming of Christ and that they correspond to the second half of the Olivet Discourse. Thus, the fall of Jerusalem to Rome/seal judgments represent the already side of the eschatological tension, while the future parousia of Christ /trumpet and bowl judgments represent the not-yet aspect of that tension.[18]

My present argument, however, now alters that thesis by suggesting rather that the scope of the judgments portrayed in Revelation 6 go beyond what happened in the Jewish Revolt of A.D. 66–73, for they envision God's wrath poured out worldwide and even cosmically. In other words, the seal judgments pertained to more than the past fall of Jerusalem. More particularly, I contend here that the seal judgments draw on the Olivet Discourse/fall of Jerusalem (however they are to be connected) but with a view to forecasting the future fall of the Roman Empire. The second change to my original thesis, which is admittedly somewhat unsettling to me as an evangelical, is that the author of the Apocalypse believed that the Second Coming of Christ would coincide with the fall of Rome. Such an argument is not new of course, because "liberal" preterists have longed argued that John expected Jesus to return in the first century and destroy the Roman Empire, which in fact did not occur.

As a conservative interpreter, however, I have made peace with this second change of my original thesis by agreeing with those scholars who say in this regard that John, like Paul or any other New Testament author, hoped that the parousia would come in his lifetime but would not be overly distraught if it did not. Rather they were comforted by the realization that in the first coming of Christ they had already experienced the dawning of the kingdom of God.[19] So, to restate my current thesis: Revelation 6 is John's reapplication of the Olivet Discourse/past fall of Jerusalem to the future parousia of Christ/destruction of Rome. I now examine the seal judgments in the light of that thesis.

---

18. *Four Views of Revelation,* edited and contributed by C. Marvin Pate (Grand Rapids: Zondervan, 1998), 146–61 and in C. Marvin Pate and Calvin B. Haynes, *Doomsday Delusions, What's Wrong with Predictions about the End of the World,* 34–57.

19. The following is based on my article published with permission, "Revelation 6: An Early Interpretation of the Olivet Discourse," In *Criswell Theological Review,* vol. 8, no. 2, Spring 2011, 45–56.

The White Horse Judgment (Rev. 6:2) and the Olivet Discourse

The cavalier on the white horse, with bow and crown, finds two possible connections with the Olivet Discourse. It could be the triumph of the gospel that Jesus predicted would occur on earth before his return (see Matt. 24:14//Mark 13:10//Luke 21:12). This feature of the Olivet Discourse, however, seems to be ruled out because it is decidedly positive in meaning in contrast to the consistently negative connotations of the other seal judgments in Revelation 6. Second, the white horse rider could be equated with the false messiahs Jesus forecast in the Olivet Discourse would come before his return (see Matt. 24:4–5, 11, 23// Mark 13:5–6, 21–23//Luke 21:8). Indeed, Josephus recorded that ten Jewish messianic claimants eventually brought about the Jewish Revolt, thus demonstrating that they were false messiahs (*J.W.* 1.10.6/209; *Ant.* 10.1.3/19). The latter interpretation is certainly a foreboding eventuality and it fits nicely with the negative connotations of the other seal judgments in Revelation 6. For John's part, in the light of history he reduces the plurality of false messiahs in the Olivet Discourse to one— Nero/Domitian the antichrist.

The "already" aspect of the fulfillment of the first seal in Revelation 6 is, on this reading, the Jewish false messiahs who were the catalyst to the fall of Jerusalem to Rome in A.D. 70. The "not-yet" aspect of the fulfillment would then be Nero, as the following discussion reveals.

In a classic turning of the tables, John seems to be alluding to Rome's future defeat at the hands of its former emperor—Nero, especially if Revelation 6 draws on the Roman fear of a Parthian invasion. The Parthians were expert horsemen and archers, and they posed a constant threat to the Roman Empire in the first century. They were always poised to cross the Euphrates River, and in A.D. 62 their military leader, Vologesus, did attack some Roman legions. The Parthians rode white horses, and their founder, Seleucus, was named Nikator, "the victor." Furthermore if, as a number of scholars believe, the beast of 13:3 (cf. 17:11), who received a mortal wound in the head but was revived draws on the *Nero Redivivus* (revived) story, then the Parthian background of 6:2 is strengthened.

Although Nero's first five years as emperor were relatively good, it was downhill after that. He perpetrated one monstrosity after another, including the murders of foes, friends and family, sodomy, tyranny, and persecution of Christians (beginning in A.D. 64). Indeed, the title "beast" was a fitting one for him (13:1). So unpopular was Nero that toward the end of his reign (A.D. 67–68), there were open revolts against his authority in Gaul and Spain. Eventually, the Praetorian Guard and the Senate proclaimed him to be a public enemy and approved Galba as his successor. Nero fled and reportedly committed suicide by thrusting a sword through his throat on June 9, A.D. 68. Despite that fact, the rumor spread that he had not died but escaped to Parthia and would return with the Parthian army to regain his throne—hence the story of *Nero Redivivus*. This fearful expectation of the return of Nero, the antichrist, leading the Parthian cavalry riding on white horses with bows and arrows, going forth to conquer, makes good sense of the first horseman of the Apocalypse (cf. *Sibylline Oracles* 4:119–27).

This reading, then, of Revelation 6:2 takes into account both the fall of Jerusalem in A.D. 70 to the Romans (due to the false messiahs) the "already" aspect and a future fall of Rome to Nero *Redivivus* (see Revelation 13) and the Parthians the "not-yet" aspect.

The Red Horse Judgment (Rev. 6:3–4) and the Olivet Discourse

In the Olivet Discourse, Jesus acknowledged the certainty of war but added that that was not necessarily the sign that the end had totally arrived (Matt. 24:6–7//Mark 13:7–8//Luke 21:9–10; Rev. 6:3–4). It, like the other signs of the times, was only the beginning of "birth pains" (see Mark 13:7–8 and parallels). Many interpreters believe that Jesus's reference to the increase of wars here and in Revelation 6:3–4 (the second horseman) alludes to the first century. The already/not-yet eschatological tension helps explain this dynamic.

The peace that Caesar Augustus (31 B.C.–A.D. 14) established (*pax Romana*) throughout the Roman Empire was short-lived. Wars broke out in Britain, Germany, Armenia, and Parthia under Emperor Claudius (between A.D. 41 and 54). The period following Nero's death (A.D. 69) saw three emperors, Otho, Galba, and Vitellius, quickly rise and fall, amid civil upheavals and political chaos. So devastating was the period following Nero's death that it threatened to reduce the Roman Empire to rubble (Josephus, J.W. 4.9.2; cf. Tacitus *Histories* 1.2–3; Suetonius *Lives*, "Vespasian" 1). Especially relevant to the end time sign of wars and rumors of wars was the Jewish Revolt against Rome, which culminated in the fall of Jerusalem (A.D. 66–73). The Jewish war against Rome witnessed the deaths of thousands and thousands of Jews in Judea and the enslavement of thousands more. Josephus estimates that as many as 1,100,000 Jews were killed at that time (though he undoubtedly exaggerated the figure). Titus, the Roman general, razed the city to the ground and took 50,000 more Jewish captives back to Rome to form a part of his triumphant processional (*J.W.*, preface to 1 and 4; cf. 7.1.1).

For John, the Jewish Revolt was but one of a number of civil wars that threatened to undo the Roman Empire, and no Roman emperor could stop it; not Vespasian, Titus, or Domitian. Added to this foreboding concern was the ever-ready Parthian cavalry stationed across the Euphrates River, which was poised to strike at the heart of the Roman Empire (see Rev. 8:13–9:21).

Stated in terms of the already/not-yet fulfillments: the disruption of *pax Romana* in the first century was the "already" aspect of the unleashing of the rider on the red horse, a judgment that would soon culminate in the fall of Rome. The total collapse of her claim to peace is the "not-yet" aspect of divine wrath. To put it another way: since Rome destroyed the city of Jerusalem (the already aspect), then God will destroy the city of Rome when Jesus returns (the not-yet aspect).

The Black Horse Judgment (Rev. 6:5–6) and the Olivet Discourse

The inevitable consequence of war is famine, nowhere so starkly depicted as in Revelation 6:5–6 (cf. vv. 7–8), with its description of the third horseman. It would have been easy for the seer of the Apocalypse to envision war and famine. The Olivet Discourse does the same (Matt. 24:7//Mark 13:8//Luke 21:11). During Claudius's reign, famine occurred in Rome in A.D. 42, and food shortage was reported in Judea in 45–46, in Greece in 49, and in Rome again in 51, and quite often in Asia Minor including the time of Domitian, 92. The reference to the pair of scales and the inflated prices for food in 6:5–6 cannot help but recall the severe famine that occurred in Jerusalem during its siege by the Roman army (Matt. 24:7//Mark 13:8//Luke 21:11). During that time the inhabitants of Jerusalem had to weigh out their food and drink because of the scarcity of those necessities. So severe was it that even a mother could eat her child (*J.W.* 6.3.4; see also *J.W.* 5.10.5; cf. 6.5.1; Luke 21:23).

The fall of Jerusalem and the resulting famine may also explain the ironic statement in Revelation 6:6, "and do not damage the oil and the wine." The command to spare the oil and the wine is possibly an allusion to General Titus's order that even during the ransacking of Jerusalem, olive trees (for oil) and grapevines (for wine) were to be spared. If so, the fall of Jerusalem serves as the perfect backdrop for the third seal judgment (6:5–6), Indeed, Jesus's statement in the Olivet Discourse that such horrors were but the beginning of the end (Mark 13:7), the initiation of the messianic woes (13:8), points in that direction. We should also refer to the similar edict of Domitian restricting the growing of vines in Asia in A.D. 92. For John, such famines well could have signaled to him that the parousia of Christ was near and with it the fall of Rome. Thus we may say that the famine in Jerusalem occasioned by the siege of that city by Roman legions along with the other famines that plagued the Roman Empire constituted the "already" aspect of the judgment of the black horse, which served as a forecast of doom at the return of Christ, and the ultimate famine to be inflicted upon Rome constituted the "not-yet" aspect of that judgment.

The Pale Horse (Rev. 6:7–8) and the Olivet Discourse

There is no explicit mention of death in the Olivet Discourse, but that reality accompanied wars and famines, as we saw above.

The fourth seal judgment is death personified (cf. Rev. 1:18; 20:13–14). As mentioned above, thousands and thousands of Jews were killed in the first revolt against Rome. But, according to Revelation 6:7–8, the four horsemen of the Apocalypse will one day retaliate against the Roman Empire, killing one-fourth of its people. And that would only be the beginning (see Revelation 8–16). Here, again, we see the already/not-yet eschatological tension: the already—the thousands of Jews killed in the Jewish Revolt/the not-yet—the future death of a significant portion of the Roman Empire at the return of Christ.

Christian Martydom (Rev. 6:9–11) and the Olivet Discourse

There are three interlocking destinies delineated in the Olivet Discourse and the fifth seal judgment of Revelation: the persecution of Jesus's disciples, Jesus's crucifixion, and the destruction of Jerusalem. The apparent connection to be made from these three destinies is that Israel's crucifixion of Jesus and subsequent persecution of his disciples brought about divine destruction on Jerusalem. Rome, too, must be factored into the fifth seal judgment.

The Olivet Discourse ominously predicts that Jesus's disciples will be persecuted (Matt. 24:9–10//Mark 13:9–19//Luke 21:12–19). Luke's second volume, Acts, records the fulfillment of Jesus's prediction, describing the persecutions of Peter and John (Acts 4:1–12; cf. 12:3–19), Stephen (Acts 6:8–7:60), James (Acts 12:1–2), Paul (Acts 16:22–30; 21:27–23:35), and many other Jewish Christians (Acts 8:1–4). In being "delivered up" to the Jewish and Roman authorities, the disciples were repeating the destiny of Jesus (notably, his suffering and death).

Later church tradition understood that the fall of Jerusalem in A.D. 70 came about as a result of divine judgment because of the Jewish persecution of Jesus's followers. For example, Eusebius, the fourth-century church historian, refers to the belief of many that God judged Jerusalem because it killed the half-brother of Jesus, James the Just (*Eccl. Hist.* 2.23). Even Josephus attributed Jerusalem's fall to divine judgment. Writing of the burning and destruction of the temple in late August/early September A.D. 70, he observes that the fire was not ultimately ignited by the Romans: "The flames . . . owed their origin and cause to God's own people" (*J.W.* 6.4.5).

The same threefold intertwined destinies surface in Revelation 6:9–11, the fifth seal judgment. It is clear that the martyrs described therein are Christians. Corresponding descriptions of these saints occur in 7:9–17 and 14:1–5. Their exemplar in suffering for righteousness is Jesus, the Lamb that was slain (5:6–14). One may ask, "Who were the perpetrators of such injustice and violence on the people of God"? Revelation 6:10 provides a clue: It was "the inhabitants of the earth" (cf. 3:10; 11:10). That is the "earth-dwellers" may have been Jerusalemites who killed Jesus.

Rome too had a hand in persecuting early Christianity, beginning with Nero, as the preceding references in Revelation suggest. Moreover, it is probably the case that Revelation 6:9 (cf. 12:11) alludes to the Neronian slaughter of Christians in Rome in A.D. 64 as a scapegoat for the emperor's burning of that city. Indeed, the reference in Revelation 6:10 to God as *despotēs* is an affront to the emperor's claim to be *despotēs* (lord/master) (see Philo, *Flacc.* 4.23; Dio Chrysostum, *Or.* 45.1).

For the apostle John, one day the tables will be turned: Christ will avenge the blood of his followers (Rev. 6:10). Such divine retaliation will happen when the divinely predetermined number of Christians are martyred (cf. *1 Enoch* 47:4; *4 Ezra* 4:36; *2 Apoc. Bar.* 23.5, Rom. 11:25; *Mart. Pol.* 14; Eusebius, *Hist. Eccl.* 5.1.13).

We see in the Christian martyrs of Revelation 6:9–11 the already/not-yet pattern. The former is reflected in the fact that ancient Jews persecuted Jesus and his followers, as did Nero and the Roman government (cf. Rev. 6:9–11 with the Synoptic references [Matt. 24:9–10//Mark 13:9–19//Luke 21:12–19] and the Acts material). Consequently, God judged Jerusalem at the hands of the Romans. The latter aspect—the not-yet—is assumed in Revelation 6:9–11. If Jerusalem paid the price for spilling the blood of the martyrs, then so will Rome pay the price for its shedding of the blood of the followers of Christ at the parousia.

Cosmic Upheaval (Rev. 6:12–17) and the Olivet Discourse

The Old Testament associated cosmic disturbances with the coming of divine judgment, especially the Day of the Lord (Isa. 34:4; Ezek. 32:7; Joel 3:3–4; Hab. 2:6, 21). That Jesus should use such apocalyptic imagery to describe the fall of Jerusalem (see Matt. 24:29//Mark 13:24//Luke 21:11, 25–26) was not unusual. Josephus did the same (*J.W.* 6.5.1.3). The sixth seal judgment of the Apocalypse (6:12–17) seems to also utilize apocalyptic language to rehearse cosmic disturbances in the first century. The opening of the sixth seal (6:12–17) introduces several spectacular physical phenomena that strike terror into people of every social rank, so that they seek to hide from God and the Lamb. These phenomena may refer to various earthquakes in the first century, three mentioned by Tacitus (*Annals* 12.43, 58; 14.27)—in A.D. 51, 53, and 60—and others during the seventh decade (mentioned by Seneca, *Naturales Quaestiones* 6.1; 7.28). The darkening of the sun perhaps refers to solar eclipses that occurred between A.D. 49 and 52, or to phenomena associated with the eruption of Vesuvius in A.D. 79. Possibly the islands being moved from their places (Rev. 6:14) is connected with "the sudden formation of new islands" (e.g., Thera and Terasia; cf. Seneca *Naturales Quaestiones* 6.2, 6). One might also call attention to the connection between Revelation 6:16 and Luke 23:30, both of which allude to the destruction of Jerusalem in A.D. 70. Indeed, the cosmic upheaval promised in Revelation 6:12–17 is reminiscent of Roman prodigies, pagan prophetic warnings of the coming divine judgment upon Rome because of her impiety (so, for example, Tacitus, *Hist.* 1.3.3; 1.86; *Annals* 12.64; 14.12; 15.47). Revelation 6:12–17, then, is John's way of applying apocalyptic judgment to Jerusalem and Rome.

The preceding material also follows the already/not-yet pattern that runs throughout Revelation 6 with reference to the connections between the Olivet Discourse and the fall of Jerusalem to the Romans, and the future parousia of Christ, in the following way: If God judged Jerusalem for persecuting followers of Jesus, then he will certainly judge Rome for doing the same. Indeed, according to John, the first-century portents of earthquakes, eclipses, and the eruption of Vesuvius anticipate the future demise of Rome at the parousia. Understanding, then, the magnitude of such events could only be described in cosmic terms.

John's Ambiguity Regarding the Fall of Jerusalem in A.D. 70

The final brief point to be made in this section relates to the apostle John's ambiguity regarding the fall of Jerusalem to the Romans in A.D. 70. A review of the seal judgments of Revelation 6 indicates that John, a Jewish Christian, sometimes interprets Rome's future fall as receiving its just dessert for destroying the holy city. In line with this attitude, did Rome perpetrate war (second seal judgment), famine (third seal judgment), and death (fourth seal judgment) on Jerusalem? Then God will avenge the Jewish people by destroying the Roman Empire at the *parousia* of Christ. The other three seal judgments, however, seem to view Jerusalem as deserving of the divine punishment it received at the hands of the Romans. Thus, the holy city allowed false messiahs to bring about the Jewish Revolt (first seal judgment) and Jerusalem's persecution of Jesus and his followers incurred God's wrath as spelled out in seal judgments numbers 5 and 6. How, then, are we to account for John's ambiguity regarding Jerusalem's fall to the Romans?

The Old Testament story of God's relationship with Jerusalem seems to provide the answer, especially as it is related in Habakkuk. There the reader learns that God promised to raise up pagan Babylonia to judge Jerusalem because of its (Israel's) idolatry, but by way of contrast in the future God will destroy Babylonia (through Persia) for harming Jerusalem. The same dynamic, I suggest, is at work in the seal judgments of Revelation 6 thereby accounting for John's ambiguity toward the fall of Jerusalem in A.D. 70. Thus God raised up Rome (the new Babylon, see Revelation 17–18) to destroy Jerusalem because of its idolatry (manifested through rejecting Jesus and his followers), but in the near future God will raise up a new Persia (*Nero Redivivus* and the Parthians) to punish the Romans. This Old Testament phenomenon nicely explains John's perspective toward Jerusalem in the seal judgments, as indeed it also explains the trumpet and bowl judgments of Revelation.

Conclusion to the Olivet Discourse and Revelation 6

This section made three points regarding the seal judgments of Revelation 6 and the Olivet Discourse. First, we echoed those scholars connecting the seal judgments and the Olivet Discourse. All of the seal judgments, except death (but even that is implied), parallel Jesus's predictions about the future as recorded in the Synoptic Gospels. Second, we argued that Revelation 6 is John's reapplication of the past fall of Jerusalem/Olivet Discourse to the future fall of Rome at the parousia of Christ. Third, we suggested that the apostle John's ambiguity toward the fall of Jerusalem to Rome is explained by the Old Testament phenomenon recorded in a book like Habakkuk—God used Babylonia to punish Jerusalem but later raised up Persia to destroy Babylonia for doing so. For John's day that meant that even though God punished Jerusalem through the hands of Rome He will shortly destroy Rome for doing so through a new Persia, Nero, and the Parthians.

That Israel's story informs all of the above three points is clear: Israel's sin brought about God's judgment of the Jerusalem temple by the Romans in A.D. 70. Thus, even though Israel had long since returned to her land in 539 B.C., she was very much still in exile. The hope, however, for an imminent destruction of Rome by God in return for destroying Jerusalem, undergird the Olivet Discourse and Revelation 6 as well. The positive counterpart to the judgment of Jerusalem will occur at the return of Christ and the re-gathering of Israel to embrace him as their anointed one (see Mark 13:24–27 and parallels).

Furthermore, the four apocalyptic features occurring in Daniel recur in the Olivet Discourse: false Christs form the background to the antichrist (Mark 13:21–23 and parallels); the abomination of desolation of the Jerusalem temple (Mark 13:1–4 and parallels); the anointed one (the true Christ, Mark 13:26–27 and parallels [drawing on Daniel 7]); who re-gathers the elect, the twelve tribes of Israel (Mark 13:27).

Revelation

In dealing with Revelation we offer three comments. First, we will apply the genre of apocalypticism to Revelation. This approach will also come in handy for the next chapter when we focus on themes in apocalypticism, including Revelation. Second, we will show that the story of Israel thoroughly informs the Apocalypse. Third, we will call attention to the four eschatological features therein. [20]

---

20. Because Aune has provided a thorough explanation of each of these categories we repeat here only a selection of texts to provide a feel for the taxonomy. See Aune, *Revelation 1–5*, 52A, lxxviii–lxxix.

Revelation and the Genre of Apocalypticism

Component	Revelation	Comments
Manner (Form)	1. Medium: 1.1 Visual 1.1.1 Visions: 4:1–22:9	When John is caught up to heaven, the official apocalyptic visions begin.
	1.1.2 Epiphanies: 1:9–3:22	Two epiphanies present themselves in this passage: the appearance of Jesus, the heavenly Son of Man who is also the Ancient of Days (recall Daniel 7) and Jesus's dictation of proclamations to the seven churches.
	1.2 Auditions: 1.2.1 Discourse: 2:1–3:22; 21:5–8	Jesus's letters to the seven churches and the short discourse attributed to God constitute discourses, respectively.
	1.2.2 Dialogue: 7:13–17; 17:6b–18	There is a short dialogue between the seer and one of the 24 elders and a long dialogue between one of the bowl angels and the seer, respectively.
	1.3 Otherworldly journey: 4:1–22:9	The main otherworldly journey of John is described in this passage, with differing heavenly perspectives being presented.
	1.4 Writing: 5:1–8:1; 10:2, 8–11	The first of these passages is the book of the seven-sealed document, while the second is the little book the seer is commanded by the angel to eat.
	2. Otherworldly mediator: 1:2; 22:8–16	Although numerous angels appear in Revelation, only in 1:2 and 22:8–16 does this angel fulfill the role of the *angelus interpres*.
	3. Human recipient: 1:1,4,9; 22:8 3.1 Pseudonymity	The author identifies himself as John. Revelation does not fit this category since the author explicitly calls himself "John."
	3.2 Disposition of recipient: 1:9–10	John suffers the messianic woes like his fellow Christians; he is in a state of ecstasy.
	3.3 Reaction of recipient: 1:17; 5:4–5; 17:6; 19:10; 22:8–9	In these texts John falls as dead before the risen Lord, weeps that no one can open the seven-sealed book, is amazed at the allegorical figure of the whore, attempts to worship the angel speaking to him but is rebuffed for doing so, respectively.

Component	Revelation	Comments
Temporal Axis (Content)	4. Protology: 12:7–9: 12:10–11	This passage reflects the origin of evil in the world via the fall of the Serpent/Satan. In 12:10–11 it becomes an end-time event, creating an Urzeit-Endzeit *topos*.
	4.1 Cosmogony: 3:14; 4:11; 10:6; 14:7	The first passage asserts Christ's existence prior to creation while the other texts say the same of God.
	4.2 Primordial events: 12:7–9	Satan's protological expulsion from heaven.
	5. History, reviewed either: 5.1 Recollection of past: 17:9–11	An allusive reference to the past Roman Caesars.
	5.2 *Ex eventu* prophecy	There does not seem to such a category in Revelation.
	6. Present salvation through knowledge	This category does not seem to occur in Revelation.
	7. Eschatological Crisis: 6–18	A classic statement of the signs of the times or the messianic woes.
	7.1 Persecution: 2:10, 13; 6:9–11; 17:6; compare 1:9; 7:9, 14; 11:3–13; 12:11; 13:7; 14:13; 16:6; 18:24; 20:4	As 17:14 makes clear these persecutions are a part of the messianic woes/great tribulation.
	7.2 Other eschatological upheavals: 6:1–8:1; 8:2–9:21; 11:15–18; 15:1–16:21; 18:1–19:10	These passages attest to the judgments of the seals, trumpets, bowls, and the fall of Babylon.
	8. Eschatological judgment or destruction: 6–19	These chapters record the judgment and destruction that will come upon through the seal, trumpet, and bowl judgments.
	8.1 The wicked: 17:12–14/19:17–21; 1–24;18:1–24; 19:21; 20:11–15; 21:8	The first passage (a doublet) speaks of judgment on the Beast and ten allied kings. Rome is destroyed in 18:1–24, as are the Beast and the False Prophet in 19:21. The lost are cast into the lake of fire in 20:11–15 as is the second death in 21:8.
	8.2 The world: 20:11; 21:1	The old earth is destroyed and replaced by the new world in these two passages.
	8.3 Otherworldly beings: 19:20; 20:10	In 19:20 the Beast and False Prophet are thrown in the lake of fire as is Satan in 20:10.

Component	Revelation	Comments
Temporal Axis (Content)	9. Eschatological salvation: 9.1 Cosmic transformation: 21:1; 21:2–4; 21:9–22:5	In these passages the creation of the new heaven and a new earth are described.
	9.2 Personal salvation: 9.2.1 Resurrection: 1:5; 20:4–6; 20:11–15	In 1:9 all believers are promised resurrection while in 20:4–6 the martyrs are resurrected to reign in the temporary messianic kingdom and in 20:11–15 the general resurrection is described.
	9.2.2. Other forms of afterlife: 2:7; 22:14; 3:5, 22; 22:14; 7:13–17; 21:3–14; 22:3–5	In order, the righteous will eat of the tree of life, wear white robes, be exalted with Christ in heaven, have access to the New Jerusalem, and will dwell with God (7:13–17; 21:3–14; 22:3–5).
Spatial Axis (Content)	10. Otherworldly elements:	The entire book: heavenly son of man, ancient of days, angels, 144,000, two prophets, seven personages, New Jerusalem.
	10.1 Otherworldly regions: 4:1–5:14; 7:9–17; 8:2–5; 11:16–18; 12:10–12; 15:1–16:1; 19:1–8	These references present the heavenly hosts praising God.
	10.2 Otherworldly beings: 1:9–3:22; 4–5; 13; 16; 19; etc.	To the previous beings should be added Satan before he is cast out of heaven (12:7–9).
Parenesis (Content)	11. Parenesis: 1:1–3:22; 22:10–21 (framing sections of Revelation)	These instructions challenge the righteous to remain faithful and predict the coming judgment upon the wicked.
Concluding Instructions (Form)	12. Concluding Elements: 12.1 Instruction to recipient: 22:10	The angel tells John to keep the scroll open with the challenge to the wicked to keep doing so and receive their just judgment and to the righteous to remain so and receive God's blessing.
	12.2 Narrative conclusion: 22:10–21	A longer, more intense statement of 22:10.

Component	Revelation	Comments
Group in Crisis (Function)	13. Group in Crisis 13.1 Covenant curses:	
	1:7 [Zechariah 12:10]	
	1:9; 1:12–16 [Daniel 7: Son of Man who will bring the covenant curses to an end; cf. Daniel 9:1–27]	
	6:17 [day of God's wrath]	
	7:2–3 [Ezekiel 9:4]	
	6–7 [the past fall of Jerusalem; cf. 8–9; 15–18]	
	11:2; 14:14–20) with the messianic woes (1:9; 2:10; 2:13	
	6:9–11; compare 1:9; 7:9, 14; 11:3–13; 12:11; 13:7; 14:13; 16:6; 18:24; 20:4)	
	13.2 Covenant blessings: 1:3	blessing pronounced on the faithful
	7:14–17; 11:2, 15, 19	heavenly temple and the ark of the covenant
	21–22	New Jerusalem
	21:3–4	covenant formula, with the kingdom of God
	20	temporary messianic kingdom[22]

The Story of Israel in Revelation

Earlier in this chapter, we analyzed the seal judgments in Revelation 6 relative to the story of Israel. The same can be said of the trumpet and bowl judgments.

Trumpet Judgments of Revelation 8–9

John's parody of the fall of Jerusalem to Rome continues in the trumpet judgments of Revelation 8–9. The seven trumpet judgments mix together at least two images: Israelite history (the Egyptian plagues, but also the prophet's Joel's prediction of the coming locust invasion of Israel) and recent events in Rome's history (the eruption of Mount Vesuvius and an imminent Parthian invasion). The seer of Revelation uses these past hap-

---

21. Recall from the first chapter that I have added the function category with its inclusion of the covenant curses/messianic woes and the covenant blessings/kingdom of God/Messiah.

penings as the backdrop to foretell the coming fall of the Roman Empire. Since I have documented the following material elsewhere,[22] I simply summarize the summary of those findings in chart form:

Revelation 8–9	History (Already)	Prophecy (Not Yet)
8:1–13: 1–4 Trumpet Judgments	Egypt's enslavement of Jews/compare Roman destruction of Jerusalem (A.D. 70)	Future destruction of Rome using imagery of the eruption of Mt. Vesuvius/against backdrop of Egyptian plagues
9:1–19: 5–7 Trumpet Judgments	Babylon defeated Jerusalem (586 B.C.); Medo-Persian defeat of Babylon (539 B.C.)/Rome-now Babylon-defeated Jerusalem (A.D. 70)	Future end-time invasion of Rome by new Medo-Persian army (demonic, Parthian attack, with locust-like effort)

Bowl Judgments of Revelation 15–18

Our thesis for interpreting Revelation 15–16 is that the bowl judgments, like the trumpet judgments (Revelation 8–9), portray the imminent fall of Rome against the backdrop of the falls of Jerusalem in 586 B.C. and A.D. 70.

Did ancient Egypt enslave Israel? Then, consequently God defeated Egypt through the plagues of Moses and the Exodus. So will God upend the Romans with a new, unprecedented barrage of Egyptian-like plagues for defeating Jerusalem in A.D. 70 and carrying away into slavery thousands (50,000) of Jews (Bowls 1–5; Rev. 16:1–11). Added to this, did Babylonia destroy Jerusalem and its temple in 586 B.C.? Then, consequently God defeated Babylonia through Cyrus and the Medo-Persians. So will God defeat Rome through a new Medo-Persian empire—the Parthian empire from east of the Euphrates (bowls 6–7; Rev. 16:12–21).

The new material related to the bowl judgments—the battle of Armageddon (Rev. 16:16)—furthers the above connection. Did Rome invade Israel and destroy the holy city and the temple (A.D. 66–73)? Then God will soon regather the Roman Empire in Israel at Armageddon for the purpose of destroying that arrogant nation (cf. Rev. 16:12–21; Rev. 19:10; 20:9 with the Gog and Magog oracle in Ezekiel 38–39 [especially 38:8; 39:2, 4, 17]; cf. also Joel 3:2; Zech. 14:2; *4 Ezra* 13:34–35; *1 Enoch* 56:5–8; *Sibylline Oracles* 3.663–68; *2 Baruch* 70:7–10; 1 QM 1:10–11; 15:2–3). God will destroy Rome through the Parthians ("the kings of the earth" (Rev. 16:12); the New Medo-Persians.

---

22. C. Marvin Pate, *The Writings of John: A Survey of the Gospel, Epistles and Apocalypse* (Grand Rapids: Zondervan, 2011), 429.

Another way to express this divine retribution is that the seal judgments announce *that* Rome will fall shortly; the trumpet judgments proclaim *how* that will happen—through Egyptian-like plagues and a Parthian invasion; while the bowl judgments tell *where* the defeat of Rome will occur—at Armageddon in Israel.

All of these aspects bespeak the divine turning of the tables on Rome. Did she defeat Jerusalem? Then God will defeat her.

The Structure of Revelation and the Story of Israel

Aune proposes that the Apocalypse came together in two editions, the first being the most comprehensive.[23] The first edition (which may date to right before the fall of Jerusalem to Rome in A.D. 70) was Revelation 1:7–12a; 4:1–22:5. The second edition consisted of adding 1:1–6; 1:12b–3:22; 22:6–21. Aune argues that the first edition, the most extensive of the two, came about in two stages. John integrated six self-contained oracles (7:1–17; 10:1–11; 11:1–13: 12:1–7; 13:1–18; 14:1–20) into the three sets of seven judgments. Thus 7:1–17 was inserted between the sixth and seventh seal judgments; 10:1–11; 11:1–13 were inserted between the sixth and seventh trumpet judgments; with 12:1–7; 13:1–18; 14:1–20 being inserted right before the bowl judgments. Thus:

Seals (4:1–8:1)	Trumpets (8:2–11:18)		Bowls (15:1–16:21)
6th 7th	6th 7th		
7:1–17	10:1–11 12:1–7		
	11:1–13 13:1–18		
	14:1–20		

The second stage of the first and largest unit, according to Aune, consisted of inserting six more self-contained oracles this time between the contrasting visions of the Harlot of Rome (17:1–19:10) and the New Jerusalem, the pure Bride of Christ (21:9–22:9), which we signify by bold in order to serve as bookends to the other passages. Thus:
17:1–19:10; **19:11–21; 20:1–3; 20:4–6; 20:7–10; 20:11–15; 21:1–8;** 21:9–22:9
We agree with Aune and offer the following rationale behind these stages of the first edition, namely, they indicate that the story of Israel is driving the message of Revelation, a theory I have not seen suggested by scholars. These passages naturally unfold along the lines of sin and

23.   Aune, *Revelation 1–5*, cxx–cxxxiv.

judgment of Israel, the remnant as the beginning of the restoration of Israel, with the events accompanying the return of Christ as the completed restoration of Israel. We now proceed to unpack this thesis.

Sin and Judgment of Israel (6:1–17; 8:1–9:21; 15:1–16:21)

We have argued that the three sets of seven judgments in Revelation—seals, trumpets, bowls—were John's way of applying Rome's past destruction of Israel in A.D. 70 to a future fall of Rome. This conviction was the apostle's foundational message. Such a conviction bespeaks the story of Israel: sin, exile/judgment, and restoration.

The Remnant of Israel (7:1–17; 10:1–11; 11:1–13; 12:1–7; 13:1–18; 14:1–20)

We summarize here what we have developed at more length elsewhere, namely, that the tie that binds these six oracles is that of the remnant, Jewish Christians who survived the fall of Jerusalem in A.D. 70.[24]

The background of the sealing of the 144,000 faithful in **Revelation 7:1–17** is Ezekiel 9, where God put a mark (the letter *taw* in Hebrew) on the foreheads of those Jews who would survive the fall of Jerusalem to Babylon in 586 B.C. Likewise, Revelation 7 envisions that the Jewish Christians who escaped the fall of Jerusalem in a lull in the war in A.D. 68 were the protected remnant. The 144,000 is an obvious allusion to the twelve tribes of Israel (12 x 12,000).

In **Revelation 10:1–11** John eats the scroll of the covenant, which was sweet going into his mouth but bitter in his stomach. This symbolic act taps once again into Ezekiel 2:9; 3:3, whose same reactions of sweet and bittern correspond to the faithful remnant who would survive the fall of Jerusalem to the Babylonians and those who would not, respectively. So it is with John in A.D. 70. The same note is sounded in **Revelation 11:1–13**. There the temple falls to the Romans, but two witnesses emerge to preach the gospel, Moses and Elijah.[25] The one

---

24. See C. Marvin Pate, *The Writings of John*, 411–420, 431–436, 437–446, 447–454, 465–470, 465–470.

25. The task of identifying the two witnesses of Revelation 11:3–14 must take into account the Old Testament background drawn upon therein. Zechariah 3–4 and 6:19–24 speak of two eschatological figures in terms of two olive trees and two menorahs, which were probably Joshua the High Priest and Zerubbabel the Davidic prince. Revelation 11:4 presumes this background. Furthermore, the miraculous preaching and works of the two witnesses in Revelation 11 recall Elijah (cf. vv. 5–6a and the shutting up of the heavens from raining and consuming enemies with fire from heaven with 1 Kings 17–18; 2 Kings 1, respectively) and Moses (cf. v. 6b and turning water into blood and other plagues with Exod. 7:14–19; 7:14–11:10). Some futurists believe Moses and Elijah will return during the tribulation period to preach against the antichrist once the eschatological temple has been rebuilt. Others—some preterists—think the two witnesses were Peter and Paul who met with martyrdom in Rome under Nero (A.D. 64–68). Many interpreters, however, view the two witnesses to be

gave Israel its law and the other is associated with the remnant—the faithful 7,000 who would not succumb to idolatry.

In **Revelation 12:1–7** the remnant (the woman and her children represent true Israel suffering the messianic woes) escapes the wrath of Satan with God's new exodus into the wilderness. We will deal with **Revelation 13:1–18** in a later chapter, but here we simply note that Emperor Nero is called 666, using gematria. The proconsuls of Asia Minor were responsible for enforcing Caesar worship but there were those who resisted such idolatry and rather worshipped Christ. Revelation 13:9–18 anticipates that these true believers will go into captivity for their faith. Such language distinctly reminds one of the Jews' captivity to Babylon, but a remnant eventually returned home to Israel. Revelation 13 envisions such language as applying to the Jewish Christian remnant. In **Revelation 14:1–20** we meet once again with the sealed 144,000 remnant as we did in Revelation 7. The difference is that now the remnant accompanies Christ as holy warriors against Rome.

If we are accurate in our understanding of these six self-contained oracles, their placement into the three sets of judgments makes perfect sense. In between each set of judgments John inserts the hope that despite the fall of Jerusalem to Rome, a remnant will escape and live to fight another day. Indeed, the Jewish Christian remnant constitutes the beginning of the promised restoration of Israel (cf. Romans 11).

The Restoration of Israel (19:11–21; 20:1–3; 20:4–6; 20:7–10; 20:11–15; 21:1–8)

It is no accident that John places these six self-contained oracles between his two visions of Rome the harlot and the New Jerusalem the bride of Christ. They combine to illustrate the restoration of Israel in terms of God defeating the Romans in return for Rome's destruction of Jerusalem. Such judgment is a theme we saw earlier at work in this chapter, namely, that in the end of time God will defeat Israel's enemies on the way to restoring the holy city. In that light we offer a brief summary of these six passages.

Revelation 19:1–11 comes on the heels of Revelation 17–18's portrayal of Rome as a harlot that God will destroy as he did to Israel's oppressor Babylonia long ago. The presentation of Jesus's return is presented in terms of the Old Testament's prediction that Yahweh as a

---

a symbolic portrayal of the prophetic witness of the church in the first century A.D.. Thus, the two olive trees/menorah picture the witness of the church in its priestly (Joshua) and kingly (Zerubbabel) functions. Indeed, Revelation 1:6; 5:10; 20:6 describe the church as "a kingdom and priests." And the church also fulfilled the roles of the law (Moses) and the prophets (Elijah) in its testimony to Christ. We think it possible that John intended to call to mind Peter and Paul as representatives of the church there in Rome while drawing on the Moses and Elijah typology.

warrior would defend Israel in the end-time by defeating her enemies. That final victory would be followed by the messianic banquet.

In **Revelation 20:1–3**, Satan is bound during the temporary messianic kingdom. Recall that the eternal kingdom of God and the temporary messianic kingdom are the covenant blessings intensified at the end of history. **Revelation 20:4–6** indicates that those who are faithful to Christ will reign with him in that kingdom.

Revelation 20:7–10 uses the language of Ezekiel 38–39 to depict the final destruction of the enemies of the people of God—Gog and Magog—who stage one last stand, only to be finally destroyed. In **Revelation 20:11–15** the enemies of the church, the true Israel of God (see Gal. 6:16), are judged by almighty God.

Revelation 21:1–8 paints a beautiful picture of Israel's restoration as the New Jerusalem in whom God's covenant will be fully realized. A voice from God's throne proclaims, "Behold the tabernacle of God is among men, and He will dwell among them, and they will be His people, and God Himself will be anong them" (vv. 3–4, cf. v. 7). This promise taps into the new covenant formula. Furthermore, just as Isaiah 56–66 prophesied, the restoration of Jerusalem will be a new creation, with the old things passing away (v. 4).

Our thesis seems confirmed. In the midst of Israel's sin and judgment, God provided a remnant as a foretaste of the coming restoration of Israel.[26]

Four Apocalyptic Features in Revelation

The four apocalyptic features that we have seen in Daniel and the Olivet Discourse along with Revelation 6 also manifest themselves in the Apocalypse. (1) The abomination of the Jerusalem temple is described in Revelation 11:1–6 but is replaced by the New Jerusalem temple in Revelation 21–22. (2) Connected with the destruction of the temple is the beast, the antichrist (Nero/Domitian) in Revelation 13–18. (3) The anointed one is, of course, Jesus Christ, the heavenly Son of Man (Rev. 1:12–18) the hero of the book (see Rev. 1:1–3). (4) It is he who will return to regather the twelve tribes of Israel (Rev. 7, 14) to their land (Rev. 16).

---

26. My view here has significant agreement with the dispensational interpretation of Revelation: the 144,000 are Jewish Christians, while the members of the unnumbered group are Gentile Christians; the millennium will witness the restoration of Israel; Revelation 20 is best understood as affirming a temporary millennial kingdom on earth; Israel's Gentile enemies will be destroyed. My reading of Revelation, however, also significantly differs from dispensational interpretation in that the timing of the great tribulation according to Revelation is *now*, There will be no rapture of the church before the messianic woes, because that along with the kingdom of God are occurring at the present time. There will be no need for a rebuilt Jerusalem temple, because God the Father and the Son will replace that temple with their presence.

Chapter in Review

This chapter has attempted to uncover the historical background of the biblical prophetic-apocalyptic material which is the story of Israel. We have tracked four responses to that story, especially concerning the national crises in Israel.

First, we examined apocalyptic retellings of the story of Israel in light of the imminent end/actual fall of Jerusalem to the Babylonians in 586 B.C.: Isaiah 24–27; 56–66; Joel 2–3; Ezekiel 38–39.

Second, we then examined an apocalyptic retelling of the story of Israel in light of the extension of the Babylonian exile from 70 to 490 Years: Daniel 9–12.

Third, we investigated an apocalyptic retelling of the story of Israel in light of the failure of the restoration of Israel under Cyrus the Persian: Zechariah 9–14.

Fourth, we considered the Olivet Discourse and Revelation 6 as well as Revelation as a whole to be apocalyptic responses to the fall of Jerusalem to Rome in A.D. 70.

In the chapter to follow, we will take a step back and discuss the themes of apocalyptic literature that emerge from both Daniel and Revelation, as well as from famous Second Temple Jewish writings that are apocalyptic in genre.

3

THE FUNCTION OF APOCALYPTICISM AND THE THEME OF ISRAEL'S STORY

The Chapter at a Glance

In this chapter we will use the function category of the genre of apocalypticism as a grid through which to interpret the eschatological themes occurring in seven typical apocalyptic works. Accordingly, this chapter will unfold in six points.

- Israel's story as the key to interpreting the genre of apocalypticism
- Israel's exile as the intensification of the covenant curses into the messianic woes
- The covenant blessings as culminating in the arrival of the kingdom of God/Messiah
- Present salvation
- The condition for entering into the eschatological covenant blessings
- The assurance of the coming covenant blessings/kingdom of God or Messiah

IN THIS CHAPTER WE HIGHLIGHT RECURRING ESCHATOLOGICAL themes found in apocalyptic literature, both canonical and non-canonical.

We will do so by using the third component we suggested in our first chapter that completes the genre of apocalypticism, namely, the function of that type of literature. The reader will recall that the function component of apocalypticism is none other than Israel's story placed in an apocalyptic setting: the writer believes Israel is living in the last days—the covenant curses have intensified into the messianic woes which will precede the culmination of the covenant blessings into the eternal kingdom of God or the temporary messianic kingdom. We supply here in chart form the occurrence of the function component in seven typical apocalyptic books pertinent to our study, both canonical and non-canonical. In another study not published I have applied the entire taxonomy of the genre of apocalypticism to these seven works.

COVENANT CURSES/MESSIANIC WOES: EXHORTATIONS

Apocalyptic Book:	Covenant Curses and Messianic Woes:
Daniel	Covenant curses (9:1–26) Messianic woes (8:19; 12:1, 11–12)
1 Enoch	Covenant curses (103:9–104:8) Messianic woes (62:4–6)
Dead Sea Scrolls	Covenant curses and messianic woes are intermingled: 1QM 1:1–6; 3:6; 12:14–15; Temple Scroll (11Q 19; 55:15; 56:8; 59:1–9; 64:7–9).
Revelation	Covenant curses (1:7 [Zechariah 12:10]; 1:9; 1:12–16 [Daniel 7-Son of Man who will bring the covenant curses to an end Daniel 9:1–27]; 6:17 [day of God's wrath]; 7:2–3 [Ezekiel 9:4]; 6–7 [the past fall of Jerusalem; compare 8–9; 15–18]; 11:2; 14:14–20) Messianic woes (1:9; 2:10; 2:13; 6:9–11; compare 7:9, 14; 11:3–13; 12:11; 13:7; 14:13; 16:6; 18:24; 20:4)
Testament of Moses	Covenant curses (2-sin/Deuteronomy 28:15; 5:1–6:1/Deut. 32:15–18; punishment–3:1–4/Deut. 28:16–68; 8/Deut. 32:19–27; 9:1–5) Messianic woes (10:1–10)
4 Ezra	Covenant curses (3:1–5:20; 5:23–30; 6:35–9:26) Messianic woes (3:23–30; 6:35–9:26; 9:28–10:24)
2 Baruch	Covenant curses (1:4–5; 4:1; 5:1–4; 6:1–8; 7:1–8:5; 10:1–11:7; 19:1; 84:1–6); Messianic woes (26:1–29:8; 35:1–43:3; 53–70:10)

COVENANT BLESSINGS/KINGDOM OF GOD/ CONSOLATION[1]

Apocalyptic Book:	Covenant Blessings and Kingdom of God/Messiah:
Daniel	Compare 9:27–30 (covenant blessings/restoration of Israel with 2:44 [the kingdom of God]; 12:1–3 [resurrection of the righteous])
1 Enoch	Covenant blessings (1–5; 81–82; 91; 92–105) Age to come in heaven reached temporarily via mystic ascent (14; 70–71)
Dead Sea Scrolls	Compare the covenant blessings with the restoration of Israel/kingdom of God (1QM 1:1–2, 9; 12:3; Temple Scroll (11Q 2:1–15; 29:7–9)
Revelation	Covenant blessings (1:3 [one of seven blessings pronounced on the faithful]; 7:14–17; 11:2, 15, 19 [the heavenly temple and the ark of the covenant]; 21–22 [the new Jerusalem]; 21:3–4 [covenant formula] Kingdom of God (7:14–17; 11:2, 15, 19) Temporary messianic kingdom (20)
Testament of Moses	Covenant blessings (3:5–4:4/Deut. 30:2; 9/Deut. 32:28–34; 4:5–9/Deut. 30:3–10; 10/Deut. 32:35–43) Kingdom of God/restoration of Israel (10:1–10)
4 Ezra	Covenant blessings (6:25–28; 6:38–59; 10:38–59; 11–13) Restoration of Israel (9:28–13) Temporary messianic kingdom (7:26–44; 12:31–34)
2 Baruch	Covenant blessings (4:1–7; 30:1–5; 82–86) Glories of the age to come (31:5–32:7; 44:3–15; 46:5–6; 51:7–10; 77:5–7, 13–15) Temporary messianic kingdom (29:3–30:1; 40:1–4; 72:2–74:3)

In what follows we will use the function category as a grid through which to interpret the eschatological themes occurring in the above seven books. Accordingly, this chapter will unfold in six points: (1) Israel's story as the key to interpreting the genre of apocalypticism; (2) Israel's exile as the intensification of the covenant curses into the messianic woes; (3) the covenant blessings as culminating in the ar-

---

1. The reader will recall from chapter 1 that the function component of the genre of apocalypticism corresponds to the group in crisis, 14.1/14.2, respectively.

rival of the kingdom of God/Messiah; (4) present salvation; (5) the condition for entering into the eschatological covenant blessings; and (6) the assurance of the coming covenant blessings/kingdom of God or Messiah. When it is all said and done, this chapter will have applied the story of Israel to all fourteen features of the genre of apocalypticism.

ISRAEL'S STORY AS THE KEY TO INTERPRETING THE GENRE OF APOCALYPTICISM

In this section we offer three observations: Moses and Israel's story; the purported authors of the preceding apocalyptic books and Israel's story; the summary of Israel's story that each of those books provides.

Moses and Israel's Story

Thus far we have defined Israel's story as her sin, exile, and restoration. It is important that we see where that story of Israel officially began, namely, with Moses and, in particular, the book of Deuteronomy. Moses is of course the originator of Israel's story, which is spelled out in the book of Deuteronomy. That book, following the Suzerain-Hittite treaty, provides the structure of God's covenant with Israel.

Hittite Treaty	Deuteronomy
Preamble	1:1–5
Historical Dialogue	1:6–3:29
Stipulations	4:1–26:19
Curses/Blessings	27:1–30:8
Document clause	31:9, 24–26
Appeal to witnesses	31:26–32:47

Components 3 and 4 highlight Israel's story. The stipulations specify that Israel is to keep the Torah and, in doing so, experience the covenant blessings. Should Israel sin against the Torah, however, her fate will be the covenant curses expressed in terms of judgment and exile. For our purposes, we note that all of the apocalyptic literature included in this study presuppose the covenant format of Deuteronomy. Indeed, *Testament of Moses* explicitly follows such a structure as it forecasts Israel's story of sin, exile, and restoration.

The Purported Authors of the Preceding Apocalyptic Books and Israel's Story

Choosing these heroes of the Hebrew faith did more than legitimate the pseudonymous[2] authors of their respective works (Daniel, Enoch, the Old Testament prophets appealed to by the Dead Sea Scrolls, Revelation, Moses, Ezra, and Baruch). These appealed to authors were deeply involved in Israel's story. Here we include those Old Testament authors from our last chapter whose writings are not apocalyptic in genre per se, but which do include apocalyptic themes: Isaiah 24–27; Isaiah 56–66; Joel 2–3; Ezekiel 38–30, and Zechariah 9–14. We also include Jesus's Olivet Discourse. In what follows we will list the authors according to their respective relationships to the phases of Israel's story: sin, exile, restoration, after which we will offer an explanation.

Sin	Exile	Restoration
Enoch	Baruch	Enoch
Moses	Ezekiel	Dead Sea Scrolls
Isaiah	Daniel	Olivet Discourse
Joel	Zechariah	Revelation
	Ezra	

Before looking at all the details, however, it is worth noting that the five books comprising *1 Enoch* tell Israel's story.

Sin	**The Book of the Watchers** (1–36) describes the above story of Israel regarding the fallen angels.
	The Astronomical Book (72–82), among other astronomical secrets, presents the sin that the Watchers taught humanity in general and Israel in particular, namely, to worship God according to the solar calendar rather than the divinely approved lunar calendar. Thereby the Watchers deceived the world and even Israel in worshipping the wrong calendar.[3]
Exile	**The Animal Apocalypse** (83–90) envisions the unfolding in history of the sin, exile, and restoration of Israel, with emphasis on sin and the resulting exile.

2. Again, I question that Daniel is pseudonymous, and I take it that the apostle John is the author of Revelation.

3. Jubilees and the Dead Sea Scrolls also follow the solar calendar in contrast to the lunar calendar of mainline Judaism.

| Restoration | **The Parables of Enoch** (37–71) predict that the Son of Man/Messiah/Elect One (all the same) will restore Israel in the eschatological future. |
| Exhortation | **The Apocalypse of Weeks** (91–105) challenges the reader to remember the two ways tradition of Deuteronomy 30:15: Choose life by obeying the covenant law, or choose death by disobeying that covenant law. This passage is the nub of Israel's story. |

Sin

Enoch: In Genesis, the chronological order from Enoch on runs as follows: Enoch (Genesis 5), the fallen angels (Genesis 6), the flood (Genesis 6–9), the table of nations and the tower of Babel (Genesis 10–11), Abraham and the patriarchs (Genesis 12–50).[4] *First Enoch* interprets this sequence as follows: the fallen angels are called the Watchers because they beheld women and cohabitated with them producing giants/demons which caused the need for the flood to cleanse the earth. Moreover, these Watchers constituted the seventy fallen angels who controlled the seventy nations of the then known world. Enoch is raptured to heaven and has a vision of the big picture of the influence of the Watchers, which was twofold. First, the Watchers taught the human race sin which resulted in the divine judgment of the flood. Second, the Watchers also influenced Israel to sin, setting in motion Israel's story of sin, exile, restoration.

Testament of Moses: *The Testament of Moses* is structured on the pattern of the story of Israel—sin, exile, restoration—as spelled out in Deuteronomy, Moses' farewell speech to Israel. The emphasis on Moses' farewell speech is on the inevitability of Israel's sin and exile.

Isaiah and Joel: The classical prophets, including Isaiah, considered their calling to be that of enforcing the covenant. Thus Isaiah presumes Israel's story, with Isaiah 1–40 announcing that Israel's sin will lead her into captivity while chapters 24–27/56–66 envision Israel's future restoration. Joel 2–3 does the same.

Exile

Baruch: In the Old Testament, Baruch was the prophet Jeremiah's secretary, who was directed by his mentor to send a letter to the Jewish exiles in Babylonia telling them that their stay in captivity was going to last seventy years. Later in the second century B.C., the Old Testament apocryphal book Baruch was composed to elaborate on the exilic letter

---

4. The *Testaments of the Twelve Patriarchs* consists of apocalyptic predictions by each of Israel's patriarchs, all of which deal with the story of Israel.

by rooting Israel's experience in the sin, exile, and restoration pattern. The apocalyptic book of *2 Baruch* does the same but it is dated to the first century A.D.

Ezekiel: The book of Ezekiel sends the message to the Jews in Babylonian exile that God is with them even though the Jerusalem temple is in ruins. It too rehearses Israel's story under the rubric of sin, exile, and restoration.

Daniel: As we saw in our chapter 2, the book of Daniel presupposes Israel's story; indeed it spells it out in chapter nine. That chapter is interesting because it signals that Israel's exile will last not 70 years, but 490 years!

Zechariah: Technically, the prophet Zechariah was written after Israel returned to her homeland; in other words, after the exile. Yet, the realization was dawning on Zechariah, Haggai, and Malachi that even though Israel had returned to her land, she was still in exile.[5]

Ezra: The same could be said of Ezra–Nehemiah as well. Indeed, Ezra the scribe began a renewal movement to obey the Torah like never before, culminating in the some 6,000 oral laws of the later Pharisaic tradition.

Restoration

Enoch: Not only does the apocalyptic seer predict the whole panorama of Israel's sin, exile, and restoration (*a lá 1 Enoch*), but according to chapter 14 Enoch actually experienced the restoration proleptically via mystic ascent to heaven. *First Enoch* 14 is the first written experience of *merkabah* mysticism, a religious encounter that granted the seer a temporary view in heaven of the coming restoration of Israel coming to earth.

Dead Sea Scrolls: The authors of the Dead Sea Scrolls claimed to experience through mystic worship with the angels in heaven around the divine throne the coming restoration of Israel (see Songs of the Sabbath Sacrifice). Indeed, according to the *Damascus Covenant* (CD) and the *Community Rule* (1QS) becoming a member of the Essene community involved them in the annual new-covenant renewal service. These considerations indicate that the authors of the Dead Sea Scrolls believed themselves to be the new-covenant community, the *avant garde* of the restoration of Israel.

The Olivet Discourse: As is commonly now recognized by New Testament scholars, Jesus announced that in his works and words the kingdom of God had dawned. The Olivet Discourse assumes that, predicting the signs of the times and the return of Christ in glory to institute the long-hoped-for restoration of Israel, though considerably redefined.

---

5. A thesis made famous by N. T. Wright in his works, for example, *The New Testament and the People of God, Jesus and the Victory of God*, and now in his *Paul and the Faithfulness of God*.

Revelation: John the prophet (to be equated with, I believe, John the apostle) is also an enforcer of the Old Covenant now replaced with the new covenant of Jesus. Revelation therefore announces that the new covenant blessings belong to followers of Jesus while the covenant curses are falling upon the followers of the beast.[6]

The Summary of Israel's Story That Each of Those Books Provides

Here we simply note that Israel's story informs the history category of the content section of the genre of apocalypticism. In other words, Israel's sin, exile, and restoration, or some part of it, inform every text we have included. We simply list, therefore, the passages and make the connections with Israel's story.[7]

Recollection of the Past

Daniel: Daniel 7:9–14 recalls the history of Adam and the fall using the imagery of the heavenly Son of Man and the four beasts. Israel's story is reflected in the following way: Israel has repeated Adam's sin, sending her away into exile but in the end time the heavenly Son of Man, the true Israel, will rescue God's people.

1 Enoch: Enoch receives a vision that remembers the primordial past of the appearance of the heavenly Son of Man (48); a short history of the fall of Jerusalem (56:1–57:3); followed by the dream visions which rehearse the time from the fall of the Watchers (also called "stars") all the way up to the Maccabean Revolt, the presumed restoration of Israel (83–90); with the apocalypse of weeks rehearsing Israel's history up to the fall of Jerusalem (93).

Dead Sea Scrolls: CD (*Damascus Covenant*) and 1QS (*the Community Rule*) provide a covenant renewal service in which Israel's story (sin-exile-restoration through the Qumran community) is rehearsed while 4QMMT (*Some Works of the Torah*) offers its understanding of what separates its authors from Jerusalem, namely, adherence to the Torah through the perspective of the Teacher of Righteousness.

Revelation 4–22: These chapters recall the sin and exile of Israel with the parousia of Christ providing the true restoration of the people of God, as we argued in chapter two.

Testament of Moses: In 1:1–18, Moses says that God planned before creation to create the book of the covenant (Deuteronomy), so that Israel will remember God's law after Moses is gone. *Testament of*

---

6. This overall point on the authors and the background of the story of Israel correspond to the genre of apocalypticism of form 3./3.1, human recipient and pseudonymity, respectively.

7. This summary of the story of Israel obviously corresponds with the history section of the content in the genre of apocalypticism—5/5.1/5.2

Moses is an eschatological reading of the sin, exile, and restoration of Israel.

4 Ezra: In 3:1–27, Ezra recalls the past history of Israel: the creation and fall of Adam, the patriarchs, the exile, the propagation of Adam's evil heart even in Israel thus precipitating the fall of Jerusalem to the Babylonians.[8]

2 Baruch 5:1–9:2; 53–72: *Second Baruch* 5:1–9:2 recalls the fall of Jerusalem to Babylonia while chapters 53–72 summarize Israel's history, from the creation to Abraham to the fall of the temple to the coming of the Messiah.

Ex Eventu Prophecy

Daniel: Many scholars think chapters 2 and 7 portray the four kingdoms as predictions from the past that are actually recent events in history. The same is true of chapters 8–12, with their predictions of the fate of Israel relative to the tension between the Ptolemaic and Seleucid empires, along with the coming restoration of Israel. In other words, the sin, exile, and restoration of Israel undergirds these chapters as it does all of Daniel 9.

1 Enoch: In 89:10–90:42, Enoch is presented as predicting the unfolding of history from his day onwards, including the flood, exodus, entrance into Canaan land, to the building of the temple to its destruction, to the return of the exile, through the Hellenistic period to the establishment of the messianic kingdom through the Maccabees.

Dead Sea Scrolls: The *Pesharim* interpret the Old Testament prophecies regarding the new covenant as predicting that the Qumran community will be the fulfillment of those predictions. *Pseudo-Daniel* does essentially the same thing. These Dead Sea Scrolls writings document their history as though it was predicted in the Old Testament. In other words, Israel's sin and exile will be reversed in the restoration by which God honors true Israel, the writers of the DSS (most likely the Essenes).

Testament of Moses: Chapters 2–11 present Moses as predicting the future of Israel to Joshua, from the possession of Canaan to the Babylonian destruction of the temple to the persecution by Antiochus Epiphanes to the rule of Herod the Great and ultimately to the future restoration due to renewed obedience to the Torah.

4 Ezra: In 11:12–39, Ezra is presented as predicting that Rome will be the fourth kingdom of Daniel 2 and 7.

2 Baruch 1:2–5; 5:1–9:2; 53–72: The prophecies of 1:2–5; 5:1–9:2, and 53–72 as well as a good portion of *2 Baruch* present past history as if it were still future, from the fall of the Babylonians (to the Romans in A.D. 70) to the messianic restoration of Israel.

---

8. *4 Ezra* consists of a Jewish apocalypse, chapters 3–14, with chapters 1–2 and chapters 15–16 representing Christian interpolations.

There can be little doubt from the history category of the content component that Israel's story is the major player in the genre of apocalypticism.

ISRAEL'S EXILE AS THE INTENSIFICATION OF THE COVENANT CURSES INTO THE MESSIANIC WOES

In this section we make two points based on the genre of apocalypticism: (1) protology, the origin of sin that precipitated Israel's story;[9] (2) which produced the judgment and exile of Israel, the covenant curses, that now has intensified into the messianic woes.

Protology: The Origin of Sin That Precipitated Israel's Story

Although other matters are touched upon in the apocalyptic texts falling into this section, the overriding concern of this material is to explain the origin of sin. Three explanations are offered, each of which impacts Israel in some way: the fall of Adam, the fall of the Watchers, and the fall of Satan.

The Fall of Adam

Perhaps the majority of the apocalyptic texts in the protology category concerned with the origin of sin point the finger of blame for sin in the world at Adam. Three things are blamed on Adam. First, Daniel 7:13–28 alludes to Adam's sin in the Garden of Eden as reverting the cosmos back into chaos. This retrogression is seen in the way that Daniel portrays the heavenly Son of Man as the replacement of Adam and the four beasts as representing primordial chaos rising up against Israel in the last days. Second, Adam's sin caused him to lose his divine glory. The Dead Sea Scrolls claim that they are the new recipients of Adam's lost glory because they are the true humanity; see *The Community Rule* (1QS 4:7–8, 23); *The Damascus Covenant* (CD 3:18–20); *The Hymns* (1QH 17:18).[10] Third, N. T. Wright has persuasively argued that the Old Testament presents Israel as God's intended replacement of Adam.[11] Regretfully, however, Israel's fall in the wilderness connected to the golden calf incident demonstrated that Israel,

---

9. 4.44.1/4.2 consists of cosmogony and primordial events, both of which we subsume under the main title, protology.

10. My first two books argue this point as relating to much of Second Temple Judaism, not just the Dead Sea Scrolls, *Adam Christology as the Exegetical and Theological Substructure of 2 Corinthians 4:7–5:21* (Lanham, MD: University Press of America, 1991) and *The Glory of Adam and the Afflictions of the Righteous: Pauline Suffering in Context* (New York: Edwin Mellen Press, 1993).

11. N. T. Wright, "Adam in Pauline Christology." *Society of Biblical Literature Seminar Papers* (Chico, CA: Scholars Press, 1983): 259–89

too, had repeated Adam's sin.[12] Such a disaster was in reality the beginning of the sin part of Israel's story. *Fourth Ezra* 3:5–11; 4:30; 6:56; 7:116–127 make the same point. These texts recall the creation and fall of the world, the evil seed of Adam's heart as the root of Israel's sin, the inferiority of the other nations stemming from Adam compared to Israel, and the depravity that Adam's sin has caused for all of humanity even Israel, respectively.

The Fall of the Watchers

Second only to the fall of Adam as the preferred explanation of the origin of sin is the blame placed on the Watchers of Genesis 6. *First Enoch* focuses on this theory. In *1 Enoch* 2:1–5:4; 6:1–36:4, Enoch is granted visions of the divine creation of the earth with all things set in their regular course, except the Watchers, the angels in Genesis 6 who cohabitated with women producing a race of giants and evil. That is to say, they lost their divine place in heaven due to their lust for women on earth. Opposing these Watchers are the seven archangels. *First Enoch* 2:1–5:4; 6:1–36:4; 10:1–22 relate that the fall of the Watchers was the cause of the judgment upon the world. Even so, they were not destroyed by the flood but incarcerated in the nether world, with one tenth of the fallen angels left to mislead the world (see *Jubilees* 10:1–11). Their influence, nonetheless, continued in history causing Israel itself to fall into sin, which once upon a time was thought to be the replacement of Adam (*1 Enoch* 90:19, 30, 37).

The Fall of Satan

Still other writings based on Genesis 3 attributed the origin of sin to the fall of Satan.[13] Isaiah 27:1 alludes to the fall of Satan under the well-known primordial combat tradition. In the Isaiah passage, a single monster is described using three designations: Leviathan the twisting serpent, Leviathan the crooked serpent, and the dragon.[14] In our

---

12. I discuss Wright's theme and amplify it in my article, "Genesis 1–3: Creation and Adam in Context," *Criswell Theological Journal,* 10, (2013): 3–26.

13. Isaiah 14:10–15 and Ezekiel 28:1–9 are much debated as to whether they allude to the fall of Satan before creation or rather to the fall of ancient near east kings such as the king of Tyre.

14. These personages reflect the widespread combat myth in the ancient near east. The Canaanite rendition of the theme portrays creation as resulting from the struggle between Baal and Yamn or Mot against Chaos (*Chaoskampf*); see this tradition behind Psalms 74:12–17; 89:9; Job 26; Daniel 7. In Israelite poetry, these conflicts were transposed into stories of Yahweh's conquest of Rahab and Leviathan; see Isaiah 27:1; Psalms 74:13–14; 89:9–10; Job 7:12. In the prophets, the primordial combat myth is applied metaphorically to Israel's historical enemies (Isaiah 14:10–15; Ezekiel 28:1–9; etc.). For a helpful discussion of this subject, see David E. Aune, *Revelation 6–16.* Word Biblical Commentary 52b (Nashville: Nelson, 1998), 667–74, along with his bibliography.

writings, Revelation 12:7–11 reflect the origin of evil in the world via the fall of the Serpent/Satan. In 12:10–11 it becomes an end-time event, creating an *Urzeit-Endzeit* topos (cf. Luke 10:18; John 12:31). Ezekiel 38–39 and its description of Gog and Magog may also turn the primordial fall of Satan into the end-time battle with God. Similarly, in *Testament of Moses* 10:1; 12:9 God determined before creation to have His kingdom defeat Satan and the kingdom of this world at the end of history. Most likely Daniel reflects this tradition, pitting the heavenly Son of Man against the four beasts from the sea.

There are Jewish texts that report Satan as accusing Israelites before God in heaven (Job 1:6–12; 2:1–6; *Jubilees* 1:20; 17:15–16; 48:15–18; *1 Enoch* 40:7; cf. Zech. 3:2). The classic passage relating Satan to Israel is 1 Chronicles 21:1–22:1, where Satan incited David to take a military census of Israel, which provoked divine judgment on all of Israel. Here we have David, leader of Israel, being manipulated by Satan to sin against God. No doubt we are to see in David's sin and God's subsequent judgment on Israel a foreshadowing of Israel's sin and exile, except God stops short of destroying Jerusalem in David's day because he repented of his sin.

We should also call attention to *1 Enoch* 37–71, the *Parables of Enoch*, which offer a different account of the origin of sin. Rather than the Watchers, as the rest of 1 *Enoch* does, the Parables blame a group of Satans, with a ruling Satan, as their leader (53:3; 54:6). It is these Satans who lead humanity to sin (40:7; 69:6). In *1 Enoch* 69:4–12 a list of five Satans is given, together with an account of their misdeeds.

The Covenant Curses Now Intensified into the Messianic Woes

In the introduction to this chapter we provided a summary chart that correlated the covenant curses with the presence of the messianic woes in the seven apocalyptic works we are examining. Here we spell out the eschatological crises that the messianic woes posed for the authors and recipients of these books.[15] We shall do so by dividing that category into its two constituent points—persecution of God's people by the enemies of Israel (actually the remnant of Israel) and eschatological cosmic upheavals upon the earth. In all we make three comments below.

Eschatological Crisis/Messianic Woes
Here we simply include key statements in each of the seven works that refer to the nature of the present crisis that faces Israel as the eschatological crisis of the messianic woes. According to Daniel 12:1, Israel is experiencing the end-time messianic woes because of the intensification of the covenant curses due to her disobedience to God. In *1 Enoch* 1:1; 37:4;

---

15. The eschatological crisis section is 7./7.1/7.2 in the catalogue of the genre of apocalypticism.

100–108, the first two passages state that Enoch is writing in view of the messianic woes/great tribulation of the last days, while chapters 100–108 spell out the end-time destinies of the righteous and the wicked. Israel will undergo the end-time messianic woes because of the intensification of the covenant curses due to her disobedience to God. In the *Hymns* of the Dead Sea Scrolls—1QH 3:7–10; 5:30; 7:2–21; 10:1:5–11—these verses locate the community in the midst of the messianic woes, using the imagery of labor pangs that will bring forth the messiah.

Revelation 6–18 is a classic statement of the signs of the times or the messianic woes, portraying them as the seal, trumpet, and bowl judgments.[16] In *Testament of Moses* 9:1–7, Taxo's martyrdom precipitates the advent of the messianic woes. Two passages in *4 Ezra*—4:26–32; 6:13–28—predict the end of the age will come with the signs of the times, the messianic woes, using the topos of the labor pangs. *Second Baruch* 26:1–30:5; 58–76 relate the presence of the messianic woes in terms of dark and bright waters (the former representing the wicked and the latter depicting the righteous). *Second Baruch* 26:1–30:5 predicts that the Messiah will appear at the end of the messianic woes. This category of eschatological crisis/messianic woes may be divided into two points.

Persecution

All seven of the preceding works lament the persecution that has come upon Israel as the culmination of the covenant curses: Daniel 2:19–27; 7:21–26; 12:1–3 attribute Israel's persecution to the messianic woes poured out upon Israel by her enemies. *1 Enoch* 1:1–2 envisions that the righteous will be persecuted by the wicked up through the last days. The Dead Sea Scrolls documents CD 1:5–11 (*The Damascus Covenant*); 26:12–15; 1QH 3:17–4:22 (the *Hymns*); and 1QM 1:1–2 (*The War Scroll*) present the end-time holy war perpetrated upon them (the DSS authors) by apostate Jews and Gentiles in the last days. As Revelation 7:14 makes clear, 7.1 2:10, 13; 6:9–11; 17:6; cf. 1:9; 7:9, 14; 11:3–13; 12:11; 13:7; 14:13; 16:6, relate that the persecutions are a part of the messianic woes/great tribulation. *Testament of Moses* 8:1–9:7 is a collage of history in which the author predicts eschatological persecution on Israel that is greater than that of the Babylonians, Antiochus, and Pompey the Roman's capture of Jerusalem. *Fourth Ezra* 5:23–30; 10:7–24 lament the fact that Zion, God's chosen city, has been destroyed by Babylonia. *Second Baruch* 10:1–19 presents the days accompanying the fall of Jerusalem as the messianic woes.

---

16. For a full discussion of the messianic woes as the signs of the times, see C. Marvin Pate and Douglas K. Kennard, *Deliverance Now and Not Yet: The New Testament and the Great Tribulation* (New York: Peter Lang, 2004). Craig S. Keener provides a nice succinct chart containing the occurrences of the various signs of the times in the Bible and in Second Temple Judaism in his, *The Historical Jesus of the Gospels* (Grand Rapids: Eerdmans, 2009), 366–71.

Eschatological Upheavals

Daniel 2:19–27 and 2:44 predict that the invasion of the kingdom of God upon this earth causes cosmic upheavals. *First Enoch* 1:3–9; 62:4 speak of the coming cosmic upheavals. The first passage predicts that the last days will witness cosmic upheaval, which in 62:4 is numbered as one sign of the birth pangs of the Messiah. The Dead Sea Scrolls *War Scroll* (1QM) prophesies that in the end-time holy war, God will fight on behalf of the Qumran community like He did against the ancient Egyptians, Canannites, Philistines and now the Kittim (Romans). According to the *War Scroll*, the enemy will be destroyed and God will restore true Israel, the Qumran community, to Israel's original beauty and bounty. Revelation 6:1–8:1; 8:2–9:21; 11:15–18; 15:1–16:21; 18:1–19:10 attest to the cosmic judgments of the seals, trumpets, bowls, and the coming fall of Rome. *Testament of Moses* 10:1–7 states that at the appearance of (Michael?) the Messiah, the earth will undergo cosmic upheaval as the kingdom of God replaces it. According to *4 Ezra* 5:4–13; 9:1–13, cosmic upheavals will come as a part of the signs of the times. In *2 Baruch* 10:1–19 the destruction of the temple is presented as cosmic upheaval.

THE COVENANT BLESSINGS AS CULMINATING IN THE ARRIVAL OF THE KINGDOM OF GOD/MESSIAH[17]

Our third major point of this chapter presents the covenant blessings as culminating in the arrival of the kingdom of God/Messiah; recall again our introductory chart establishing this claim. This topic consists of two parts: eschatological judgment or destruction upon Israel's enemies and the covenant blessings/restoration upon Israel.

Eschatological Judgment or Destruction upon Israel's Enemies

As we noted above, Daniel 2:44 and 7:27 envision the coming kingdom of God as crushing the kingdoms of this world in cosmic fashion. *1 Enoch* 62:3–16 predicts that destruction will come upon the wicked because they rejected the heavenly Son of Man/people of God. 1QM; 1QH 13:33–37 of the Dead Sea Scrolls predict the defeat of Israel's enemies at the hand of God. Revelation 6–19 records the judgment and destruction that will come upon the earth through the seal, trumpet, and bowl judgments. *Testament of Moses* 10:1–7 prophesies that at the appearance of (Michael?) the Messiah, the earth will undergo cosmic upheaval as the kingdom of God replaces it (recall our comment above). *Fourth Ezra* 7:26–74 observes that with the advent of the temporary

---

17.   This section corresponds to components #8–10 of the genre of apocalypticism.

messianic kingdom the wicked will be thrown to the place of judgment that God foreordained for them. *Second Baruch* 13:1–12 proclaims that at the advent of the Messiah the nations who helped to destroy Jerusalem will be destroyed in retaliation.

This eschatological judgment/destruction may be subdivided into three categories: (1) judgment on the wicked or ignorant, (2) judgment on the world, and (3) otherworldly beings who dispense those judgments.

Judgment on the Wicked or the Ignorant

Four passages in Daniel describe divine judgment on the wicked or ignorant (2:44; 4; 5: 12:1–3). The first passage announces the coming judgment upon the kingdoms of this earth at the advent of the Kingdom of God. Chapter 4 records the fall of King Nebuchadnezzar due to his arrogance, but his restoration is due to his repentance before the God of Israel. Chapter 5 records the judgment of King Belshazzar due to his flagrant idolatry. The last passage (Dan. 12:1–3) predicts the resurrection unto judgment for the wicked.

Three passages in *1 Enoch* fit this category (62:3–16; 94–95, 97–100). The first text we noted above; the other two sets of passages spell out the judgment that will fall upon the wicked. In the Dead Sea Scrolls, 1QH 3:27 and *Enoch* (4Q 204 1:1–5) are typical of the judgment pronounced upon the wicked or ignorant therein: the wicked and ignorant of the laws of Qumran will be destroyed like the summer sun burns up all in its path.

Revelation 17:12–14/19:17–21; 1–24; 18:1–24; 19:21; 20:11–15; 21:8 all speak of the coming judgment of Rome. The first passage (a doublet?) speaks of judgment on the Beast and ten allied kings. Rome is destroyed in 18:1–24, as are the Beast and the False Prophet in 19:21. The lost are cast into the lake of fire in 20:11–15, as is the second death in 21:8.

According to *Testament of Moses* 10:1–7, the enemies of God and Israel will be destroyed. *Fourth Ezra* 7:35–87 focuses on the judgment of the righteous at the advent of the Messiah. Recall from above that *2 Baruch* 13:1–12 predicts that at the advent of the Messiah the nations who destroyed Jerusalem will be destroyed in retaliation.

Judgment on the World

Daniel 2:44 predicts the destruction of the kingdoms of men by the advent of the kingdom of God. *First Enoch* 62:4 forecasts the destruction of the world and the wicked that indwell it. According to 1QH 3:33–36 in the Dead Sea Scrolls, the world as inhabited by the wicked will meet with divine judgment. In Revelation 20:11; 21:1, the old earth is destroyed and replaced by the new world in these two passages. In *Testament of Moses* 10:1–7, the enemies of God and Israel will be destroyed. *Fourth Ezra* 7:116–131 envisions that at the advent of the Messiah all will be judged according to Deuteronomy 30:15: Choose life by obeying the Torah, or choose death by disobeying it. Ezra laments that God allowed Adam's sin to corrupt the ability of people to choose the former, especially Israel. According to *2 Baruch* 68, at the advent of the Messiah, Jerusalem will be honored and the nations will be judged.

Otherworldly Beings

Included in this category are statements to the effect that God will judge the evil world via otherworldly/heavenly beings or conversely that His judgment will fall on evil supernatural beings: In Daniel 10:1–20 Michael helps Gabriel the angel to defeat the prince (the angel of Persia) from hindering Daniel's prayers. If we take *1 Enoch* as a whole, we find God judging the Watchers via his good angels, while the heavenly Son of Man and divine Wisdom judge Israel's enemies. In the Dead Sea Scrolls, the liturgical texts of 4Q 400–405 present the true worshippers as joining the angels around the divine glorious throne in praise to God. In Revelation 19:20; 20:10, the Beast and False Prophet are thrown into the lake of fire as is Satan, respectively. According to *Testament of Moses* 10:1–10, the Devil will be defeated at the advent of the Messiah. According to *4 Ezra* 7:28–30; 12:31–33; 13:1–58, the Messiah (7:28–30; 12:31–33) is none other than the Son of Man (13:1–58) who will destroy Israel's enemies. According to *2 Baruch* 6:1–9:2; 29:4, heavenly beings include angels (6:1–9:2) and the Messiah, along with the evil Behemoth and Leviathan (29:4), with the Messiah killing the last two and feeding them to the saints at the messianic banquet.

Before moving on to the restoration of Israel, we must include two final remarks on the covenant curses/messianic woes and eschatological judgments that fall on the evil enemies of Israel. First, what the first topic is describing consists of the messianic woes/signs of the times. We may supplement our data here with a list of five portents found both in some of the texts we are discussing and in other texts from Second Temple Judaism, including the New Testament.

Earthquakes	*As. Mos.* 10:41; *T. Levi* 4:1; *4 Ezra* 9:3; *2 Baruch* 2:7; *Apoc. Ab.* 30; cf. Mark 13:8 [and parallels]
Intense Famine	*4 Ezra* 6:22; *2 Baruch* 27:6; 70:8; *Apoc. Ab.* 30; cf. *b. Sanh.* 97a; Mark 13:8 [and parallels]; Rev. 6:8
Wars	*1 Enoch* 90; *4 Ezra* 9:3; *2 Baruch* 27:4; 48:32, 37; 70:3, 6, 8; cf. *Sanh.* 97a; b. *Meg.* 17b; Mark 13:8 [and parallels]; Rev. 6:4

Internecine Strife	*1 Enoch* 100:1–2; 56:7; *4 Ezra* 6:24; *2 Baruch* 70:3–7; *m. Sota* 9:15; *b. Sanh* 97a; cf. *Jub.* 23:16; Mark 13:12 [and parallels]
Cosmic Disturbances	*Sib. Or.* III. 796–808; *1 Enoch* 80:4–6; *As. Mos.* 10:5–6; *4 Ezra* 5:4, 5; cf. *Sanh.* 99a; Mark 13:24–25 [and parallels]; Rev. 6:10[18]

Second, we return to a topic we identified in chapter two, namely, the idea in the Old Testament and Second Temple Judaism that Israel's endurance of the messianic woes atoned for her sins and would be the basis for her hoped-for restoration. Since we have devoted a whole book to this subject elsewhere, we supply here only the results pertinent to our current topic.[19]

We saw in chapter two that most of the Old Testament prophetic-apocalyptic texts pin the hope of Israel's restoration on the suffering of the righteous servant of the Lord.[20] This suffering servant personage took its point of departure from the individual suffering of the servant of the Lord in Isaiah 40–55, but was expanded to include other suffering servants. We find the latter category in Isaiah 24–27; 56–66; Daniel 11:31–12:10; and Zechariah. The idea of a corporate suffering servant continues in Second Temple Judaism; see, for example, *1 Enoch* 37–71, the Dead Sea Scrolls, and *Testament of Moses* 9. Other texts in the apocalyptic taxonomy, such as *4 Ezra* and *2 Baruch*,[21] seem to equate Israel in some way with the suffering servant.

Building on the work of others, I have argued elsewhere that the Synoptic gospels present Jesus as the suffering servant who endures the messianic woes for the people of God.[22] Here, for example, we connect Mark 13 (the signs of the times) with Mark 14–15 (Jesus's passion). Note the parallels between the two: (1) both Jesus and his disciples are described as being "handed over" to the authorities (cf. 14:18–21 with 13:9, 11–12); (2) both are associated with the hour of God's timing (cf. 14:32–42 with 13:32–33); (3) both must be watchful (cf. 14:34, 37–38 with 13:32–33); (4) both settings predict the glory of the coming Son of Man (cf. 14:62 and 13:26); and (5) both use the same chronological

---

18. Pate and Kennard, *Deliverance Now and Not Yet*, 31. *The Assumption of Moses* is the same as *The Testament of Moses*. Moreover, *Babylonia Sanhedrin, Babylonia Megillat, Mishnah Sota* are rabbinic books dating to the second century A.D. and beyond. *Testament of Levi* (a part of the Twelve Patriarchs), *Apocalypse of Abraham, Jubilees,* and *Sibylline Oracles* are all second-century Jewish apocalypses.

19. Pate and Kennard, *Deliverance Now and Not Yet.*

20. The exceptions are Joel 2–3 and Ezekiel 38–39, where no trace of the individual suffering servant seems to occur, but Israel does in fact suffer for her sin. One wonders from this if Joel and Ezekiel apply the suffering servant to Israel as a nation?

21. In these books the suffering servant is not to be equated with the Messiah.

22. Pate and Kennard, *Deliverance Now and Not Yet,* 302–481.

references (cf. 14:17, 72; 15:1 with 13:35). Dale C. Allison adds five additional parallels between Mark 14–15 and chapter 13[23] along with suggested interpretations,[24] and Kennard and Pate have amplified how Schweitzer's concept of atoning tribulation relates to this idea.[25]

The Covenant Blessings/Restoration of Israel

Two points must be made regarding this section. First, eschatological salvation consists of cosmic transfiguration and personal salvation. Second, personal salvation includes both resurrection and other forms of afterlife.

Eschatological Salvation as Cosmic Transfiguration

Daniel 2:44 and Daniel 7 state that the kingdom of God will defeat the kingdoms of men and transform the cosmos for the better. According to *1 Enoch* 45, the righteous will inhabit the new heaven and new earth. In the Dead Sea Scrolls, the *New Jerusalem Text* (2Q24) like no other Scroll presents the New Jerusalem as the future home of the righteous. Revelation 21:1; 21:2–4; 21:9–22:5 like no other literature, describes the creation of the new heaven and a new earth as the future home of the righteous. According to *Testament of Moses* 10:1–10, this earth with be replaced by the kingdom of God. *Fourth Ezra* 7:26–31 4:35; 8:1–37 depict the messianic kingdom on earth as the restoration of paradise; both righteous and evil will be resurrected, one for eternal joy the other for eternal sorrow. According to *2 Baruch* 26:1–30:5; 40:1–4; 72–74, in the temporary messianic kingdom Paradise will be restored in terms of health, harmony, and holiness.

Eschatological Salvation as Personal Resurrection or Some Form of the Afterlife

The righteous are destined to inhabit a resurrection body. Daniel 12:1–3 is perhaps the only clear promise of a future bodily resurrection of the righteous in the Old Testament. According to *1 Enoch* 5:7; 39–40, the righteous will receive a glorious resurrection body in the last days. According to 4Q 385 2:1–9; 1QH 3:5–6 of the Dead Sea Scrolls, the righteous will receive a glorious resurrection body in the last days. Revelation 1:5; 20:4–6; 20:11–15 speak of the future resurrection. In 1:5 it is implied that all believers are promised resurrection by way of participation in the kingdom of God, while in 20:4–6 the martyrs are resurrected to reign in the temporary messianic kingdom and in 20:11–15 the

23. Dale C. Allison, *The End of the Ages Has Come: An Early Interpretation of the Passion and Resurrection of Jesus* (Philadelphia: Fortress, 1985), 37.

24. Ibid., 38.

25. See *Deliverance Now and Not Yet.*

general resurrection is described. According to *Testament of Moses* 10:8–9, the righteous will be raised on high which implies that they will be resurrected. According to *4 Ezra* 7:34–44, both the righteous and the wicked will be raised to live forever in their respective places of reward or punishment. In *2 Baruch* 50:3–4; 51:1–16 it is said that the righteous will receive glorious resurrection bodies at the advent of the Messiah.

Eschatological salvation is also promised as some form of afterlife. In Daniel 2:44–45; 7:26–27 it is the life of the kingdom of God. In *1 Enoch* 14, the age to come/kingdom of God can be experienced temporally now through merkabah mysticism. In 1QH 3:3–4 of the Dead Sea Scrolls, the righteous will live in heaven joining the angels in praising God forever. Revelation 2:7; 22:14; 3:5, 22; 22:14; 7:13–17; 21:3–14; 22:3–5 present the following order: the righteous will eat of the tree of life, wear white robes, be exalted with Christ in heaven, have access to the New Jerusalem, and will dwell with God (7:13–17; 21:3–14; 22:3–5). According to *Testament of Moses* 10:8–10 the righteous will be raised on high to join the ranks of the stars/angels (cf. Dan. 12:1–3). According to *4 Ezra* 4:35; 8:1–37, the righteous will dwell in their heavenly chambers and the wicked will dwell in the chambers prepared for them in judgment. In *2 Baruch* 68, one reads that Zion will be rebuilt, the priesthood restored, and Israel will be honored by the nations.

Further Considerations

We conclude this section on eschatological salvation by making a number of points not spelled out so far in this particular discussion. First, *4 Ezra* provides the explicit nomenclature for the temporal framework for these apocalyptic themes we are examining, namely, the two ages—this age and the age to come (*4 Ezra* 7:50; 7:113; 8:1; cf. *1 Enoch* 71:15). The doctrine of the two ages is the sub-structure of the entire New Testament, starting with the already/not-yet aspects of Jesus's preaching of the Kingdom of God.[26] Second, the doctrine of the two ages can be illustrated in a more nuanced fashion as: this age>the end of the age=messianic woes>the age to come, begun by the temporary messianic kingdom>completed by the eternal kingdom of God.

Third, the doctrine of the two ages presupposes divine determinism, that is, that God is in control of history. Fourth, this in turn accounts for the *Urzeit-Endzeit* schema that characterizes much of apocalyptic literature, none more beautifully than in Revelation 21–22, as we saw in chapter one. Fifth, the future of the Gentiles in the eschaton differs from writer to writer, from utter destruction to subservience to Israel to joint worship

---

26. See George E. Ladd and Donald Hagner for the classic book on the subject, *A New Testament Theology* (Grand Rapids: Eerdmans, 1974; 1991). Kennard and I try to offer a more nuanced theme of the overlapping of the two ages, in *Deliverance Now and Not Yet*.

of God with Israel in Jerusalem. We saw this in our chapter 2, and such variation also accompanies the material examined in this chapter as well.

PRESENT SALVATION

In this section we cover two points—the intersection of heaven, earth, and hell[27] which provides the backgound of present salvation through mystic ascent to heaven.[28]

The Intersection of Heaven, Earth, and Hell

There are three spatial locations in the apocalyptic works we are examining: heaven, earth, and hell. There is a commonality among these places in that there is an intersection of otherworldly elements, regions, and beings. In other words, there is constant traveling among these three locations by otherworldly beings. Such mobility, then, sets the stage for these worldly beings to ascend to heaven or to be cast into in to hell. A closer look at this material, however, also reveals that each aspect—otherworldly elements, otherworldly regions, otherworldly beings—makes its own respective point, and all in relationship to Israel. We will proceed in this section by making two points on each of the three dimensions: its thesis, and then a chart supporting that thesis.

Otherworldly Elements
Our thesis here is that the otherworldly elements are at the service of Israel. The following chart indicates this thesis to be the case:

OTHERWORLDLY ELEMENTS
ARE AT THE SERVICE OF ISRAEL

Daniel 9:20–27	The future restoration of Israel will be on earth
1 Enoch 42	Pre-existent Wisdom desires to dwell in Israel which will constitute her (Israel) restoration on earth.
The DSS *New Jerusalem Texts*: (4Q 554–555); *1QM* 12; *Aramaic Apocalypse* (4Q 246); (4)	The New Jerusalem is the future home of true Israel, where she will worship with the angels and the heavenly Son of God.

---

27. This corresponds to category #10 of the genre of apocalypticism, which is divided into otherworldly elements, otherworldly regions, and otherworldly beings.

28. This intersection of heaven, earth, and hell corresponds to category #6 of the genre of apocalypticism, the spatial/vertical axis of the content.

Daniel 9:20–27	The future restoration of Israel will be on earth
Revelation	Throughout the book there are heavenly elements that work to bring about true Israel's salvation: Son of Man, Ancient of Days, angels, 144,000, 2 prophets, New Jerusalem (the essence of true Israel's salvation).
Testament of Moses 10:1–10	God will appear at the end of history to deliver Israel, who will live in heaven.
4 Ezra 4:33–43; 9:26–10:59	In the age to come (4:33–43), fallen Jerusalem will be replaced by the heavenly Jerusalem (9:26–10:59).
2 Baruch 4; 6:1–9:2; 29:4	*2 Baruch* 4; 6:1–9:2; 29:4, as we noted earlier, delineates the heavenly Jerusalem (4), angels (6:1–9:2), Messiah, Behemoth, Leviathan, and the treasury of manna (29:4). All of these otherworldly elements will serve Israel, even the two monsters who will be slayed by the Messiah to feed Israel at the heavenly messianic banquet.

Otherworldly Regions

Our second thesis adds a moral component to the discussion: One's response to Israel determines the otherworldly region of one's destiny. The following chart supports this thesis:

ONE'S RESPONSE TO ISRAEL DETERMINES ONE'S OTHERWORLDLY REGION

Daniel 2, 7, 9:24–27	The kingdom of God will descend to earth to defeat Israel's enemies (the four kingdom topos) and to rule earth through Israel.
1 Enoch 21	*First Enoch* 21 is typical of the passages in *1 Enoch* that describe the location in heaven for the righteous (Israel) and the location of hell for the Watchers and the wicked, the latter group having strived to lead Israel astray.
DSS: *Songs of the Sabbath* texts and 1QM (*The War Scroll*)	The Songs of the Sabbath texts present the Essenes, the true Israel, as being caught up to heaven to worship God with the angelic hosts. Indeed, the mystic ascent turns the worshipper into an angel. At the end of history they will descend to earth to defeat the rest of humanity (non-Essenes and Gentiles).
Revelation 4:1–5:14; 7:9–17; 8:2–5; 11:16–18; 12:10–12; 15:1–16:1; 19:1–8	These passages present the heavenly hosts praising God in anticipation of the final deliverance of true Israel (Jewish and Gentile believers in Jesus) from their enemies.

Testament of Moses 10:1–10	This text predicts that the heavens and the stars will be the future home of the righteous after God defeats Israel's attackers. It seems to be assumed that Israel's enemies will not be in heaven.
4 Ezra 7:32–44	Somewhat surprisingly assigns heavenly dwellings for the righteous *and* wicked in the afterlife, the former for blessing but the latter for torment due to their persecution of Israel. So, even though Israel's enemies will be in heaven, they will be confined to a place of judgment.
2 Baruch 22:1–23:7; 24:1–4	According to 22:1–23:7/24:1–4, in heaven the books of the deeds of the wicked (persecutors of Israel) and the righteous (Israel) are kept for safekeeping. It seems to be assumed that Israel will be in heaven but her enemies will not be there.

Otherworldly Beings

Our thesis here is that there is a spiritual warfare component revealed in the following passages, namely, the heavenly spiritual war between Israel's defenders and Israel's oppressors parallels the earthly struggle between Israel and her enemies. The data for this thesis can be offered in chart form:

THE EARTHLY CONFLICT BETWEEN ISRAEL AND HER ENEMIES REFLECTS THE HEAVENLY CONFLICT BETWEEN THE HEAVENLY FORCES OF GOOD AND THE FORCES OF EVIL

Daniel 3:28; 5:5–25; 7; 8–12	These passages refer to key heavenly beings. Thus Daniel 3:28 refers to the Son of God in the fiery furnace with the three Hebrew young men. Daniel 5:5–25 describes the divine hand writing judgment on the wall of the palace. Chapter 7 presents the heavenly Son of Man while Daniel 8–12 records the appearances of a number of angels, both good and bad. In all of these texts the good angels are delivering exilic Jews. Daniel 8–12 is perhaps the classic text in the Old Testament which reveals that there is a heavenly battle between good angels defending Israel against bad angels which corresponds to the earthly struggle Israel has with her enemy nations.

1 Enoch 62–63	*1 Enoch* 62–63 with their emphasis on the pre-existent Son of Man as currently both in heaven and yet suffering with Israel on earth as the Suffering Servant, seem to correlate a heavenly battle and an earthly battle: heavenly Son of Man suffering with Israel on earth as the Suffering Servant.
DSS: 4Q 400–405; *Aramaic Testament of Levi* (4Q 213)—two messiahs are mentioned (Levitic and Davidic), angels along with the two messiahs—Levitic and Davidic—will join the righteous in heavenly worship. Add to these texts 1QM (*The War Scroll*).	These supernatural beings currently fight for Israel against Belial, another name for Satan (cf. 2 Cor. 6:15). 1QM reveals that this heavenly spiritual war over Israel will play out on earth at the end of history, even as it occurs simultaneously in heaven (see 1QM 17:7).
In Revelation, the entire book describes heavenly beings and entities: heavenly Son of Man, ancient of days, angels, 144,000, two prophets, seven judgments, New Jerusalem. To the previous beings should now be added Satan, before he is cast out of heaven (12:7–9).	Revelation 12:7–9 reveals that there is a heavenly battle between Michael and Satan, but Michael defeats Satan (probably with the aid of the other heavenly good beings) and casts him to earth. At that point Satan pours out his fury on true Israel on earth. Thus it can be seen that Revelation presents more of a sequential heavenly battle leading to an earthly battle. Still, the two battles—heavenly and earthly—are related.
Testament of Moses 10:1–10	According to this text, God through His Messiah will wage war against Satan and destroy him at the end of history. But perhaps there is the implication that such a battle is now occurring also in heaven, as in Revelation 12:7–9.
In *4 Ezra* 7:28–30; 12:31–33; 13:1–58, Messiah (7:28–30; 12:31–33) and Son of Man (13:1–58) receive significant attention.	While they are in heaven now, at the end of history these two supernatural beings will defeat Israel's enemies. Like *1 Enoch* 62–63, *4 Ezra's* emphasis on the pre-existent Messiah and Son of Man as currently both in heaven and yet suffering with Israel on earth as the Suffering Servant seems to correlate a heavenly battle and an earthly battle.

2 Baruch 4; 6:1–9:2; 29:4 speak of the heavenly Jerusalem (4), angels (6:1–9:2), Messiah, Behemoth, Leviathan, and the treasury of manna (29:4).	As we noted before concerning these passages, at the end of history these good heavenly beings will feed the two monsters to Israel at the messianic banquet. Yet the fact that there exists now both good beings in heaven (heavenly Jerusalem, angels, Messiah, manna) and bad beings in heaven (chaos monsters Behemoth and Leviathan, who will be killed by the Messiah and fed to Israel at the messianic banquet) seems to imply some type of supernatural struggle that will culminate in Israel's deliverance at the end of history.

Present Salvation through Mystic Ascent

The previous three points combine to show the interplay between heaven, earth, and hell, and that supernatural beings journey from one location to the next. Heaven, earth, and hell are not hermetically sealed compartments. This background prepares the way for the next claim, namely, that righteous earthly beings can travel to heaven from earth via mystic ascent and thereby experience salvation temporarily in the present in the heavenly dimension. This idea is expressed in *1 Enoch* 14, 37–71; the Dead Sea Scrolls (1QH 3; 4Q 400–405); Revelation 4–22. Such a mountain top experience ceases, however, when the believer returns back to the cruel world of the messianic woes. The good news is that the mystic ascent/temporary deliverance does give hope in that it anticipates the full arrival of the kingdom of God to earth. We see, then, that just as the genre of apocalypticism contains the temporal/historical story of Israel, in some cases it also contains a spatial/vertical dimension of Israel's story; that is, one that is the heavenly counterpart of the historical story of Israel.

The basic point to be made in this section relative to the spatial/vertical axis is that the tie that binds together the spatial/vertical axis, or the heavenly realm, is Israel's story. Thus the texts falling into the spatial/vertical category present Israel's sin-exile-restoration-restoration in the following way: First, the origin of the sin that caused Israel to stumble was the pre-existent fall of Satan, the Watchers, or Adam, whichever the case may be for the respective passages below. Second, the exile of Israel is portrayed as a current ongoing spiritual battle between the good and fallen angels in heavenly warfare. Third, the restoration of Israel is still in the future from heaven's perspective for all of the texts in this category, but in some passages there is a present aspect as well of that restoration; this is the already/not-yet eschatological tension that even heaven experiences at the moment. These three points combine to indicate that Israel's story in heaven overlaps with Israel's story on earth. One thinks here of the film *Avatar* with its interconnected parallel worlds. Israel's story in heaven proceeds as follows:

Sin

All three of the theories of the origin of sin occur in this category. (1) Adam's fall is drawn on in those Dead Sea Scrolls texts that envision that the Qumran community constitutes the restoration of Adam's lost primeval glory. Recall our discussion in the protology section: the *Community Rule* (1QS 4:7–8, 23; *The Damascus Covenant* (CD 3:18–20); 1QH 17:18. The Dead Sea Scrolls consider its authors to be the true Israel who is the real replacement of Adam. (2) The fall of the Watchers and their subsequent spread of sin to the world including Israel is portrayed in *1 Enoch* 1–36, as we saw earlier. (3) Revelation 12 alludes to the fall of Satan (cf. *Test. of Moses* 10:1–10).

Exile

Israel's exile on earth is concurrent in heaven in the form of spiritual holy war. To put it another way, the attack on Israel and subsequent control over Israel by enemy nations during her earthly exile is the counterpart of the heavenly war between the fallen angels energizing Israel's enemies and those good angels defending Israel in heaven. Recall our third point in the last section. See again Daniel 10–12, where the fallen angels controlling Persia and Greece are called the "prince of Persia" and the "prince of Greece" (10:20), while the good angels Gabriel and Michael defend Israel in the heavenly realm both now (so Gabriel) and during the messianic woes (so Michael). Revelation 12 presumes the same drama. We might also call attention to Ephesians 6:10–18 and its description of believers as participating in the heavenly warfare between bad and good angelic beings. We might also mention again in this regard that *1 Enoch* 62:3–16 presents the heavenly Son of Man as suffering with Israel during the exile on earth but that at the advent of the kingdom of God Israel's enemies will be destroyed.

Restoration

In the heavenly axis, there is an amazing eschatological tension at work that Andrew Lincoln has identified in ancient Jewish and Christian apocalyptic literature, namely, like the New Testament as a whole so too Judaism knew of the overlapping of the two ages in heaven.[29] That is to

---

29. See Andrew T. Lincoln, *Paradise Now and Not Yet: Studies in the Role of the Heavenly Dimension in Paul's Thought with Special Reference to his Eschatology.* Society for New Testament Studies Monograph Series 43 (Cambridge: University Press, 1981), though he does not connect the overlapping of the two ages in heaven with the story of Israel as I am doing here. We should

say, the age to come has already dawned in heaven but it is not yet complete. We can chart this dynamic as follows:

Age to come dawned in heaven	Age to come not complete in heaven
Present salvation experienced in mystic ascent temporarily	Future salvation to be experienced on earth eternally

THE CONDITION FOR ENTERING INTO THE ESCHATOLOGICAL COVENANT BLESSINGS

The overall purpose of Second Temple apocalyptic literature was to challenge its readers to be faithful to God despite the intense pressure that the enemies of God brought to bear upon the true believer. By being faithful, believers ensure their entrance into the kingdom of God. This reality can be seen in the seven writings we have been examining. The actual authors of the aforementioned works believed themselves to be the true followers of the Torah, however they defined it. This point is easily made: Daniel (or a later redactor of Daniel) believed that the true Jew in the Maccabean period practiced circumcision, Sabbath keeping, and the dietary laws. It was those very Jewish badges of faith that Antiochus Epiphanes tried to eradicate in Hellenizing Judaism (see also 1–4 Maccabees).

The authors of *1 Enoch* also lived in the Maccabean period but they maintained that one could not properly practice Sabbath keeping and any other Jewish festivals unless one followed the solar calendar. The Dead Sea Scrolls authors (150 B.C.–A.D. 68) believed that the majority of Jews had committed apostasy and they, the Essenes, alone properly adhered to the Torah, one redefined by the Teacher of Righteousness (founder of the community); and that also followed the solar calendar as well. John, in Revelation, accused Jews of rejecting their messiah and as forming a league with the Roman imperial cult (Rev. 17–18). Consequently, the covenant curses were being hurled upon them by the very one they rejected. So John replaces obedience to the Torah with following Jesus as the condition for entering the eschatological covenantal blessings. The authors of *Testament of Moses, 4 Ezra,* and *2 Baruch* adhered to the Pharisaic interpretation of the Torah and lamented that many Jews did not; hence the fall of Jerusalem in A.D. 70.[30]

---

add to this discussion the fact that the proof that the age to come is not complete even in heaven is that a spiritual holy war continues to take place there.

30. This point corresponds to the form component of the genre of apocalypticism: the disposition of the author (3.2/3.3), medium (1.4), and in the parenesis point of the content component (11).

THE HOPE OFFERED IN APOCALYPTIC LITERATURE[31]

The overall purpose of the various manners or means by which the heavenly message was communicated to the respective authors was to instill hope and assurance in the audience that God knew of Israel's plight (exile resulting from sin) and would indeed act to deliver His people (restoration). Indeed, heaven had a vested interest in what was happening on earth to Israel, especially those Jews faithful to the Torah, however understood. Of the many passages making that point in the "form" section of the taxonomy, we provide a sampling.

Visions

Daniel 2:1–45 and 7:1–28

These visions present the four kingdoms topos. There are two possible scenarios of identifying the four kingdoms. The first scenario is Babylonia, Medo-Persia, Greece, and Rome. The second scenario is Babylonia, Media, Persia, and Greece. Whichever might be the case, for our present purpose, Daniel 2 and 7 rehearse the exile of Israel in the unfolding of four world empires (sin, exile) while instilling hope in the coming kingdom of God (the restoration of Israel). Moreover, the exile and restoration are located in the end times. Elsewhere, the entire *Testament of Moses* records Moses' vision of the future of Israel in terms of the covenant curses/messianic woes and the covenant blessings/kingdom of God.

Epiphanies

Daniel 10:1–12:4 and 12:5–13

These sections of Daniel record two epiphanies. The first is that of an angel laying out in detail the future history pertaining to Israel from the time of Babylonia, Persia, Greece, and the Ptolemies and Seleucids down to Antiochus Epiphanes, as we saw in the last chapter. The second epiphany, a shorter one, involves two angels swearing to the truth of the previous angel's forecast of history. These epiphanies bring assurance to the audience of Daniel because they demonstrate that history is "His story"; that God knows exactly how the future will play out in terms of the exile/covenant curses/messianic woes leading to the restoration/covenant blessings/kingdom of God.

---

31. This section corresponds to the form component of the genre of apocalypticism, notably the manner: visions, epiphanies, discourses, dialogues, otherworldly journey, otherworldly mediator, and medium: 1./1.1/1.1.1./1.1.2./1.2./1.2.1./1.2.2./1.3/2/1.4.

4 Ezra 3–5:20; 5:21–6:34; 6:35–9:26; 9:27–10:59; 11:1–12:39; 13:1–58; 14:1–48

In the first three visions, the angel Uriel appears to Ezra; in the next vision the old/new Jerusalems appear to Ezra; in visions five and six the four kingdoms and the Son of Man appear to Ezra (recall Daniel 7, except that the fourth kingdom in *4 Ezra* is Rome, not Antiochus Epiphanes); in the final vision the Lord himself speaks to Ezra. Once again, the heavenly epiphanies reveal to Ezra the future unfolding of the exile of Israel/covenant curses/messianic woes along with her restoration/covenant blessings/kingdom of God. The latter is to be implemented by the heavenly Son of Man/Messiah/Elect One (all names for the same salvific personage).

Discourses

Daniel 10:1–12:4

After an intense spiritual struggle to break through in prayer an angel appears to Daniel, providing a lengthy discourse on future events. The content of that discourse elaborates upon the build up to the fourth kingdom, something that Daniel 2 and 7 only hint at, but which will be replaced by the coming kingdom of God.

1 Enoch 37–71

In the parables of Enoch, Enoch receives three discourses about the coming vindication of the righteous (who are identified with the heavenly Son of Man) as well as the approaching judgment of the evil ones (the Watchers in the past and Jews influenced by them to disobey the Torah). This vindication and judgment are two sides of the same coin of restoration for Israel in the last days.

Testimonia (4Q 175)

This famous text in the Dead Sea Scrolls envisions Moses speaking to the children of Israel regarding the coming prophet (the Teacher of Righteousness who was involved in the founding of the Qumran community), who will enable Israel to obey the covenant stipulations and thereby initiate the eschatological restoration.

Dialogues

2 Baruch 1:1–5:7; 13:1–30:5; 48:1–76:5

God and Baruch dialogue over Israel's fate (1:1–5:7; 13:1–30:5). The same occurs in 48:1–76:3, except God gives Baruch the vision of the dark and bright clouds that recalls the checkered history of Israel's relationship with God but ends with the promise of Israel's restoration in the last days.

Revelation 7:13–17 and 17:6b–18
There is a short dialogue between the seer and one of the twenty-four elders and a longer dialogue between one of the angels who pours out the bowl judgments and the seer, respectively. The two dialogues pit the remnant of the covenant (the first passage) against the enemies of Christ (the second passage). The remnant of the covenant are the victors.

Otherworldly Journeys

Daniel 9:20–27; 10:1–12:4; 12:5–13
Three otherworldly journeys are recorded in these passages, respectively: Gabriel to Daniel, an unknown angel to Daniel, two more unknown angels to Daniel. These heavenly trips to earth contextualize the sufferings that Israel is undergoing, namely, they are the covenant curses culminating in the messianic woes. Daniel 12:1–4 also predicts a future otherworldly appearance by Michael in defense of Israel during those messianic woes.

The Hymns (1QH 3:19–22)
In this famous passage from the Dead Sea Scrolls, the Essene worshipper of God languishes in the midst of the flood of the messianic woes but God temporarily delivers him by raising him to heaven where he experiences salvation and communion with the angels. This temporary spatial relief is not the final earthly vindication of the Essenes.

2 Baruch 4:1–9:27
Baruch is lifted up presumably to heaven, from where he can watch the destruction of Jerusalem by the Babylonians (i.e., the beginning of the exile). The vision of the New Jerusalem descending to earth, however, holds out hope for faithful Jews.

Otherworldly Mediators

Daniel 7:13–28; 10:1–12:4; 12:5–13
The last two texts contain the angelic mediators' answers to Daniel's prayer regarding the lengthening of the exile to cover the four world empires. The first passage unveils the heavenly Son of Man who intercedes/mediates on behalf of the people of God. In effect, then, these two passages juxtapose the exile and restoration of Israel in the last days.

Medium

The content of the heavenly revelation is the apocalyptic secrets that were to unfold in the telling of Israel's story by each apocalyptic author.

In other words, the heavenly writings referred to in our list of books offered an apocalyptic reading of Israel's story, locating themselves in the exile of the covenant curses/messianic woes and on the verge of the restoration of the covenant blessings/kingdom of God/Messiah.

Dead Sea Scrolls

The Dead Sea Scrolls as a whole are claimed by their authors to be inspired interpretations of Old Testament prophecy, asserting that the Essene community is the eschatological fulfillment of the new covenant and that in the precepts of the Teacher of Righteousness they have the right interpretation of the Torah. The Essenes perceive themselves as in the covenant curses/messianic woes but about to enter the covenant blessings/restoration/kingdom of God.

Revelation 5:1–8:1; 10:2, 8–11; 22:18–19

The first of these passages is the book of the seven-sealed document while the second is the little book the seer is commanded by the angel to eat. These two references to sacred writings in Revelation contain the covenant curses/judgment of God on the followers of the beast but the covenant blessings/kingdom of God on the followers of the Lamb. The last text warns that no one should add or take away from the book of Revelation, reminding one of Deuteronomy 13:2–6 and its warning against following the advice of false prophets.

4 Ezra 14:15–48

Ezra is led by the Lord to write twenty-four books summarizing the Law regarding its past, present, and future relative to Israel and the nations; in essence Israel's story interpreted eschatologically. Despite the terrible days ahead for Israel, the end-time restoration lay just around the corner.

Chapter in Review

In this chapter we have used the function category as a grid through which to interpret the eschatological themes occurring in the above seven apocalyptic books. Accordingly, the chapter unfolded in six points: Israel's story as the key to interpreting the genre of apocalypticism; the exile of Israel as the intensification of the covenant curses into the messianic woes; the covenant blessings as culminating in the arrival of the kingdom of God/Messiah; present salvation through mystic ascent to heaven; the condition for entering into the eschatological covenant blessings; and the assurance of the coming covenant blessings/kingdom of God or Messiah. These six points are tied into the function component of the genre of apocalypticism.

Actually, Israel's story informs all of the components of that genre. The form component (1–3) introduces the supposed author of the work, one who was deeply involved at some point in the past with the sin and exile stages of Israel. This person with heaven's backing assured the recipients that God was in control of Israel's destiny; that is, her restoration would surely come.

The temporal axis (4–9) charts Israel's sin, exile, and future restoration along historical lines while the spatial axis (10) reveals that Israel's story on earth is paralleled by Israel's story in heaven. The parenesis (11) challenges the readers to continued obedience to the Lord, however that obedience is defined.

The final form component (12–13) reinforces the parenesis section by challenging the readers to renew their covenant with the Lord and in doing so choose life over death. The function component (14) expressly connects the covenant curses with the messianic woes and the covenant blessings with the restoration of Israel (kingdom of God/ Messiah) in encouraging the readers to be faithful to God because this evil age is at its end and about to give way to the age to come. Moreover, the overall evidence of this chapter that Israel's story undergirds the genre of apocalypticism overwhelmingly supports the claim that covenantal and apocalypticism go hand in hand.

4

PREPARING TO
INTERPRET THE TEXT

The Chapter at a Glance

This chapter is devoted to two preliminary steps for interpreting the text: text criticism and translation.

- A survey of the subject of text criticism addresses three subjects: the witnesses to the Greek New Testament, the history of text criticism of the Greek New Testament, and the principles used to decide among variant readings in the Greek manuscript evidence.

- A discussion of how to translate the entire passage from the Greek text into English offers two points. We begin with a more general and foundational concern: reviewing two major theories of Bible translation. Then, we tackle the task of translating the Greek into English, following four steps: (1) deciding upon the text (assuming there are textual variants in the passage under examination, which is the case in Revelation 1:1–3, our sample passage); (2) punctuating the passage to delimit the sentences; (3) providing a preliminary translation of the Greek passage by parsing verbs, identifying nouns and pronouns, and moving word by word through the sentences; (4) providing two translations: first a more formal translation, then a more functional translation that smooths out the first.

WE MOVE NOW TO A DISCUSSION OF INTERPRETING canonical prophetic-apocalyptic material, most notably Revelation. The next two chapters cover two constituent topics: preparing to interpret the text (Chapter 4) and interpreting the text (Chapter 5). This chapter is devoted to two preliminary steps for interpreting the text, namely, surveying the subject of text criticism and providing a tentative translation of the text. The goal of the former step is to identify or establish the text to be studied while the latter step translates that text. We begin with the process of establishing the text through text criticism.

TEXT CRITICISM: ESTABLISHING THE TEXT

In this the foundational study of the Greek New Testament, we address three subjects: the witnesses to the Greek New Testament, the history of text criticism of the Greek New Testament, and the principles used to decide among variant readings in the Greek manuscript evidence.[1]

The Witnesses to the Greek New Testament

There are four lines of ancient manuscripts that have enabled scholars to reconstruct the original Greek New Testament: Greek manuscripts, ancient versions, patristic quotations, and lectionary readings.

Greek Manuscripts

There are some 5,700 Greek manuscripts of the Greek New Testament, almost an embarrassment of riches compared to the meagre number of Hebrew manuscripts that form the basis of constructing the Old Testament/Hebrew Bible.[2] Moreover, we have the early

---

1. The classic treatment of the subject is that by Bruce M. Metzger, *The Text of the New Testament: Its Transmission, Corruption, and Restoration*. Third Edition (Oxford: Oxford University Press, 1992). See also Stanley E. Porter's smaller but nevertheless significant updated treatment of the subject, *How We Got the New Testament: Text, Transmission, Translation* (Grand Rapids: Baker, 2013).

2. Simply stated, we only possess six major Hebrew manuscripts from which the Old Testament has been compiled, and they all date to no earlier than ca. A.D. 900. Those manuscripts are:

Name	Date
The Cairo Codex (book) of the Prophets (Former and Latter)	Ca. A.D. 900
Aleppo Codex (complete copy of the Hebrew Bible)	Ca. A.D. 900
Leningrad Codex (complete Hebrew Bible; the basis of the present Hebrew Bible)	Ca. A.D. 1000
British Museum Codex of the Pentateuch	Ca. A.D. 950

translations of the Greek New Testament along with the church fathers' quotations to aid the process, as well as thousands of lectionary readings. In this section, we will briefly cover these various sources from which text critics have reconstructed the original text.

Byzantine Family (Constantinople)	Alexandrian Family (Egypt)	Western Family (Rome)
95% Miniscules (2,700 mss.)	Uncials: Sinaiticus, Vaticanus	Uncial: Bezae
8th–9th centuries	4th century	5th century
Smoother readings, harmonized, conflated readings	Shorter, harder readings	Longer readings, especially in the book of Acts
King James	ASV, NASB, NIV, RSV	No translation, but RSV includes some readings in its footnotes in Acts

Several comments can be made based on this chart. First, the Greek manuscripts are written on two types of writing materials: papyri and codexes/books. Second, the variant readings in the Greek manuscripts fall essentially into three families: Alexandrian/Egypt (the oldest mss

Name	Date
Leningrad (formerly St. Petersburg) Codex of the Prophets	Ca. A.D. 900
Reuchlinianus Codex of the Prophets	Ca. A.D. 1100

For Hebrew mss later than these six see Paul D. Wegner, *A Student's Guide to Textual Criticism of the Bible* (Downers Grove, IL: InterVarsity Press, 2006), 122. Also to be added to this list are: the Silver Amulets (Num. 6:24–26, 700 B.C.), the Dead Sea Scrolls (150 B.C.–A.D. 68), the Nash Papyrus (Exod. 20:2–17, 100 B.C.), Cairo Geniza (a storage room for Jewish sacred books, which contains some 200,000 Hebrew fragments dating to A.D. 1000). Though it is not as old as the pre-Christian Hebrew texts noted here, we must for poetic justice mention the Severus Scroll. According to Rabbi Meir, the Torah Scroll General Titus brought to Rome after the fall of Jerusalem in A.D. 70 (which Josephus mentions in connection with the Triumphant Procession bringing back Jews as slaves and temple furniture; see our later discussion) was returned to Israel to be housed in a new synagogue that Emperor Severus (222–235 A.D.) permitted to be built! We should also mention that one of the reasons Hebrew manuscripts of the Old Testament have been scarce was on purpose: out of reverence for the sacred texts, those placed in the storing room for old texts in the synagogues (Genizas) when full were buried in the ground in a sacred ceremony. Of course, the destructions of Jerusalem in 587 B.C. and in A.D. 70 also witnessed the destruction of untold Hebrew texts of the Old Testament as well.

and which divide into second century papyri and fourth century co-
dexes), the Western/Rome text (which dates to the second century)
and Byzantine/Turkey (which date to no earlier than the third century
[but most date to the eighth century]). Third, in terms of reliability,
the Alexandrian family provides the most reliable texts since they date
to the fourth and second centuries; after that come the Western and
Byzantine families. Moreover, rarely do the Byzantine and Western
texts by themselves represent the original reading.

Ancient Versions

Name	Date	Description
Old Latin versions	Mid–second century	A primary translation of the Greek New Testament that reflects a Western text
Latin Vulgate version	382–405	Jerome's translation which incorporated much of the Old Latin mss
Old Syriac versions	Second to fifth centuries	Comprised of the Diatessaron (Tatian's harmony of the four gospels, A.D. 170) and the Syriac Peshitta (fifth century)
Coptic (Egyptian) versions	Third to fifth centuries	Comprised of the Sahidic and Bohairic versions based mostly on the Alexandrian family, except for certain passages in the Gospel and Acts, where they reflect the Western family
Gothic version	Fourth century	Based on the Byzantine family
Armenian version	Mid–fifth century	Based on either Greek or Syriac mss
Georgian translation	Mid–fifth century	Tertiary translation based on the Armenian version and the Greek or Syriac
Ethiopic translation	Fifth to sixth ceturies	Uncertainty pertains to the family of mss it is based on
Arabic translation	Eighth century	Based on a mixture of family texts
Old Slavonic translation	Ninth century	Based on both Byzantine and Western families

Early Church Fathers (Patristic) Quotations of the Greek New Testament
The early church fathers quoted the Greek New Testament thousands of times in their preaching and teaching. Indeed, if we had no Greek manuscripts of the New Testament itself, we still could reproduce all of the Greek New Testament except for about twelve verses just from this category alone.

Lectionary Readings
There are about 2,280 readings of the New Testament that occurred in private or public worship services. They date from the fourth to the sixteenth centuries.

The History of Text Criticism of the Greek New Testament

Following Metzger's outline of this topic, we divide it into three stages: the pre-critical period of text criticism of the New Testament (from Ximenes to Erasmus to the Textus Receptus); the modern period of text criticism of the New Testament (from Griesbach to the Nestle/Aland text[3]); recent debates in New Testament criticism.

The Pre-Critical Period of Text Criticism of the New Testament
Cardinal Ximenes de Cisneros organized and implemented the printing of the first Greek New Testament in 1514, some sixty years after the invention of movable-type printing. It was part of a huge joint Bible publishing project in Spain carried out in the town of Alcala, which also carried the Latin name "Complutum." Ximenes produced a printed polyglot bible with Hebrew, Aramaic, Greek, and Latin texts, called the Computensian Polyglot. The fifth volume out of six (the sixth had a Hebrew lexicon and grammar), and the first of the six to be printed, contained the Greek New Testament (along with a bilingual Greek-Latin lexicon), while the first four volumes contained the Old Testament in Hebrew, the Latin Vulgate, and the Septuagint. Although this text was printed in 1514, it was not distributed or published until 1522 because of political delays in getting papal approval of the project. The textual basis of this Greek New Testament has never been firmly agreed upon, although it probably made use of Vatican manuscripts. These manuscripts appear to have been dated from the thirteenth to the fifteenth centuries, and were based on the Byzantine text, that is, the text that had come to be used throughout the eastern Roman or Byzantine Empire and was

---

3. Metzger, *The Text of the New Testament*, 95–123. For the third point mentioned above we will rely on Porter (*How We Got the New Testament*) on various pages in which he deals with more recent issues than Metzger's text covers.

reflected in the vast majority of extant manuscripts, especially those known at the time.[4]

The Dutch scholar **Desiderius Erasmus** has the distinction of being the editor first to publish, even if not to print, the Greek New Testament. In 1514 he apparently was finally convinced by the publisher Froben to produce such a text while on a trip to Basel. In Basel, where he undertook to produce this text, he made use of a total of about a half dozen minuscule manuscripts dating from the tenth to the twelfth centuries. He relied primarily upon two twelfth-century minuscules with the Byzantine text type. In a few places, such as the last six verses of the book of Revelation, and some other places (e.g., Acts 8:37; 9:5–6) where his manuscripts had muddled text and commentary, Erasmus reverted from the Latin Vulgate into Greek. The end result was not only a book full of numerous typographical errors, no doubt due to haste and the difficulty of the typesetters working off of the edited manuscripts themselves, but also a book that contains numerous instances of Greek devised by Erasmus and not found in any actual ancient Greek manuscript. Not only did Erasmus produce an eclectic text, but he also created one that introduced readings into the Greek New Testament that have been retained in some subsequent editions to this day. Nevertheless, Erasmus published this volume in 1515, and then a further four editions (1519, 1522, 1527, 1535).

One important story regarding Erasmus and the preparation of his edition bears repeating. When his first edition appeared, he was accused by Stunica (Diego Lope de Zuniga) (c.1531), one of the editors of the Complutensian Polygot and the chief editor of the New Testament, of excluding the Trinitarian words found in 1 John 5:7–8: "the Father, the Word, and the Holy Ghost: and these three are one. And there are three that bear witness in earth." Erasmus's response was that these words were not found in any of the manuscripts that he had consulted for his Greek New Testament or subsequently. One of the manuscripts that he apparently consulted subsequently was Codex Vaticanus (B), which Erasmus asked a friend to examine for him, after which he received a letter, dated June 18, 1521, copying out the text and confirming that there was no such passage. Erasmus—precipitously and unwisely, we now see—said that he would include these words (the so-called Johannine Comma) if they could be found in a single Greek manuscript. Lo and behold, such a manuscript appeared, now known as Gregory 61, held in the Trinity College Dublin library. It appears to have been written in 1520 in Oxford by someone

---

4. Metzger, *The Text of the New Testament*, 95–98; Porter, *How We Got the New Testament*, 37–38

named "Froy" or "Roy." Erasmus fulfilled his obligation and put the Johannine passage in his third edition of 1522, but with a footnote that indicated his doubts regarding its authenticity.[5]

Textus Receptus is the name given to the manuscripts on which the Authorized Version of 1611 was based, although other published versions of Erasmus's Greek text of the New Testament preceded it. Several versions to note include the four editions published by Robert Estinenne (Stephanus) (1503–1559). The third edition (1550) followed Erasmus's later editions and included a critical apparatus that referred to other manuscripts, including Codex Bezae (D) when it was apparently located in Italy. This edition was widely used in England, and it formed the basis for the English theologian Brian Walton's (1600–1661) Polyglot Bible, with the fifth volume including the Greek New Testament (1657). The fifth volume included variant readings from Codex Alexandrinus (A), and the sixth volume, an appendix, contains a critical apparatus with variants from Stephanus's edition and fifteen other manuscripts. Stephanus's fourth edition (1551) was the first edition that included the enumeration of verses. Theodore Beza (1519–1605), the early Reformer, published nine editions of the Greek New Testament. Even though he owned a number of manuscripts, such as Codex Bezae (D) and Codex Claromontanus (Dp), these were not used in any significant way in preparing his editions, which tended to follow that of Stephanus.

The Authorized Version (1611) probably made use of Beza's editions. The famous Elzevir publishing house published an edition of the Greek New Testament that followed Beza. In the preface to the second edition (1633) they referred to "the text which is now received by all, in which we have nothing changed or corrupted" From this statement, we get the term "Textus Receptus." Due to the strength of this statement, and the fact that this and related editions had established themselves as the Greek text of the New Testament, the Textus Receptus became the basis for all of the major Protestant translations until 1881, while Roman Catholics continued to use the Latin Vulgate. John Fell (1625–1686), the English theologian during the Civil War (1642–1651), used the second Elzevir edition for an edition that included a critical apparatus with variants from over one hundred manuscripts and versions, including Codex Vaticanus (B), although a number of these manuscripts, Vatincanus included, are cited en masse rather than individually.[6]

---

5. Metzger, ibid., 98–102; Porter, ibid., 38–39.

6. Metzger, ibid., 105–106; Porter, ibid., 40–41.

The Modern Period of Text Criticism of the New Testament

Here we summarize the efforts of Griesbach, Lachmann, Tischendorf, Westcott and Hort, Nestle, and Kurt Aland. Their work firmly established the eclectic Greek text as the basis of the Greek New Testament.

Johann Jakob Griesbach (1745–1812) laid the foundation for all subsequent investigation of the Greek New Testament by departing from the Byzantine family (upon which the Textus Receptus was based) as the best witness to the original New Testament. Instead, he broadened the Greek witnesses to include three family text types: Alexandrian, Western, and Byzantine recensions. The Alexandrian text Griesbach attributed to Origen (as found, for example, in the Syriac, Bohairic, and Ethiopic versions); the Western text contained Codex Bezae (D) and Codex Claromontanus (Dp), and the Byzantine text was a later amalgamation of the other two. Moreover Griesbach developed fifteen principles of textual criticism, no doubt the most important of which was that the shorter reading was likely the most original owing to the scribal tendency to add to the text rather than take away. For example, Griesbach determined that the shorter reading of the Lord's prayer—Luke 11:3–4 ("Father, hallowed be your name)—was to be preferred over the longer reading that harmonized Luke 11:3–4 with Matthew 6:9 ("Our Father who art in heaven, hallowed be your name"); this was so even before the publication of Vaticanus which vindicated the shorter reading.

Karl Lachmann (1793–1851) made a complete break with the Textus Receptus when he published his edition of the Greek New Testament (1831) that contained only what Lachmann considered the oldest texts, those of the fourth century Eastern texts: only uncials, Old Latin, and early church fathers; and no miniscules (of which the Byzantine family essentially consisted).[7]

Constantin Tischendorf (1815–1875), the Leipzig New Testament scholar, is to this day probably the single most significant figure in New Testament textual criticism. In part because of his theological beliefs in the integrity of the Bible, he devoted his life to discovering and publishing more biblical manuscripts than any other scholar, as a means of demonstrating the reliability of the text. He also published numerous critical editions and editions of the Greek New Testament (as well as the Greek Old Testament). Tischendorf's eighth edition of the Greek New Testament (1869–1872), however, contains a comprehensive critical apparatus of all the (then) available manuscripts, versions, and ancient authorities, and it is still unparalleled in its scope and accuracy. He also developed a comprehensive set of criteria for doing textual criticism.

---

7. Metzger, ibid., 119–125; Porter, ibid., 44–45.

Tischendorf is perhaps best known for his discovery, over the course of three trips to St. Catherine's Monastery on Mount Sinai, of the Codex Sinaiticus (א), which was published in beautiful facsimile in 1862 to commemorate the millennial anniversary of the Russian Empire. There has been persistent criticism of Tischendorf, with accusations being made and repeated that he essentially stole the manuscript from Sinai. Recent research in the archives of the Russian state, however, have discovered two interesting sets of correspondence. One involves Tischendorf himself pushing the Russian authorities to ensure an equitable and timely settlement of the issue of the manuscript with the monks at St. Catherine's, and the other is the actual receipt and surrounding documents, where the monks acknowledge payment for the manuscript. Tischendorf's accomplishments and reputation remain intact.[8]

Brooke F. Westcott (1825–1901) and **Fenton J. A. Hort** (1828–1892) gained renown for their studies of New Testament manuscripts and the publication of their critical edition of the New Testament in 1881. After twenty-eight years of work, Westcott and Hort published the text of the Greek New Testament (with an introduction and appendixes) titled *The New Testament in the Original Greek*. Not being interested in simply supplying a textual apparatus with all the variant readings, they refined and applied textual principles from earlier scholars to determine what they believed to be the original Greek text.

Their goal was ambitious, but Westcott and Hort took advantage of the versions and New Testament quotations in ancient authors and the church fathers to formulate their text. Manuscripts were divided into four text types—Syrian, Western, Alexandrian and Neutral. The "Neutral Text" was represented by the fourth-century unicals, namely, Codex Vaticanus and Codex Sinaiticus, but could also be traced backed further into the mid-second century A.D. They believed the "Neutral" text-type to be closer to the original Greek text than any of the other three text types. They considered the Syrian text type (which we now call Byzantine) to be the latest since no distinctly Syrian readings were found in any of the church fathers of the third century, whereas there are numerous in the latter fourth century, especially in the area of Antioch (Syria).[9] As a result of their work, Westcott and Hort developed the following textual map:[10]

---

8. Metzger, ibid., 126–129; Porter, ibid., 44–45.

9. Metzger, ibid., 129–134.

10. Metzger, ibid., 134.

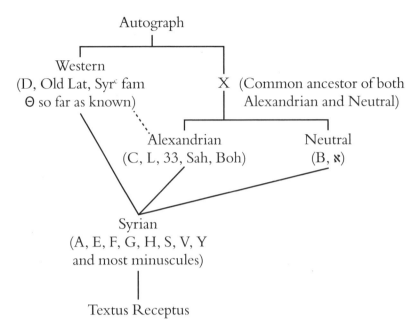

Eldon Jay Epp summarizes the conclusions of Westcott and Hort in this way:

> A major conclusion was that the Syrian text had not yet been formed by the mid-3rd century and that of the other three that lay behind it, the two oldest were competing texts in the earliest traceable period: the Western and the Neutral. (The Alexandrian text, since Westcott and Hort, has generally been classified with the Neutral, though the term "Alexandrian" has been retained to describe the combined entity.) The question that remained for Wescott and Hort concerned which of these earliest pre-Syrian text types (Neutral or Western) represented the original, since both—according to them—had 2nd-century claims. There was no way by which Wescott and Hort could bring their historical reconstruction to reveal—on historical grounds—which of the two was closer to the original New Testament text.[11]

Eberhard Nestle (1851–1913) and **Kurt Aland** (1915–1994) did the work that resulted in the most commonly used modern critical

---

11.   Eldon J. Epp, "Textual Criticism," *Anchor Bible Dictionary*, ed. David Noel Freedman (New York: Doubleday, 1992), 6.412–35; 429.

edition of the Greek text.[12] Eberhard Nestle's Greek text, the *Novum Testamentum* Graece, was published in 1898 by the Württemberg Bible Society, Stuttgart, Germany. The Nestle text went through twelve editions (1898–1923) and then was taken over first by his son, Erwin Nestle (13th–20th editions, 1927–1950). First Kurt Aland (21st–25th editions, 1952–1963), then both Kurt Aland and Barbara Aland (26th–27th editions, 1979–1993) followed the work of the Nestles. Eldon J. Epp and Gordon D. Fee critique the Nestle-Aland text as follows:

> As everyone knows, Nestle's edition—from its beginning and for many years to follow—was based simply on a majority vote among the texts in the editions of Tischendorf, Westcott-Hort, and Weymouth or (later) Weiss, that is Nestle chose among competing readings by selecting the one supported by two of these three editions. Nestle's edition put forth no other principals for determining the text and certainly offered no theory of the text—both of which are prominent features of editions like those of Tischendorf and Westcott-Hort. Furthermore, the Nestle edition paid "relatively little attention to manuscripts," as the Alands admit (19). It comes as a surprise, therefore, to discover that they call the Nestle edition a "breakthrough" which represents the "conclusive battle" against the *textus receptus*.[13]

Elsewhere Epp goes on to say, "It might be granted then that the Nestle text has been the dominant edition in terms of practical use down through the years, but it is difficult to see how it has been a major force at the theoretical level in our discipline, and to that extent their portrayal supports our characterization of their volume as a revisionist history of New Testament textual criticism."[14]

The Most Recent Debates in New Testament Text Criticism

At least three debates rage today relative to New Testament criticism: text types, criteria for evaluating variant readings, rejection of the traditional text.

---

12. See Wegner, *A Student's Guide to Textual Criticism of the Bible,* 218–219, for the following section.

13. Eldon J. Epp and Gordon D. Fee, *New Testament Textual Criticism* (Oxford: Clarendon, 1993), 18–19.

14. Eldon J. Epp, "New Testament Textual Criticism Past, Present, and Future: Reflections on the Alands' *Text of the New Testament,*" *Harvard Theological Review* 82, no. 2 (1989), 222.

Debate Regarding Text Types

Most scholars subscribe to the principle that "quality is more important than quantity" (i.e., textual evidence must be weighed and not merely counted) and that manuscripts must be evaluated as to their accuracy and grouped according to textual families so that they can be reasonably weighed. There is much less agreement, however, when it comes to determining text types or groupings. Epp voices the majority opinion of textual scholars: "It can be argued plausibly that three textual clusters or constellations can be identified in reasonably separate groups, and that each finds its earliest representatives in papyrus mss and then carries on to one or more major uncials."[15]

Kurt and Barbara Aland are strong critics of the idea of textual traditions or types. There has been significant discussion as to the validity of textual families before the fourth century. After examining in detail early manuscripts from mainly before the third and fourth centuries, Kurt and Barbara Aland have established the following five categories: [16]

Category I	Manuscripts of a very special quality that should always be considered in establishing the original text (e.g, the Alexandrian text belongs here). The papyri and uncials through the third to fourth centuries also belong here automatically, one may say, because they represent the text of the early period (if they offer no significant evidence, they are bracketed).
Category II	Manuscripts of a special quality but distinguished from manuscripts of category I by the presence of alien influences (particularly the Byzantine text), and yet of importance for establishing the original text (e.g, the Egyptian text belongs here).
Category III	Manuscripts of a distinctive character with an independent text, usually important for establishing the original text but particularly important for the history of the text (e.g, F1, F13).
Category IV	Manuscripts of the D (Western) text.
Category V	Manuscripts with the purely or predominately Byzantine text.

---

15. Epp, "Textual Criticism," 6.412–35; 431.

16. Kurt and Barbara Aland, *The Text of the New Testament. An Introduction to the Critical Editions and Theory and Practice of Modern Textual Criticism,* trans. Erroll F. Rhodes (Grand Rapids: Eerdmans, 1987), 106.

The Alands then categorize all the manuscripts according to the following notations: [17]

1	Agreement with the Byzantine Text
½	Agreements with the Byzantine Text where it has the same reading as the original text
2	Agreement with the original text
S	Independent or distinctive readings (e.g., special readings)

It is at this point that the Alands' research displays a measure of circular reasoning, for the original text is thought to be the Nestle-Aland text, though not everyone would agree that it contains the most original readings in every instances, as Epp notes:

> There is a certain measure of question-begging or circularity of argument in this schema when, for example, a MS is placed into Category I on the basis of its "incidence of agreements with the original"… but when—at the same time—MSS in Category I constitute those which possess "a very special quality which should always be considered in establishing the original text." In addition, there is a fair measure of prejudgment or arbitrariness if, for example, numerous MSS are automatically included in Category I merely because of their age and another MS (P74) is included in that same category despite its age.[18]

Criteria for Evaluating Variant Readings

There is significant disagreement concerning the weight to be given to various canons or criteria when determining textual critical issues. This debate has occurred at two levels: (1) regarding the specific criteria used when determining a specific reading, and (2) how much weight to give internal and external evidence. This latter issue has been so hotly debated that four basic methods of criticism have emerged: historical-documentary, rigorous eclecticism, reasoned eclecticism, and Byzantine-priority.[19]

---

17. Ibid.
18. Epp, "New Testament Criticism," 226.
19. See Wegner, *A Student's Guide to Textual Criticism of the Bible*, 221.

Name	Proponents	Description
Reasoned eclecticism	Bruce Metzger Kurt Aland Michael Holmes Eldon Epp	Balanced use of internal and external evidence
Radical/thoroughgoing eclecticism	George D. Kilpatrick J. Keith Elliot	Emphasizes internal evidence over external
Documentary approach	Victor Dearing Phillip W. Comfort	Emphasizes external evidence over internal
Byzantine-priority approach	Harry A. Sturz Maurice A. Robinson Zane Hodges Arthur Farstad	Emphasizes the Byzantine textual tradition [20]

The method adopted here is reasoned eclecticism, wherein the New Testament text critic examines all available evidence, both external and internal, to determine the most plausible original reading of the text. Michael Holmes states, "Central to this approach is a fundamental guideline: the variant most likely to be original is the one that best accounts for the original of all competing variants in terms of both external an internal evidence."[21]

Rejection of the Traditional Text

Bart Ehrman attended the Moody Bible Institute and Wheaton College, two of the most famous and respected conservative Christian institutions of our day (I also attended and graduated from both). He went on to train at Princeton Seminary under one of the leading New Testament text critics of the twentieth century, Bruce M. Metzger. Indeed, Ehrman was the heir apparent to Metzger's brilliant scholarship. Ehrman has gone on to become, however, one of the most vociferous opponents of conservative Christianity and, for that matter, of the

---

20. This chart is indebted to *A Student's Guide to Textual Criticism of the Bible*, 238.

21. Michael W. Holmes makes this point in, "Textual Criticism," in *New Testament Criticism & Interpretation*, eds. David A. Black and David S. Dockery (Grand Rapids: Zondervan, 1991), 112.

traditional New Testament Greek text.[22] Regarding Ehrman's publications on New Testament text criticism, we may simplify his contentions in three statements, responding to each as we proceed.

First, Ehrman deduces from the thousands of variant readings represented in our Greek New Testament manuscripts that the traditional Greek text accepted by text critics today was unstable in the first couple or so centuries of church history; it therefore is not reliable. In this connection, Ehrman makes the famous statement that there are some 5,800 Greek manuscripts of the New Testament, that contain 200,000 to 400,000 variant readings, which means that we have more variant readings than words of the New Testament itself (138,000 of them)![23] Stanley Porter refutes this sensationalist claim: "First, the vast majority of New Testament text critics rightly note that the truth is that 80–90 percent of the traditional text of the Greek New Testament is in agreement!"[24]

Second, Ehrman proceeds to argue from his sensationalist manuscript statistics that significant variant readings represent "false teachings" (i.e., in Mark 1:41, Jesus was "angry" [unorthodox] not "compassionate"[orthodox]; in Hebrews 2:9 Jesus tasted death "apart from God" [unorthodox] not "by the grace of God"[orthodox]; in John 1:18 Jesus was the "unique son" [unorthodox] not the "unique God" [orthodox]). These unorthodox readings suggest to Ehrman that there was a Greek New Testament text that was produced by the historical losers in the battle with orthodoxy. In other words, there was a Greek New Testament that was heretical from the first century on, but it was suppressed by the orthodox church and replaced by the current traditional text.[25] Two factors detract from Ehrman's claim, however. The unorthodox readings he chooses are generally recognized as being the later variant readings and therefore not the original readings of the New Testament. Further, there are not many such unorthodox variant readings that Ehrman can identify.[26]

Third, assuming his first two points are demonstrated, Ehrman asserts that there were many such unorthodox readings in the first and second centuries, but the manuscripts wore out because of frequent usage by many "heretical" communities. My response to this claim is as follows: Ehrman's assumption is based on an argument from silence and such arguments are

---

22. Probably the book most typical of Ehrman's skeptical approach to text criticism is his *The Orthodox Corruptions of Scripture: The Effect of Early Christological Controversies on the Text of the New Testament* (New York: Oxford University Press, 1993).

23. Bart D. Ehrman, *Misquoting Jesus: The Story behind Who Changed the Bible and Why* (San Francisco: HarperSanFrancisco, 2005), 88–90.

24. Porter, *How We Got the New Testament,* 65.

25. Ehrman, *Misquoting Jesus,* 68.

26. Porter, *How We Got the New Testament,* 67

seldom authoritative. If Gnosticism was so popular in early Christianity (first to mid-second centuries) why then are there no Gnostic documents *before* A.D. 170 (the Gospel of Thomas)? Put another way: If Gnosticism was so popular among early Christians, why do the church fathers quote the New Testament thousands of times but never quote a Gnostic text? The answer Ehrman is forced to offer is that the Gnostic texts were so popular that they wore out with usage, leaving no manuscripts from that time period. This answer is reminiscent of the KJ-only argument—the Byzantine texts do not occur before the 300s A.D. because the early church used them so much that they wore out from usage and are therefore no longer available![27] In brief, Ehrman's claims cannot be substantiated by the facts. Rather, the traditional Greek text is the closest to the original.

Principles of Text Criticism in Evaluating Variant Readings

Westcott and Hort essentially developed the commonly accepted principles of establishing the original text among variant readings. These principles are categorized as external and internal considerations. Regarding the former, the age and geographical distribution of a manuscript are key. Thus, for example, a reading that is in the Alexandrian family (the oldest texts) that also surfaced in Rome would be a strong candidate for the original over against a single Byzantine reading. Perhaps the most famous principle developed by Westcott and Hort was the idea that manuscripts should be weighed not just counted. That is, just because one variant reading had numerous manuscripts supporting it (i.e., the Byzantine family), sheer numbers should not eclipse the fact that another variant reading with a few manuscripts supporting it (i.e., the Alexandrian family) was earlier and, therefore, more likely the better reading.

Since it is also important to consider three issues related to internal evidence, the number of questions to ask rises to four:

1. Which variant reading is older? The reading that is closer to the original should be preferred.
2. Which reading is the shorter? Faced with deciding between two readings of a text, scribes tended to combine the readings so as not to make a choice between them that might be wrong. The Byzantine family is famous for this harmonization approach.
3. Which reading is the most difficult? Scribes tended to smooth over difficult readings.
4. Which reading most likely gave rise to the other(s) readings? Shorter readings usually give rise to longer readings.

---

27. Ehrman makes this claim in his video debate with Daniel Wallace, October 2, 2012. https://www.youtube.com/watch?v=wyABBZe5o68 (last accessed 8/22/16).

With these questions established, we may now discuss three variant readings in the book of Revelation, the most famous prophetic-apocalyptic book in the New Testament.[28]

Readers might be surprised that a variant of Revelation 13:18 reads 616 for the number of the beast, not the familiar 666. There is, however, no Greek manuscript with 616 while the best Greek texts have 666 (e.g., P47, ℵ, A). What is the source of the number 616? Most likely it originated from the Latin form of Nero Caesar which adds up to 616, while the Greek form adds up to 666.

Similarly, there is a famous variant reading in Revelation 22:19. The Textus Receptus (upon which the King James is based) has "from the book of life," while the older Greek texts have "from the tree of life." It is not necessary to follow the four questions above to ascertain the correct reading here, because there is no Greek manuscript with the reading, "from the book of life." Since Erasmus's Greek text of 1516 stopped short of the last six verses of Revelation, he simply translated the Latin Vulgate of these verses back into Greek. Thus, there is no Greek text containing the phrase, "from the book of life."

The discussion is more complicated for Revelation 22:21. There are two key variant readings in Revelation 22:21. The first is between "May the grace of the Lord Jesus be with all the saints" and "May the grace of the Lord Jesus Christ be with all the saints." Which one most likely represents the original text? The choice is essentially between the Byzantine and Alexandrian manuscripts. The following chart provides an overview.

	Byzantine reading: has "Lord Jesus Christ"	Alexandrian reading: has "Lord Jesus."
(1) Which reading is older?	Minuscules 046 and 051; later editions of the Vulgate, Syriac, and Armenian (all of these post-5th century)	Sinaiticus (fourth century) and Alexandrinus (fifth century)
(2) Which reading is shorter?	Includes "Christ"	Does not include "Christ"
(3) Which reading is more difficult?	Follows the full title, "Lord Jesus Christ"	Does not, eliminating "Christ"
(4) Which reading explains the rise of the other reading?	A pious scribe added "Christ" to follow the full name of Jesus	Seems incomplete

28. The following three examples come from Bruce M. Metzger, *A Textual Commentary on the Greek New Testament,* 2nd ed. (New York: American Bible Society, 2005).

The evidence unfolds in the following way: (1) The older reading is the Alexandrian reading; (2) the shorter reading is "Lord Jesus"; (3) the more difficult reading omits "Christ"; (4) the incomplete reading for Christ's name, "the Lord Jesus" is completed by a later editor to "Lord Jesus Christ." The best conclusion, therefore, is that the Byzantine reading is a transcriptional mistake. The Bohairic version of the Coptic translation omits the words, "the grace of our Lord Jesus," because the scribe inadvertently omitted the phrase by passing from "Jesus" (v. 20) to "Jesus" (v. 21).[29]

In concluding this first major section of this chapter, we restate the goal of New Testament text criticism. Text criticism seeks to identify the original reading of the Greek New Testament, which is made more than possible because of the treasure trove of Greek manuscripts in our possession.

TRANSLATING THE TEXT

Once the process of text criticism establishes what the text is, the next step in preparing to interpret the Greek text is to ascertain what the text says; that is, to translate the Greek passage into English. John D. Harvey writes, "There are a variety of approaches the interpreter may use in moving from the Greek text to an English understanding of it. Of those approaches, translating the entire passage provides the fullest and most direct interaction with the text and allows the interpreter to arrive at his or own independent understanding of what the text says."[30]

As we discuss how to translate the entire passage from the Greek text into English, we offer two points. First, we begin with a more general and foundational concern, namely, overviewing the two major theories of Bible translation. Second, we tackle the task of translating the Greek into English, following four steps: (1) deciding upon the text (assuming there are textual variants in the passage under examination, which is the case in Revelation 1:1–3, our sample passage); (2) punctuating the passage to delimit the sentences; (3) providing a preliminary translation of the Greek passage by parsing verbs, identifying nouns and pronouns, and moving word by word through the sentences; (4) providing two translations: first a more formal translation, then a more functional translation (the second smoothing out the first). In my opinion, questions of **structure** (determining phrases, clauses, compound sentences), **syntax** (how words are related to each other), **style** (noting literary features of the text), and **semantics** (the meaning of words as gained by lexical study), are best left for the actual interpretation of the text. We will tackle that task in the next chapter.

---

29. Such an error is called "haplography."

30. John D. Harvey, *Interpreting the Pauline Letters: An Exegetical Handbook* (Grand Rapids: Kregel, 2012), 108.

Two Theories of Bible Translation

Essentially, translators employ two theories of Bible translation today. Some English Bibles purport to practice the formal-equivalence (word-for-word in the order of the Greek text) method of translating whereby earnest attempts are made to translate word-for-word the original language into English as well as maintain the original word order and sentence structure. Although many English Bibles claim to follow a formal-equivalence theory, the New American Standard Bible is generally regarded as the most "complete equivalent" or "formal equivalent" translation of the twentieth century. In 1995, the text of the NASB was updated to reflect the most recent Greek and Hebrew texts as well as to provide greater understanding and smoother readability. In fact, the ultimate purpose of both the Authorized Standard Version and NASB has always been to provide "the most literally accurate English translation" from the original languages. Other translations that also purport to practice the formal-equivalence (complete equivalence) theory are the Revised Version (RV), the New Revised Standard Version (NRSV), the English Standard Version (ESV), and the New King James Version (NKJV).

In contrast, other Bibles practice a dynamic-equivalence (functional equivalence) theory whereby attempts are made to translate the ancient authors "thought-for-thought." This translation theory begins with an exegetical translation of the original language and then, based upon interpretations, creates a contemporary vernacular English translation that best conveys the ideas and connotations of the ancient authors. The New Living Translation (NLT), a revision of the Living Bible (LB), is based upon the most recent scholarship in the theory of translation. It proudly proclaims to be a thought-for-thought translation that seeks to be both exegetically accurate and idiomatically powerful and that is to be both reliable and readable. Thus, the emphasis is placed on being a functional-equivalent translation.

In reality, there are no completely word-for-word, formal-equivalent English translations because they would be unreadable. There are no perfect translations, which is why there are so many Bibles on the market. All translations are, in different and varying degrees, interpretations; all translations have limitations; and all translations have strengths and weaknesses. Our purpose here, however, is not to pit one Bible translation against another. It is our goal to point out how different Bible translations can assist us in preparing to interpret Revelation. As we advance, it may be helpful to identify, on a sliding scale, the degree of differences between those more formal ("formal-equivalent") English Bibles to the more functional ("functional-equivalent):

More Formal	More Functional
ASV NASB KJV NKJV RSV ESV NRSV NET NIV TNIV NLT LB	

Translations to the right tend to translate English into a more readable contemporary vernacular than those to the left.[31]

Translating the Greek Text into English

We have chosen to apply our four steps for translating a passage to Revelation 1:1–3, the opening verses of the book. Here is the text taken from the twenty-eighth edition of the *Novum Testamentum Graece*:

> **1** Ἀποκάλυψις Ἰησοῦ Χριστοῦ ἣν ἔδωκεν αὐτῷ ὁ θεὸς δεῖξαι τοῖς δούλοις αὐτοῦ ἃ δεῖ γενέσθαι ἐν τάχει, καὶ ἐσήμανεν ἀποστείλας διὰ τοῦ ἀγγέλου αὐτοῦ τῷ δούλῳ αὐτοῦ Ἰωάννῃ, **2** ὃς ἐμαρτύρησεν τὸν λόγον τοῦ θεοῦ καὶ τὴν μαρτυρίαν Ἰησοῦ Χριστοῦ ὅσα εἶδεν. **3** Μακάριος ὁ ἀναγινώσκων καὶ οἱ ἀκούοντες τοὺς λόγους τῆς προφητείας καὶ τηροῦντες τὰ ἐν αὐτῇ γεγραμμένα, ὁ γὰρ καιρὸς ἐγγύς.

Deciding upon the Text Using Text Criticism

The Nestle/Aland 28 edition reflects the original text of Revelation 1:1–3. Six key variant readings were assessed to reach this conclusion.

1. ℵ* adds ἅγιος to δούλοις αὐτοῦ in Revelation 1:1, but A does not have the modifier. Because the unmodified reading also occurs in Revelation 11:18 and 19:2, 5 our text correctly omits ἅγιος.

2. The Byzantine family texts 1611 and Andreas 2351 omit τῷ δούλῳ αὐτοῦ in Revelation 1:1, because of *homoioteleuton* where the scribe jumped from the second αὐτοῦ to the third αὐτοῦ eliminating the words in between. Our text correctly keeps τῷ δούλῳ αὐτοῦ.

3. Byzantine texts 1611 and 17, Arabic and Coptic Victorinus and Ps. Ambrose have the plural μακάριοι ὁ ἀναγινώσκων in Revelation1:3, probably in keeping with the plural forms of the beatitudes in Revelation 14:13 and 22:14. The singular form in our text seems to be the better reading.

---

31. This discussion is indebted to Herbert W. Bateman IV, *Interpreting the General Letters: An Exegetical Handbook* (Grand Rapids: Kregel, 2013), 139–141.

4. The Vulgate has the singular ἀκούων in Revelation 1:3 but the plural in our text is correct.

5. The Byzantine texts 1611, 2053, 2062 along with the Vulgate, Syriac, Coptic Bohairic insert ταύτης after προφητείας in Revelation 1:3, but our text has the better reading.

6. There are three variant readings regarding "the words" of the prophets in Revelation 1:3. A, C, the Vulgate, the Coptic, and the Syriac have τοὺς λόγους; C has τούς λόγους ταύτους; ℵ has τόν λόγον. Normally ℵ is to be preferred over A, but in Revelation A is more dependable than ℵ. Moreover, since τοὺς λόγους parallels 22:7, 10, 18, both external and internal evidence favors our text.[32]

Punctuating the Text

Revelation 1:1–3 consists of two sentences. The first sentence runs from the beginning of verse 1 to the end of verse 2. There is no main verb in the opening sentence; verse 1 simply begins with "The Revelation of Jesus Christ." The first sentence consists of three statements (containing both clauses and prepositional phrases):

—The Revelation of Jesus Christ which God gave to him to show to his servants what must come to pass quickly,

—and he made known by sending his angel to his servant John,

—who witnessed to the word of God and to the testimony of Jesus Christ, even to all that he saw.

Verse 3 is the second sentence in Revelation 1:1–3. It consists of three relative clauses and one subordinate clause (we will analyze the clauses and other syntactical features in the next chapter). The three relative clauses are:

—Blessed is the one who reads aloud,

—and [blessed are] the ones who hear the words of the prophets

—and [blessed are] the ones who keep what is written therein.

---

32. These text critical issues have been culled from David E. Aune, *Revelation 1–5*, volume 51a (Dallas: Word, 1997), 6–7.

The subordinate clause concludes the second sentence, "for the time is near."

Preliminary Translation Moving Word-by-Word through the Passage[33]

1.1 Ἀποκάλυψις	Ἰησοῦ	Χριστοῦ,	ἣν	ἔδωκεν	αὐτῷ	ὁ	θεὸς	δεῖξαι
NNSF	NGSM	NGSM	RR-ASF	VAAI3S	RP3DSM	DNSM	NNSM	VAAN
the revelation	of Jesus	Christ	which	gave	him	—	God	to show

τοῖς	δούλοις	αὐτοῦ,	ἃ		δεῖ	γενέσθαι	ἐν
DDPM	NDPM	RP3GSM	RR-APN		VPAI3S	VAMN	P
	slaves	his	the things which		must	take place	in

τάχει,	καὶ	ἐσήμανεν	ἀποστείλας	διὰ	τοῦ	ἀγγέλου	αὐτοῦ
NDSN	CLN	VAAI3S	VAAP-SNM	P	DGSM	NGSM	RP3GSM
a short time	and	communicated it[b]	sending it[c]	through	—	angel	his[1]

τῷ	δούλῳ	αὐτοῦ	Ἰωάννῃ,	²ὃς	ἐμαρτύρησεν	τὸν	λόγον	τοῦ	θεοῦ
DDSM	NDSM	RP3GSM	NDSM	RR-NSM	VAAI3S	DASM	NASM	DGSM	NGSM
to[3]	Slave		John	who	testified about	the	word	of	God

καὶ	τὴν	μαρτυρίαν	Ἰησοῦ	Χριστοῦ,	ὅσα	εἶδεν.	³μακάριος	ὁ
CLN	DASF	NASF	NGSM	NGSM	RK-APN	VAAI3S	JNSM	DNSM
and	the	testimony	of Jesus	Christ	all that	he saw	blessed is[e]	the

ἀναγινώσκων	καὶ	οἱ		ἀκούοντες	τοὺς	λόγους	τῆς
VPAP-SNM		CLN	DNPM		VPAP-PNM	DAPM	NAPM	DGSF
one who reads aloud	and	blessed are those[g]		who hear	the	words	of the

Προφητείας	καὶ	τηροῦντες	τὰ	ἐν	αὐτῇ	γεγραμμένα,	ὁ	γὰρ
NGSF	CLN	VPAP-PNM	DAPN	P	RP3DSF	VRPP-PAN	DNSM	CAZ
Prophecy	And	observe	the things	in	it[3]	written[1]	the[5]	because

καιρὸς	ἐγγύς.
NNSM	B
time	is near[h]

Two Translations: Formal and Functional

One of the most formal translations (word-by-word) is that of the New American Standard Version. It translates Revelation 1:1–3 as follows:

> —The Revelation of Jesus Christ, which God gave Him to show to His bond-servants, the things which must soon take place; and He sent and communicated *it* by His angel to His bond-servant John, who testified to the word of God and to the testimony of Jesus Christ, *even* to all that he saw.

> —Blessed is he who reads and those who hear the words of the prophecy, and heed the things which are written in it; for the time is near.

Contrast the NASB to the more functional approach of the NIV:

> —The revelation from Jesus Christ, which God gave him to show his servants what must soon take place. He made it known by sending his angel to his servant John, who testifies to everything he saw—that is, the word of God and the testimony of Jesus Christ.

> —Blessed is the one who reads aloud the words of this prophecy, and blessed are those who hear it and take to heart what is written in it, because the time is near.

Personally, I appreciate both translations of Revelation 1:1–3, but for different reasons. I like the NASB's commitment to rendering the Greek word by word for grammatical purposes. It helps me to both better grasp the original reading and its structure. Therefore, I would prefer to make my sermon outline based on the NASB (along with the Greek, of course). On the other hand, I prefer to use the NIV in preaching because it better resonates with today's audiences. Through my years of preaching, I have discovered that Christian audiences like the sound of the NIV over that of the NASB.

Chapter in Review

This chapter broached the subject of interpreting canonical prophetic–apocalyptic material, most notably Revelation. It addressed two preliminary steps for interpreting the text: surveying the subject of text criticism and providing a tentative translation of that text. The goal of the former step was to identify or establish the text under study, and the latter step translated that text. The next chapter will engage in the actual interpretation of the text by moving through four steps: examining the structure of the text which leads to ascertaining the syntax and semantics of the text, followed by relating the style of the passage to the three previous points.

5

INTERPRETING BIBLICAL APOCALYPTIC LITERATURE

HISTORICAL BACKGROUND

OF ALL THE BOOKS IN THE BIBLE, Revelation requires some introductory remarks before one can properly interpret it. Such an introduction should include, therefore, the following: the genre of Revelation; its authorship; the date and historical setting of its writing; the major schools of interpretation of the book; and the relationship among Revelation, the Epistles of John, and the Gospel of John.

Genre

Before one can properly interpret any piece of literature, the Bible included, one must determine its genre or literary type. This principle is acutely important for Revelation, and its neglect has resulted in a morass of conflicting viewpoints. The difficulty is heightened by the fact that Revelation consists of a mixture of three genres: apocalyptic, prophetic, and epistolary. Since we covered this material in our first three chapters, we need not revisit that topic here.

Author

In ascertaining the identity of the author of Revelation, two lines of evidence need to be assessed: external and internal. The external evidence consists of the testimony of the church fathers, which is nearly unanimously in favor of the opinion that the apostle John was the author of the Apocalypse. Those ancient witnesses include Papias, Justin Martyr, the Muratorian Fragment, Irenaeus, Clement of Alexandria, Tertullian, Hippolytus, Origen, and Methodius. The notable exceptions to this testimony are Dionysius, bishop of Alexandria (247–264), and Eusebius, the church historian, who himself was persuaded by Dionysius' arguments against Johannine authorship of the book (though Eusebius expressed his doubts less vigorously than did Dionysius).

In turning to the internal evidence for determining the authorship of Revelation, Dionysius' four categories continue to convince many against Johannine authorship.[1] Those categories are (1) the writer's self-identification; (2) the construction of Revelation as compared with the genuine writings of John the apostle; (3) the character of these writings; and (4) the writing style of these materials.

The first internal argument offered by Dionysius is that whereas Revelation identifies its author as "John" (1:1, 4, 9; 22:8), neither the Gospel of John nor the letters of John do the same. The assumption here is that if the apostle John had written Revelation, he would not have felt any compulsion to identify himself as its author. This reasoning, however, is an argument from silence and therefore is not convincing. Moreover, the apocalyptic nature of the book may have necessitated the

---

1. This influence can especially be seen in the monumental work by R. H. Charles, *The Revelation of St. John*, 2 vols. (Edinburgh: T. & T. Clark, 1920).

author identifying himself, even as other works fitting that genre do. Actually, the fact that the author mentions his name—John—without any appeal to credentials, suggests he was well known to the Asia Minor churches. This simple mention of "John" lends support to the claim that John the apostle authored the Apocalypse.

With regard to the construction of Revelation and that of John's Gospel and letters, Dionysius argued that the former does not begin with the identification of Jesus as the "Word" nor with the author's eyewitness vantage point whereas the latter do (cf. John 1:1–18 with 1 John 1:1–4). This observation, however, overlooks Revelation 1:2 and its connection of the word of God with Christ. It also misses the significance attached to the concept of "witness" in Revelation and in the other Johannine literature (cf. Rev. 1:2; 22:16 with John 1:19–51; 5:32; 8:18; 15:26; 1 John 1:1–4; 5:6–11).

Dionysius also maintained that the vocabulary of Revelation differs significantly from the genuine Johannine writings. Yet Dionysius' assertion does not hold up under careful scrutiny. Twelve of the nineteen Johannine terms that are supposedly not found in Revelation do in fact occur (e.g., "life," "blood," "judgment," "devil"). Moreover, three of the terms not occurring in Revelation are also absent from the Gospel of John ("forgiveness," "Antichrist," "adoption"), and one of them ("conviction") is not present in 1 John. Furthermore, although "truth" is not in the Apocalypse, its synonym "genuine" is. Also, while "joy" is absent in the Apocalypse, it only occurs once each in the three letters of John. We are left then with one term, "darkness," that occurs frequently in the other Johannine writings and not in Revelation—hardly enough evidence upon which to base a major distinction.

Finally, Dionysius claimed that Revelation is written in poor Greek, in contrast to the good Greek style of the other Johannine materials. This claim, however, overlooks three factors: (1) an author's writing style is not always consistent; (2) John, like his contemporaries, may well have used an amanuensis (a professional secretary), through whom he composed his gospel and the letters (cf. Rom. 16:22; 1 Pet. 5:12). Exiled on the island of Patmos, however (cf. 1:9), he presumably did not have access to such an individual. (3) Revelation (Apocalypse) is a different genre than John (Gospel) or the Epistles of John (Letter), which might also account for differing styles. On balance, then, the external and internal evidence seem to point to the apostle John as the author of the Apocalypse.

Date and Historical Setting

The date and historical setting of Revelation are integral to how one interprets that work. Later in this introduction, we will overview the four major schools of interpretation of Revelation, but here we observe that two major periods qualify as candidates for its historical setting: the period of the reign of Emperor Nero (A.D. 54–68), especially A.D. 64–68; and the time of Domitian's reign (A.D. 81–96), especially the last few years. We now summarize the arguments for those respective views.

A Neronian Date

Five arguments are often put forth to defend a pre-A.D. 70 date for Revelation.[2] First, Revelation 11:1–2 speaks of the Jerusalem Temple as still standing. Since the Temple was not destroyed by the Romans until A.D. 70, it is surmised that Revelation was written before that catastrophe occurred. Second, Revelation 17:10 speaks of seven kings: "five have fallen, one is, the other has not yet come." The one who is, the sixth king, is the one in power at the writing of Revelation. The kings are often identified with the Roman emperors of the first century. Beginning with Augustus, those kings were:

Augustus	31 B.C.–14 A.D.
Tiberius	A.D. 14–37
Caligula	A.D. 37–41
Claudius	A.D. 41–54
Nero	A.D. 54–68
Galba	A.D. 68–69
Otho	A.D. 69
Vitellius	A.D. 69
Vespasian	A.D. 69–79
Titus	A.D. 79–81
Domitian	A.D. 81–96

The advocates of a Neronian date for Revelation argue for one of two options regarding Revelation 17:10. One option is to equate the first king with Augustus, the first official Roman emperor and the sixth as Galba, who reigned briefly after Nero's death. The other possibility is to begin

---

2. The following discussion is indebted to Aune, *Revelation 1–5*, lvi–lxx; Keener, *Revelation. The NIV Application Commentary*, 35–39; Grant R. Osborne, *Revelation,* Baker Exegetical Commentary on the New Testament (Grand Rapids: Baker, 2002), 6–9; and G. F. Beale, *The Book of Revelation. A Commentary on the Greek Text* (Grand Rapids: Paternoster, 1999), 4–27.

with Julius Caesar, who first claimed the rights of Roman emperor (47–44 B.C.); then the sixth king would be Nero, with Galba being the seventh. Either way, these two approaches relate Revelation 17:10 to Nero.

Third, "666" (Rev. 13:18) is no doubt John's usage of the Jewish numerological technique of gematria. Gematria was a mathematic cryptogram which assigned numerical values to letters of the alphabet. More than one scholar has seen a possible referent of this number in *Neron Kaiser*. The Hebrew numerical valuation for *Nrwn Qsr* is as follows: N=50, R=200, W=6, N=50, Q=100, S=60 and R=200, which add up to 666.

Fourth, "Babylon" is thought to represent Jerusalem in Revelation (see Rev. 11:8; 18:10, 16, 18, 19, 21; cf. 14:8; 17:5). This equation is assumed because Jerusalem/ancient Judaism crucified Christ, persecuted early Christians, and was exempt from Caesar worship (see below). These actions earned her the name "Babylon," the nemesis of the people of God in the Old Testament. Finally, related to the previous point, Revelation 1:7, according to those advocating a pre-A.D. 70 date for Revelation, is a prophecy of Jesus's coming judgment on Jerusalem, which was fulfilled in A.D. 70 at the hands of the Romans (cf. Zech. 12:12).

Although these arguments are impressive at first glance, there are problems with them. First, most commentators rightly recognize that the symbolic Jerusalem Temple is being described in Revelation 11:2, not the literal Temple. In light of that allusion, a post-A.D. 70 setting better fits the description of the destruction of the outer Temple while the preservation of the true people of God as portrayed in that verse accounts for the reference to the inner Temple, Second, there are other viable ways of numbering the emperors in Revelation 17:10, if indeed they represent Roman Caesars.[3] According to R. H. Charles, one way is to begin with Augustus, the first recognized Roman emperor. Thus Nero would be the fifth king. Because the reigns of Galba, Otho, and Vitellius were brief and disputed they should be omitted in the count. This approach would make Vespasian the sixth ruler and his son, Titus, the seventh. The eighth king would be Vespasian's other son Domitian.[4]

Third, it seems that "666" is alluding to Nero, but it is Nero *Redivivus* (revived) that John has in mind (see Rev. 13:3). After Nero committed suicide on June 9, A.D. 68 (right after the Roman Senate condemned his rule), the legend developed that Nero returned from the dead and was about to lead the Parthians from the east to attack Rome. It seems that this myth did not gather force until the end of the first century A.D.

---

3. Some equate Revelation 17:10 with world kingdoms, not individual emperors; see Osborne, *Revelation*, 620.

4. Charles, *The Revelation of John* 2:69–70.

Fourth, the problem with equating "Babylon" with Jerusalem in Revelation is that there is not one example elsewhere of "Babylon" being used as a symbolic name for Israel.[5] On the other hand, "Babylon" was often used of the city of Rome in post-A.D. 70 Jewish literature (cf. Rev. 14:6; 16:19; 17:4; 18:2, 10, 21 with *4 Ezra* 3:1–2, 28–31; *2 Baruch* 10:1–3; 11:1; 67:7; *Sib. Or.* 5.143, 159). Babylon was an appropriate symbol for Rome because, just as Babylon captured Jerusalem and destroyed the temple in 587 B.C. (2 Kings 25), so Rome captured and destroyed Jerusalem and its temple in A.D. 70.[6]

Fifth, Revelation 1:7 and the other references to Jesus's parousia in Revelation better refer to his Second Coming in the future than to his past coming in judgment on Jerusalem in A.D. 70.

Domitian Date

Most scholars today argue for a Domitian date of the writing of Revelation. They offer five considerations. First, the pertinent church fathers thought so, including Irenaeus, Eusebius, Victorinus, Jerome, Clement of Alexandria, and Justin Martyr.[7] Second, Revelation 11:2 best fits a post-A.D. 70 date because it better reflects a time after the fall of Jerusalem and the destruction of the temple. Revelation 17:10 is quite capable of supporting a Domitian setting if we follow Charles's suggestion that the first emperor is Augustus, the first recognized ruler. This calculation, then, would make Vespasian the sixth ruler and his son, Titus, the seventh. The eighth king would be Vespasian's other son Domitian. "666" is better taken as an allusion to Domitian as Nero *Redivivus*. "Babylon" fits post-70 A.D. Rome and the name is never used in ancient Judaism for Israel or Jerusalem; Revelation 1:7 refers to Jesus's Second Coming, not the fall of Jerusalem in A.D. 70. The description one finds here is in keeping with the many other references to the Second Coming at the end of history (i.e., Matt. 24:30–31//Mark 13:26–27//Luke 21:27–28; 2 Thess. 2:8; Titus 2:13–14; Jude 14–15).

Third, the problem posed to early Christians by Roman emperor worship is extensive in Revelation (Rev. 2–3; 13:4, 14–17; 14:9; 15:2; 16:2; 19:20; 20:4) and such a practice gained momentum under Domitian, especially in Asia Minor, home of the seven churches of the Revelation.[8] Fourth, related to the previous point, persecution of those

---

5. See Beale, *The Book of Revelation*, 25.

6. So A. Yarbro Collins, "Dating the Apocalypse of John" *Biblical Research* 26 (1981), 35.

7. See Aune's references, *Revelation 1–5*, lx.

8. Key works analyzing the imperial cult as the immediate background to Revelation include W. M. Ramsay, *The Letters to the Seven Churches* (London: Hodden & Stoughton, 1904); C. J. Hemer, *The Letters to the Seven Churches of Asia in Their Local Setting. Journal for the Study of*

who did not worship Caesar became intense and more widespread under Domitian.[9] Such oppression was in contrast to Nero's persecution of Christians, which was restricted to Rome.

Fifth, the historical background of the seven churches in Asia Minor support a post-Neronian date for Revelation. Grant Osborne delineates six events reflected in the letters that point to a later date than the 60s. (1) The unaided recovery of Laodicea (3:17) best fits the earthquake and subsequent reconstruction of the city in A.D. 80. (2) Their great wealth reflects better the 90s than the 60s. (3) "Do not harm the oil and the wine" (6:6) most likely refers to an edict of Domitian in A.D. 92 restricting the growing of vines in Asia. (4) The "synagogues of Satan" (2:9; 3:9) can best be situated in conflicts that took place under Domitian. (5) The church of Smyrna (2:8–11) may not have existed in the 60s. (6) The idea of the beast's "mortal wound that is healed" (13:3, 12, 14) may well reflect the Nero *redivivus* legend that developed in the 80s and 90s.[10]

In our estimation, then, the date (at least the final editing) of the writing of Revelation was ca. A.D. 90–95, at a time when Christians in Asia Minor were being pressed to worship Domitian.[11]

The Major Schools of Interpretation

Traditionally, four major interpretations have been put forth in attempting to unravel the mysteries of the Apocalypse: preterist, historicist, futurist, and idealist. Except for the historicist view, the other three perspectives enjoy many followers today. The historicist view fell out of favor with interpreters of Revelation because this perspective restricted itself to the battle between the Protestant Reformation and the papacy in the sixteenth century, causing that school of interpretation long ago to fall out of favor with readers of Revelation. After discussing the three remaining interpretations, we will offer our own eclectic approach.[12]

---

the *New Testament Supplement Series* 11 (Sheffield: JSOT, 1986); S. R. Price, *Rituals and Power: The Roman Imperial Cult in Asia Minor* (Cambridge: Cambridge University, 1984).

9. See Aune for discussion of the development of the debate over whether Revelation in fact reflects the imperial cult, *Revelation 1–5*, lxiv–lxix; compare also Beale's judicious assessment of the evidence, *The Book of Revelation*, 28–33. He concludes that the Caesar cult did indeed make its presence known in Asia Minor under Domitian.

10. Osborne, *Revelation*, 9. Many assume number 6 above reflects a re-application of the title "Beast" for Nero to Domitian.

11. Aune thinks Revelation was first written before A.D. 70 and then revised in the 90s A.D.; *Revelation 1–5*, lviii.

12. This section on the schools of interpretation comes from ed. C. Marvin Pate, *Four Views on the Book of Revelation* (Grand Rapids.: Zondervan, 1998), 19–34.

The Preterist Interpretation

The preterist ("past") viewpoint wants to take seriously the historical interpretation of Revelation by relating it to its original author and audience. That is, John addressed his book to real churches who faced dire problems in the first century A.D. Two quandaries in particular provided the impetus for the recording of the book. Kenneth L. Gentry Jr. writes:

> Revelation has two fundamental purposes relative to its original hearers. In the first place, it was designed to steel the first century Church against the gathering storm of persecution, which was reaching an unnerving crescendo of theretofore unknown proportions and intensity. A new and major feature of that persecution was the entrance of imperial Rome onto the scene. The first historical persecution of the Church by imperial Rome was by Nero Caesar from A.D. 64 to A.D. 68. In the second place, it was to brace the Church for a major and fundamental re-orientation in the course of redemptive history, a re-orientation necessitating the destruction of Jerusalem (the center not only of Old Covenant Israel, but of Apostolic Christianity [cp. Ac. 1:8; 2:1ff.; 15:2] and the Temple [cp. Mt. 24:1–34 with Rev. 11]).[13]

The sustained attempt to root the fulfillment of the divine prophecies of Revelation in the first century A.D. constitutes the preterist's distinctive approach. The origin of preterism can be traced to the theological system known as postmillennialism, which teaches that Christ will return after the Millennium, a period of bliss on earth brought about by the conversion of the nations because of the preaching of the gospel. Preterists locate the timing of the fulfillment of the prophecies of Revelation in the first century A.D., specifically just before the fall of Jerusalem in A.D. 70 (though some also see its fulfillment in both the falls of Jerusalem [first century] and Rome [fifth century]). Despite the opinion of many that Revelation was written in the 90s during the reign of Domitian (81–96), much of evangelical preterism holds the date of the book to be Neronian (54–68). Recall, however, our arguments above against that view. The Preterist view might outline Revelation as follows:

---

13. Ken Gentry Jr., *Before Jerusalem Fell: Dating the Book of Revelation* (Tyler, TX: Institute for Christian Economics, 1989), 15–16. It should be remembered, however, that preterism is comprised of two camps—one that locates the fulfillment of Revelation largely in the first century relative to the fall of Jerusalem, and another that sees the fulfillment of Revelation in *both* the first century (the fall of Jerusalem) and in the fifth century (the fall of Rome).

Revelation 1	John's Vision of the Risen Jesus
Revelation 2–3	The Situation of Early Jewish Christianity
Revelation 4–5	The Heavenly Scene of Christ's Reign
Revelation 6–18	Parallel Judgments on Jerusalem
Revelation 19	Christ's Coming to Complete the Judgment of Jerusalem
Revelation 20–22	Christ's Rule on Earth

Postmillennialism (Preterist)

Christ comes after the millennium.

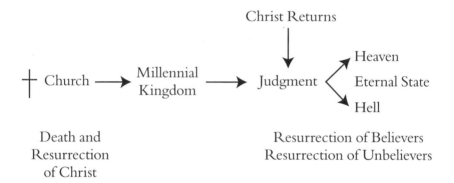

The Idealist Interpretation

The idealist approach to Revelation has sometimes been called the "spiritualist" view in that it interprets the book spiritually, or symbolically. According to this approach, Revelation is seen as representing the ongoing conflict of good and evil, with no immediate historical connection to any social or political events. Accordingly, Raymond Calkins captures the chief message of Revelation in terms of five propositions: (1) It is an irresistible summons to heroic living. (2) It contains matchless appeals to endurance. (3) It tells us that evil is marked for overthrow in the end. (4) It gives us a new and wonderful picture of Christ. (5) It reveals to us the fact that history is in the mind of God and in the hand of Christ as the author and reviewer of the moral destinies of men.[14]

Although all of the schools of interpretation surveyed here resonate with these affirmations, the idealist view distinguishes itself by refusing to assign the preceding statements to any historical correspondence and thereby denies that the prophecies in Revelation are predictive except in

14. Raymond Calkins, *The Social Message of the Book of Revelation* (New York: Woman's Press, 1920), 3–9.

the most general sense of the promise of the ultimate triumph of good at the return of Christ.[15] The origin of the idealist school of thought can be traced back to the allegorical or symbolic hermeneutic espoused by the Alexandrian church fathers, especially Clement and Origen. Akin to the Alexandrian interpretation of Revelation was the amillennial view propounded by Dionysius, Augustine, and Jerome. Thus the Alexandrian school, armed with the amillennial method, became the dominant approach to Revelation until the Reformation.

As mentioned above, the idealist does not restrict the contents of Revelation to a particular historical period, but rather sees it as an apocalyptic dramatization of the continuous battle between God and evil. Because the symbols are multivalent in meaning and without specific historical referent, the application of the book's message is limitless. Each interpreter can therefore find significance for their respective situation. There does not seem to be a hard-and-fast rule for the idealist in delineating the structure of Revelation.

Amillennialism (Idealist)

No future thousand-year reign of Christ

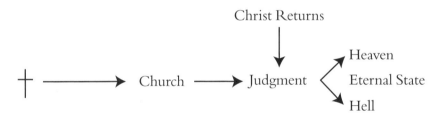

| Death and Resurrection of Christ | Both Millennial Kingdom/Tribulation Are Now | Resurrection of Believers Resurrection of Unbelievers |

The Futurist View

The most popular view regarding the interpretation of Revelation is the futurist view. *The Scofield Bible*, Hal Lindsey's *The Late Great Planet Earth,* and the *Left Behind series* have ensured that to be the case. Although the futurist view tends to interpret Revelation 4–22 as still unfulfilled (awaiting the events surrounding the Second Coming of Christ), it is not completely unified, dividing into two camps of interpretation: dispensational and historic premillennialism.

---

15. Merrill C. Tenney provides a helpful summary of the idealist interpretation of Revelation, as well as the other viewpoints, *Interpreting Revelation* (Grand Rapids: Eerdmans, 1957), 143–44.

Dispensational premillennialism derives its name from the biblical word "dispensation," a term referring to the administration of God's earthly household (KJV, 1 Cor. 9:17; Eph. 1:10; 3:2; Col. 1:25). Dispensationalists divide salvation history into historical eras or epochs in order to distinguish the different administrations of God's involvement in the world. C. I. Scofield, after whom the enormously popular *Scofield Bible* was named, defined a dispensation as "a period of time during which man is tested in respect of obedience to some specific revelation of the will of God."[16] During each dispensation, humankind fails to live in obedience to the divine test, consequently bringing that period under God's judgment and thus creating the need for a new dispensation. Read this way, the Bible can be divided into the following eight dispensations (though the names vary in this school of thought): innocence, conscience, civil government, promise, Mosaic law, church and age of grace, tribulation, millennium.[17]

The hallmark of dispensationalism has been its commitment to a literal interpretation of prophetic Scripture. This approach has resulted in three well-known tenets cherished by adherents of the movement.

First, it is essential to maintain a distinction between the prophecies made about Israel in the Old Testament and the church in the New Testament. In other words, the church has not replaced Israel in the plan of God. The promises He made to the nation about its future restoration will occur. The church is, therefore, a parenthesis in the outworking of that plan. The dispensational distinction between Israel and the church was solidified in the minds of many as a result of two major events in this century: the holocaust (which has rightly elicited from many deep compassion for the Jewish people) and the rebirth of the State of Israel in 1948.

Second, dispensationalists are premillennialists; that is, they believe Christ will come again and establish a temporary, one-thousand-year reign on earth from Jerusalem. Third, dispensationalists believe in the pretribulation rapture. That is, Christ's return will occur in two stages: the first one for his church which will be raptured to heaven before the end-time tribulation period begins; the second one in power and glory to conquer his enemies.

The dispensationalist's understanding of the time frame of Revelation and its structure go hand in hand. Because this school of thought

---

16. *The Scofield Reference Bible* (New York: Oxford, 1909), note to Genesis 1:28 heading. For an updated definition that emphasizes faith as the means for receiving the revelations in the various dispensations, see Charles C. Ryrie, *Dispensationalism Today* (Chicago: Moody, 1965), 74.

17. C. I. Scofield, *Rightly Dividing the Word of Truth* (New York: Loizeaux Brothers, 1896). Many modern dispensationalists, however, have grown uncomfortable with these periodizations, preferring rather to talk about the Bible in terms of its two divisions—the old and new covenants.

interprets the prophecies of the book literally, their fulfillment, there-fore, is perceived as still future (especially chapters 4–22). Moreover, the magnitude of the prophecies (e.g., one-third of the earth destroyed; the sun darkened) suggests that they have not yet occurred in history. The key verse in this discussion is 1:19, particularly its three tenses, which are thought to provide an outline for Revelation: "what you have seen" (the past, John's vision of Jesus in chap. 1); "what is now" (the pres-ent, the letters to the seven churches in chapters 2–3); "what will take place later" (chapters 4–22). In addition, the dispensationalist believes that the lack of mention of the church from chapter 4 on indicates that it has been raptured to heaven by Christ before the advent of the great tribulation (chapters 6–18).

Dispensational Premillennialism (Futurist)

> Christ comes **before** the Millennium and **before** the tribulation. (A modified interpretation has Christ com-ing for his Church in the middle of the tribulation.)

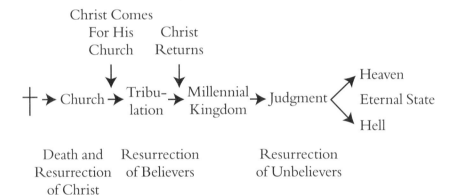

Historic Premillennialism agrees with dispensationalism that Christ will return to establish a thousand-year reign on earth at his par-ousia. Difference ensues, however, between the two approaches on the issue of the relationship of the church and the great tribulation (Rev. 18). According to historic[18] premillennialism, the church will undergo the messianic woes, the great tribulation. Accompanying this belief is the conviction that the church has replaced Old Testament Israel

---

18. The name "historic" premillennial comes from the conviction that this was the earliest view of the church fathers; see Pate and Kennard, *Deliverance Now and Not Yet*, 3. For a helpful, detailed investigation of the four schools of interpretation relative to Revelation, see Steve Gregg, *Revelation: Four Views: A Parallel Commentary* (Nashville: Nelson, 1997).

as the people of God (Rom. 2:26–28; 11; Gal. 6:16; Eph. 2:11–22; 1 Peter 2:9–10; Rev. 1:5–6; 7:1–8; etc.). Like amillennialism, the historic premillennial view is based on the already/not-yet eschatological hermeneutic: the kingdom of God dawned with the First Coming of Christ, but it will not be completed until the Second Coming of Christ. In the between period the church encounters the messianic woes, which will intensify and culminate in the return of Christ.

Historic Premillennialism (Futurist)

Christ comes **before** the Millennium and **after** the tribulation.

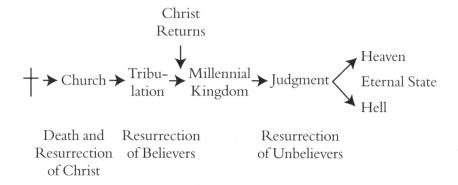

Our own view of Revelation, like many, is an eclectic approach. That is, there is an element of truth in all of the above viewpoints (with the exception of the historicist interpretation). The preterists are correct to root much of Revelation in the first century, especially the early church's battle with Caesar worship. Yet, with the futurist, we believe that the parousia did not happen at the fall of Jerusalem. Rather, it awaits the future return of Christ. The idealist perspective adds to the discussion by applying the message of Revelation throughout history until the parousia, and especially along with that the challenge therein to worship Christ alone.

The Relationship of Revelation to the Gospel and the Epistles

Although there are linguistic differences between Revelation, the Gospel of John, and the Epistles of John, it seems to us that John the apostle wrote Revelation, for at least two reasons. First, the eschatology of Revelation matches the Epistles of John—they both are characterized by inaugurated eschatology. Second, the history presumed in Revelation matches that of the Gospel of John. Thus the expulsion of

Jewish Christians from the synagogue alluded to in the Fourth Gospel continues in Revelation (especially chapters 2–3). The added feature of the Apocalypse is that now those expelled Christians face persecution from the Roman emperor cult.

Indeed, by the time John the apostle wrote Revelation (ca. A.D. 95), his churches in Asia Minor faced three opponents: (1) Jewish leadership in Asia Minor persisted in expelling Jewish Christians from the synagogues. How they did so is spelled out in Revelation 2–3. (2) With the increased emphasis on Caesar worship in Asia Minor, now John's congregations faced the other side of the coin of excommunication from the synagogues; they were forced to worship the emperor because they were no longer regarded as Jews (Judaism was exempt from the imperial cult; see again Revelation 2–3). (3) The Doceticist interpreters (those who denied the humanity of Christ based on their reading of the Gospel of John (a heresy refuted in the Epistles of John), thought they had a near at hand solution to this dilemma: Christians should go along with Caesar worship because, after all, there was only one God (1 Cor. 8:1–3). In other words, the Doceticists seem to have encouraged believers to pay lip service to Caesar. In Platonic fashion, since one's body and actions did not appear to matter to these incipient Gnostics, no harm would be done in saying "Caesar is Lord." When we look at Revelation 2–3, a part of John's counter-claim to this third group of opponents was that they were, in reality, aligning themselves with the Beast/Caesar. For those who overcome, however, by being true to Christ and refusing to worship the Beast, to them belong the blessings of the new covenant.

THE ARCH OF TITUS AND REVELATION

We mentioned in our first chapter that one of the subgenres of Revelation is *ekphrasis*, a literary description of an already existing piece of art, scene of a battle, architectural site, and more. Aune has convincingly argued, for example, that Revelation 17 is just such a subgenre, an *ekphrasis* of the *Dea Roma* coin.

An important key for identifying the harlot and the beast of Revelation 17–18 as ancient Rome is found on a coin minted in A.D. 71 in Asia Minor (the home of the seven churches mentioned in Revelation 2–3) during the reign of the Roman emperor Vespasian (A.D. 69–79). This coin is known as the *Dea Roma* Coin. One side of the coin contains a portrait of the emperor with the Latin inscription IMP CAESAR VESPASIANVS AVG PM TP PP COS III, standard abbreviations for "Emperor Caesar Vespasian Augustus, Pontifex Maximus [Greatest Priest], Tribunicia Potestas [Tribunal Power], Pater Patiae [Father of the Fatherland], Consul for the Third Time."

The reverse side of the coin depicts *Roma*, a pagan goddess of Rome, sitting on seven hills. This image of a woman sitting on seven hills was obviously a way of representing Rome in the symbolic art of the day that would have been recognized by people of this time period. John's readers would certainly have understood it that way. The goddess *Roma* wears military dress, and a small sword in her left hand rests on her left knee, symbolizing the military might of Rome. She is flanked on the left and the right by the letters S and C, which stand for *senatus consultum* (a resolution of the Senate). The river god Tiber reclines against the seven hills at the right. A group consisting of a miniature she-wolf with the twins Romulus and Remus suckling is located on the left side.

Aune makes a convincing case that Revelation 17 is a detailed description of this particular coin, an *ekphrasis*. In other words, John's vision of Babylon in Revelation is based on the *Dea Roma* coin, suggesting an ironic and not-so-subtle criticism of Rome and all that Rome represented. The resemblances between the two are indeed striking. First, the goddess *Roma*, the deity who represented and protected Rome, sits on the seven hills of that city. The harlot of Revelation likewise sits on seven hills (Rev. 17). Second, in some of the Roman legends, the she-wolf who nurses Romulus and Remus carried the connotation of a harlot. The woman in Revelation 17–18 is likewise called a harlot. Third, on the coin the woman is seated by the water of the Tiber river. The harlot in Revelation sits "on many waters" (17:1, 15).

Fourth, there is a possible connection between the phrase "Mystery, Babylon the Great, the Mother of Prostitutes" (17:5) and the label *Roma* on the coin. The city of Rome was itself regarded to be a deity with a concealed name. That "secret" name, however, was widely thought by many Romans to be *Amor* (the goddess of love and sexuality), which is *Roma* spelled backward. When John describes the goddess sitting on the seven hills but then calls her the mother of prostitutes, he seems to be consciously dragging the popular matron deity of Rome and even Rome itself down into the dirt. His portrayal is a harsh, critical parody.

Fifth, the vision of Revelation 17 presents the woman as drunk with the blood of the saints who are witnesses of Jesus (17:6). This imagery may be depicted by *Roma* holding the Roman sword, which represented the power of Rome. At the time John wrote the book of Revelation, the Roman imperial worship system was persecuting and executing Christians. The *Dea Roma* coin equates Caesar Vespasian (the obverse side) with *Roma* (the reverse side) and thereby provides John with the basis to identify the harlot of Rome with the imperial cult. This equation is so because the Roman Emperor Augustus (31 B.C.–A.D. 14) initiated the custom of building temples dedicated to both Caesar and *Roma* (the personification of Rome). Augustus commissioned the building of four temples in honor of himself and *Roma*, two in Asia (Pergamon and

Ephesus) and two in Bithynia (Nicea and Nicomedia). Thereafter, coins portraying the emperor on one side and *Roma* on the other side indicated that the two went hand in hand in implementing Caesar worship.[19]

The Roman Triumph and the Arch of Titus

Now I should like to put forth the theory that, as far as I know, has not been suggested by scholars—namely, that Revelation 4–19 is an *ekphrasis* of the Arch of Titus, itself one of many Roman Triumphs. In unpacking this thesis, we will offer three points: a description of the Roman Triumph; a description of the Arch of Titus; and then the impressive parallels between the Arch of Titus and Revelation 4–19.[20]

The Roman Triumph
We have descriptions of the Roman Triumph from a number of ancient writers, including Dionysius of Halicarnassus (30 B.C.–2 B.C.; *Roman Antiquities* II. 33.2.–34.2; VIII. 67.9–10; IX 36.3; 71.4; *Lives: Romulus* XXV. 4 [where the word for the ceremony is first called, *thriambos*]; *Aemilius Paulus* XXXLLL.1–2; and Josephus ca. A.D. 90: *Jewish Wars* VII.119–157 [who describes Titus' Triumph in Rome after defeating the Jews in A.D. 73]).[21]

In reading the above accounts of the Roman Triumph, three parts to the Triumph emerge: the pre-parade meeting of the general or emperor with his troops in the Campus Martius; passing through the Porta Triumphalis to begin the procession itself which consisted of politicos, the booty of war, models or paintings of captured cities or battles, priests to offer sacrifices, captives, and general or emperor; the killing of enemy leaders at the Capitoline Hill, and a holding of a great feast for the Senate and soldiers and the people in the city of Rome.

---

19. David E. Aune, *Revelation 17–22*. Word Biblical Commentary 52c (Nashville: Nelson, 1998), 919–928. See also the discussion in C. Marvin Pate and J. Daniel Hays in *Iraq: Babylon of the End-Times?* (Grand Rapids: Baker, 2003), 104–6.

20. Revelation 10 may also be an example of *ekphrasis,* in this case a literary description of the Colossus of Rhodes; for details, see C. Marvin Pate, *The Writings of John: A Survey of the Gospel, Epistles, and Apocalypse* (Grand Rapids: Zondervan, 2011), 432.

21. Mary Beard provides a classic description of the Roman Triumph in her work, *The Roman Triumph* (Cambridge: The Belknap Press of Harvard University Press, 2007), 81–82. Overall, Beard is skeptical of the uniformity of the Roman Triumph as portrayed in various ancient sources. For the classic study of the Roman Triumph, see H. S. Versnel, *Triumphus: An Inquiry into the Origin, Development, and Meaning for the Roman Triumph* (Leiden: Brill, 1970). For the application of the Roman Triumph to 2 Corinthians 2:14 and Colossians 2:15, see Scott Hafemann, *Suffering & Ministry in the Spirit: Paul's Defense of His Ministry in II Corinthians 2:14–3:3* (Grand Rapids: Eerdmans, 1990).

The Arch of Titus

Nigel Rodgers describes the Arch of Titus, "Among the most distinctive features of the Roman empire were the triumphal arches built to proclaim its victories. The most famous arches are in Rome itself. The Arch of Titus, dedicated in A.D. 81, is among the best preserved; it graphically commemorates Titus' capture of Jerusalem in A.D. 70, and shows the seven-branched candlestick [menorah] taken from the temple."[22]

Because it has a direct bearing on our thesis, we quote Josephus' detailed description of Titus' Triumph, picking up his description with the representations of the spoils of wars:

> Now the workmanship of these representations was so magnificent and lively in the construction of the things, that it exhibited what had been done to such as did not see it, as if they had been there really present. On the top of every one of these pageants was placed the commander of the city that was taken, and the manner wherein he was taken. Moreover, there followed those pageants a great number of ships; and for the other spoils, they were carried in great plenty. But for those that were taken in the temple of Jerusalem, they made the greatest figure of them all; that is, the golden table of the weight of many talents; the candlestick [menorah][23] also, that was made of gold, though its construction was now changed from that which we made use of; for its middle shaft was fixed upon a basis, and the small branches were produced out of it to a great length, having the likeness of a trident in their position, and had every one a socket made of brass for a lamp at the tops of them. These lamps were in number seven, and represented the dignity of the number seven among the Jews[24]; and the last of all the spoils was carried the Law of the Jews. After these spoils passed by a

---

22. Nigel Rodgers, *Roman Empire: A Complete History of the Rise and Fall of the Roman Empire, Chronicling the Story of the Most Important and Influential Civilization the World Has Ever Known* (New York: Metro Books, 2010), 174.

23. Josephus witnessed the fall of Jerusalem to the Romans having switched sides from being a leader of the Jewish forces in Galilee against the Romans to becoming the latter's ally. He no doubt also witnessed Titus' Triumph as it happened in Rome and most probably saw the Arch of Titus during and after its construction. Thus Josephus had a unique view of the Roman Triumph both as a Jew and as a (turncoat) royal historian for Emperor Vespasian.

24. Recall that the seal, trumpet, and bowl judgments number seven.

great many men carrying the images of Victory[25] whose structure was entirely either of ivory or of gold. After which Vespasian marched in the first place, and Titus followed him; Domitian [26]also rode along with them; and made a glorious appearance, and rode on a horse that was worthy of admiration.

Now the last part of this pompous show was at the temple of Jupiter Capitolinus, whither when they were come, they stood still; for it was the Romans' ancient custom to stay till somebody brought the news that the general of the enemy was slain. This general was Simon, the son of Gioras, who had then been led in this triumph among the captives; a rope had also been put upon his head, and he had been drawn into a proper place in the forum, and had withal been tormented by those that drew him along; and the law of the Romans required that malefactors condemned to die should be slain there. Accordingly, when it was related that there was an end of him, and all the people had set up a shout for joy, they then began to offer those sacrifices which they had consecrated, in the prayers used in such solemnities; which when they had finished, they went away to the palace. And as for some of the spectators, the emperors entertained them at their own feast; and for all the rest there were noble preparations made for feasting at home; for this was a festival day to the city of Rome, as celebrated for the victory obtained by their army over their enemies, for the end that was now put to their civil miseries, and for the commencement of their hopes of future prosperity and happiness.

After these triumphs were over, and after the affair of the Romans were settled on the surest foundations, Vespasian resolved to build a temple to Peace [Victory], which was finished in so short a time, and in so glorious a manner, as was beyond all human expectation and opinion: for he having now by Providence a vast quantity of

---

25. See below the notion of victory in Revelation 4–5.

26. Vespasian was the father of Titus and Domitian. General Vespasian began the attack on Israel, but when he was chosen to be the emperor of Rome his son Titus finished the campaign against Israel, destroying the holy city in A.D. 70. After Emperor Titus' death, his brother Domitian became Emperor in A.D. 81.

wealth, besides what he had formerly gained in his other
exploits, he had this temple adorned with pictures and
statues; for in this temple were collected and deposited
all such rarities as men aforetime used to wander all over
the habitable world to see, when they had a desire to see
one of them after another, he also laid up therein those
golden vessels and instruments that were taken out of the
Jewish temple, as ensigns of his glory. But still he gave
order that they should lay up their [Jewish] Law, and the
purple veils of the holy place, in the royal palace itself,
and keep them there (*Jewish Wars* 7.5.5–7).

The Arch of Titus and Revelation 4–19[27]

The Arch of Titus depicts three parts of the victor's triumph: (a) the
pre-parade, (2) the procession, and (3) the sacrifice and feast. Revelation
4–5 includes parallels to the pre-parade; Revelation 6–18 includes parallels to the procession; and Revelation 19 includes parallels to the sacrifice and feast. Here we list those parallels.

Pre-Parade and Revelation 4–5

Just as the Roman general's troops sang songs to him in honor of his
recent heroics in battle, so the hosts of heaven sing honorific hymns to
God/Christ in light of Jesus's battle[28] (Rev. 5:5–14; cf. 4:8, 10–11). Just
as the Roman general gave part of the spoils, often crowns, to his troops
in appreciation for their daring service, the crowns for the service of the
saints in heaven are given to Jesus (Rev. 4:10).

As H. S. Versnel has shown, the Latin word "*triumpe*" was a verb
the Roman soldiers used to proclaim that the general/emperor was not
only victorious but an epiphany of the god Jupiter.[29] These two points
seem to connect with Revelation 5, where Jesus is said to have "tri-
umphed" (*nikē* v. 5)[30] and therefore is worthy to be praised as God (vv.

---

27. I am glad to thank here Dr. Danny Hays, Dean of Pruet School of Christian Studies at
Ouachita Baptist University, for his initial interest in the Arch of Titus and Revelation 4–19
and, in particular, his agreement that the bowl judgments may well be a part of the *ekphrasis*
of the Arch of Titus. Since our initial discussion about the subject a number of years ago,
however, our academic pursuits have not allowed us any further collaboration on the thesis
here. So, for better or for worse, all remainder of the proposed parallels between the Arch of
Titus and Revelation 4–19, unless otherwise specified, are my own.

28. The similar doxologies to God and Christ in Revelation 4–5 indicate that John equates Jesus
with God.

29. Versnel, *Triumphus*, 1–55.

30. The word *thriambos* is not used but rather *nikaō*, but the latter is John's favorite term for
triumphing by being faithful to Christ. Paul actually uses *thriambos* in 2 Corinthians 2:14

9–14). Indeed, seated with Caesar in his chariot was the winged goddess Victory (Nikē).

Most notable in the pre-parade was that the Roman general covered his face with red lead/paint signifying that the general was both king and the god Jupiter. Ironically, however, also seated in the chariot behind the general was a slave with a bell and a whip whose job it was to remind the hero that he was also a man and one would day die (the bell and whip symbolized death). This remarkable paradox—god and dead man walking—distinctly reminds one of Revelation 5:5–10, where Jesus is portrayed as a slain lamb and yet a lion; that is, God yet mortal man by virtue of his life, death by crucifixion, and resurrection.

The Procession and Revelation 6–18

The most amazing parallels between the Arch of Titus and Revelation 6–18 are the three symbols for divine judgment in Revelation 6–18: seal, trumpet, and bowl judgments. We will argue below that these symbols John records were the sacred furniture Titus took from the Jerusalem temple at its fall in A.D. 70.

Josephus says that Titus took the temple furniture, including the bowls of incense and the trumpets, along with the Menora. These items are clearly depicted on the Arch of Titus. One recalls that Revelation 2–3 presents Jesus as in the midst of the seven churches, symbolized by the seven-branched menora that was in the temple. We will analyze the trumpet and bowl imagery in order of the presentation for this section, but what do the **seal judgments** of Revelation 6–7 represent?

With regard to the Arch of Titus, Josephus notes that the Torah, the "Law of the Jews," is the last of the spoils in the procession. Then, the Jewish author says that Titus ordered that the Torah and the purple veils of the temple should be placed in the royal palace. These details suggest that the seven-sealed scroll mentioned in Revelation 5:1–14 symbolizes the Torah.

Most scholars agree that the scroll is an *opistograph*, an ancient document written on the front and back, signifying fullness and completeness (cf. Ezek. 2:9–10). All agree that the function of the opening of the scroll by the exalted Jesus is to equate himself with God: Christ alone is worthy to open the contents of the heavenly book. As such, Revelation 5 is the investiture of the Lamb—the public acknowledgment of who he is, namely, God.[31] Beyond that point, however, the identity of the scroll is disputed. The possibilities include: the book of the destiny of the world with emphasis on its eschatological finale; the Lamb's book

---

and Colossians 2:15. It should be noted that the Roman deity Victory did accompany the conquering general in his quadriga.

31.   See Aune, *Revelation 1–5*, 319–74.

of life; Yahweh's bill of divorce of Israel; a Roman legal document; a last will and testament; a covenant promise.

To us, while all of the preceding theories are good possibilities and not necessarily mutually exclusive, we find the last suggestion especially attractive and, in what follows, we bring out that nuance of meaning. The contents of the scroll unfold in Revelation 6–18, and it is none other than the blessings of the covenant promised to those who worship Christ, and the curses of the covenant pronounced upon those who worship the Beast (Caesar). More particularly, like the blessings uttered over the obedient in Deuteronomy from Mount Gerizim and the curses pronounced on the disobedient from Mount Ebal (chapteers 28–30), so God's blessings rest on those whose deaths for Christ usher them to heaven while God's curses fall on the disobedient earth-dwellers.

The scroll (βιβλίον, book) opened by Christ was written on the front and the back, which the commentators recognize to be an allusion to Ezekiel 2:9–10. There the prophet Ezekiel is shown a divine book written on the front and the back which contained the Deuteronomic curses of the Old Covenant now realized in Israel's exile (ca. 586 B.C.). The old covenant would give way to the blessings of the new covenant (Ezekiel 36). This background seems to match the scroll of Revelation 5 with its blessings and curses. Moreover, it is interesting that Deuteronomy, which contains the covenantal blessings and curses (especially chapters 28–30), later became known as the "Book of the Covenant" (*Sirach* 24:3).[32] The seal judgments, therefore, represent the Torah, the Book of the Covenant. More particularly, the seal judgments are the reapplication of the fall of Jerusalem to Rome in A.D. 70 to the future fall of Rome.[33]

We suggest that the first four seal judgments constitute a parody of the four horses of the "quadriga," the special chariot of the Roman general in the Triumph. That chariot held a number of people (the general, his children, and the aforementioned slave) and was pulled by four white horses. The first four seals of Revelation 6:2–8 also include four horses. The white horse symbolizes the antichrist/Caesar; the red horse symbolizes war; the black horse symbolizes famine; and the pale horse symbolizes death. As Titus destroyed Jerusalem, soon Christ will unleash his destruction on Rome by way of his own "quadriga." The *quadriga* of the four horsemen of the Apocalypse had only one white horse to start with to symbolize Rome's supposed victory while the next three horses were different colors to symbolize war, famine, and death. That is, the four horsemen of the Apocalypse were mocking the

---

32. The preceding discussion comes from Pate, *The Writings of John*, 392–94.

33. The following remarks regarding the seal judgments come from my article, "Revelation 6: An Early Interpretation of the Olivet Discourse," *Criswell Theological Review*, (2011), 45–56.

peace of Rome in the aftermath of war. Added to these seal judgments are the martyred Christians at the hands of Caesar (fifth seal) and divine vindication of those persecuted ones via cosmic catastrophe (sixth seal). The seventh seal turns into the seven trumpet judgments. The Arch of Titus, therefore, makes perfect sense of why John labels the first seven judgments "seals." Titus destroyed Jerusalem and disrespected the Torah, but the seven seals of the Book of the Covenant/Torah is Christ's revenge upon Rome.

The parody of the Arch of Titus and what it represents continues in the **trumpet judgments** of Revelation 8–9. One of the pieces of furniture that Titus stole from Jerusalem and is pictured on the Arch of Titus is the temple trumpet. Revelation 8–9 can then be seen as turning those stolen properties against the future emperor. The seven trumpet judgments mix together at least two images: Israelite history (the Egyptian plagues, but also the prophet's Joel's prediction of the coming locust invasion of Israel) and recent events in Rome's history (the eruption of Mount Vesuvius and an imminent Parthian invasion). Revelation uses these past happenings as the backdrop to foretell the coming fall of the Roman Empire.

That we are on target in our theory that the trumpet judgments of Revelation 8–9 are a parody of the stolen temple trumpets displayed on the Arch of Titus seems confirmed by Revelation 10:1–11:15, for there the former, destroyed temple of Jerusalem in A.D. 70 is the backdrop of the heavenly temple from where judgment will fall on Rome.

The **bowl judgments** of Revelation 15–18 continue the theme of divine retribution on Rome. John again focuses on furniture Titus stole from the Jerusalem temple—the bowls containing incense, but in a polemical way. Our thesis for interpreting Revelation 15–16 is that the bowl judgments, like the trumpet judgments (Revelation 8–9), portray the imminent fall of Rome against the backdrop of the falls of Jerusalem in 586 B.C./A.D. 70.

The Sacrifice and Feast and Revelation 19

Aune has made a convincing case that Revelation 19 portrays the return of Christ as that of a Roman Triumph.[34] We agree with Aune's thesis, except that he misses the two main components of the third and final part of the Triumph: the killing of the captive enemies as a sacrifice to the gods and the great feast held. These two components dominate Revelation 19. In verses 1–10: the killing of the beast, the false

34. Aune, *Revelation 17–22*, 1050–52. Aune however does not apply the Roman Triumph to all of Revelation 4–19 as I do. He only applies it to Revelation 19, but does not develop the Arch of Titus background as I do here. Aune also rightly sees the Old Testament theme of Yahweh as a warrior as informing Revelation 19; Aune, *Revelation 17–22,* 1048–50.

prophet, and the whore (all symbols of Rome) are portrayed as a sacrificial offering to God and Christ in heaven. In verses 11–21 the great feast is celebrated by Christ and his followers. (Even the birds participate in the feast as they feed off of the dead bodies of Christ's enemies!) So it is highly likely that the third part of the Roman Triumph—the sacrifice and the feast—informs Revelation 19 and the return of Christ. Note the following comparisons between Revelation 19:11–21 and the Roman Triumph:

The prominence of the white horse (v. 11) and the white horses (v. 14)

The diadems worn by the rider (v. 13)

The name or title inscribed on the rider (vv. 12–13, 16)

The warrior-character of the rider suggested by his robe dipped in blood (v. 13)

The armies accompanying the rider (v. 14)

The predominately military imagery, which reflects a decisive victory (v. 15)

The killing of the captive enemies as a sacrifice to God (vv. 19–21)

The great feast for Christ and his followers (vv. 17–18)[35]

Below we put in chart form the parallels we have identified between the Arch of Titus and Revelation 4–19:

Arch of Titus	Revelation 4–19
Pre-Parade: Songs to the Victorious General/Emperor	Revelation 4–5: Songs to the Victorious Jesus: 5:5–14; compare 4:8, 10–11
Spoils of war/crowns	Saints give their crowns/spoils of war back to Jesus: 4:10
Triumpe (Latin) uttered of the General	"triumphed" (Greek *nikē* 5:5) uttered of Jesus

---

35. Aune calls attention to the above parallels, except the last two, which are my own suggested parallels (*Revelation 17–22*, 1050–52).

Arch of Titus	Revelation 4–19
General both god and mortal man	Jesus both God and mortal man: 5:5–10
Procession: The captured Menorah	Christ in the Menorah: Revelation 2–3
The captured Torah	Revelation 6: the Seal Judgments
The captured temple trumpets	Revelation 8–9: the Trumpet Judgments
The captured bowls for temple incense	Revelation 15–18: The Bowl Judgments
The Sacrifice and the Feast: The prominence of the white horses that comprised the quadriga on which the Roman general rode	Revelation 19: 11, 14: Christ rides a white horse (cf. the four horsemen of the seal judgments/Christ's *quadriga* Rev. 6)
The diadems worn by the Roman general rider	Christ wears divine diadems (v. 13)
The name or title inscribed on the Roman general	The secret name inscribed on Christ (vv. 12–13, 16)
The warrior-character of the Roman general suggested by the red paint covering his face	The warrior-character of Christ suggested by his robe dipped in blood (v. 13)
The armies accompanying the Roman general in his Triumph	The armies accompanying the Jesus general in his Triumph (v. 14)
The predominately military imagery, which reflects a decisive victory by the Roman general	The predominately military imagery, which reflects a decisive victory by the Jesus the Kings of Kings and Lords of Lords (v. 15)
The killing of the captive enemies as a sacrifice to the Roman general's gods	The killing of the captive enemies as a sacrifice to the one true God (vv. 19–21)
The great feast for the Roman general and his followers	The great feast for Christ and his followers (vv. 17–18)

LITERARY ANALYSIS OF REVELATION 1:1–3

Four steps are involved in doing a literary analysis of a New Testament text: structure, syntax, style, and semantics. We now apply these four steps to Revelation 1:1–3.

The Structure of Revelation 1:1–3

In this section we tackle two tasks pertinent to analyzing the structure of Revelation 1:1–3: a summary of clauses in general and then the structure of the clauses in Revelation 1:1–3.

A Description of Clauses

Herbert W. Bateman IV provides a helpful summary of the twofold types of clauses: independent and dependent.[36]

Three Types of Independent Clauses:	Four Types of Dependent Clauses:
(1) Coordinating conjunctive clauses are introduced by:	**(1) Relative clauses are introduced by:**
Simple connective (καί or δέ)	A relative pronoun (ὅς)
Contrastive conjunction (δέ, πλήν)	A relative adjective (οἷος, such as; ὅσος, as much/many as)
Correlative conjunction (μέν... δέ or καί...καί)	A relative adverb (ὅπου, where; ὅτε, when)
Explanatory conjunction (γάρ)	**(2) Conjunctive clauses are introduced by a subordinate conjunction that denotes:**
Inferential conjunction (ἄρα, διό, οὖν, γάρ)	Time (ὅνε; ὅτον); reason and cause (διό, ὅτι, ἐπεί); purpose and result (ἵνα, ὥστε); comparison (καθώς, ὡς, ὡσεί, ὥσπερ)
Transitional conjunction (δέ or οὖν)	**(3) Participial clauses are introduced by a participle**
(2) Prepositional clauses are introduced by:	**(4) Infinitival clauses are introduced by a participle**
"for this reason" (διὰ τοῦτο)	
"for this reason" (ἐπὶ τοῦτο)	
"as a result of this" (ἐκ τοῦτο)	
"why (εἰς τίνα)	
"in this" (ἐν τοῦτο)	
(3) Asyndeton clauses are not introduced by a conjunctive word or phrase	

---

36. Herbert W. Bateman IV, *Interpreting the General Letters: An Exegetical Handbook* (Grand Rapids: Kregel Academic, 2013), 173–74.

The Structure of the Clauses in Revelation 1:1–3

Verses 1–2 = one sentence

Independent Clause:	Ἀποκάλυψις Ἰησοῦ Χριστοῦ (supplying the verb "is")
Relative Clause:	ἣν ἔδωκεν αὐτῷ ὁ θεὸς
Infinitival Clause:	δεῖξαι τοῖς δούλοις αὐτοῦ
Relative Clause:	ἃ δεῖ
Infinitival Clause:	γενέσθαι ἐν τάχει
Relative Clause:	καὶ ἐσήμανεν (καὶ functions as a relative pronoun)
Participial Clause:	ἀποστείλας διὰ τοῦ ἀγγέλου αὐτοῦ τῷ δούλῳ αὐτοῦ, Ἰωάννῃ[37]
Relative Clause:	ὃς ἐμαρτύρησεν τὸν λόγον τοῦ θεοῦ
Relative Clause:	καὶ τὴν μαρτυρίαν Ἰησοῦ Χριστοῦ[38]
Relative Clause:	ὅσα εἶδεν

Verse 3 = one sentence

Independent Clause:	Μακάριος[39]
Participial Clause:	ὁ ἀναγινώσκων
Participial Clause:	καὶ οἱ ἀκούοντες τοὺς λόγους τῆς προφητείας
Participial Clause:	καὶ τηροῦντες τὰ ἐν αὐτῇ γεγραμμένα[40]
Relative Clause:	ὁ γὰρ καιρὸς ἐγγύς

---

37. Ἰωάννῃ stands in apposition to δούλῳ αὐτοῦ.

38. Καὶ is most likely a relative pronoun that distinguishes the word of God from the testimony of Christ. The other option is an appositional clause that equates the word of God with Christ.

39. The verb is supplied "is" with the subsequent dependent clauses serving as the complement.

40. One article [οἱ] governs ἀκούοντες and τηροῦντες thereby equating the two groups.

The Syntax of Revelation 1:1–3

We divide syntax into two categories: analyzing the syntactical function of the dependent clauses (the larger unit of thought) and then analyzing the syntactical relationship of the words (the smaller unit of thought). Dependent clauses function in one of three ways: (1) substantively, whereby the dependent clause functions like a subject of a verb, predicate nominative, direct object of a verb, or in apposition to a noun or pronoun, (2) adjectivally, whereby the dependent clause modifies a noun or pronoun, noun phrase, or another substantive, and (3) adverbally, whereby the dependent clause modifies a verb. We now apply these three syntactical functions of dependent clauses to Revelation 1:1–3:

Ἀποκάλυψις Ἰησοῦ Χριστοῦ (IC)

ἣν ἔδωκεν αὐτῷ ὁ θεὸς	(RC functions adjectivally as modifying the noun phrase, Ἀποκάλυψις Ἰησοῦ Χριστοῦ)
δεῖξαι τοῖς δούλοις αὐτοῦ	(IC functions substantively as a predicate nominative of ἔδωκεν)
ἃ δεῖ	(RC functions substantively as a direct object of δεῖξαι)
γενέσθαι ἐν τάχει	(IC functions substantively as a predicate nominative of ἃ δε)
καὶ ἐσήμανεν	(RC functions adjectivally as modifying the noun phrase, Ἀποκάλυψις Ἰησοῦ Χριστοῦ)
ἀποστείλας διὰ τοῦ ἀγγέλου αὐτοῦ τῷ δούλῳ αὐτοῦ, Ἰωάννῃ	(PC functions adverbally modifying the verb ἐσήμανεν)
ὃς ἐμαρτύρησεν τὸν λόγον τοῦ θεοῦ	(RC functions adjectivally modifying the noun Ἰωάννῃ)
καὶ τὴν μαρτυρίαν Ἰησοῦ Χριστοῦ	(RC functions adjectivally modifying the noun Ἰωάννῃ)
ὅσα εἶδεν	(RC functions adjectivally modifying the noun Ἰωάννῃ)

Μακάριος (IC)

ὁ ἀναγινώσκων	(PC functions substantively as a predicate nominative to Μακάριος)

καὶ οἱ ἀκούοντες τοὺς λόγους τῆς προφητείας	(PC functions substantively as a predicate nominative to Μακάριος)
καὶ τηροῦντες τὰ ἐν αὐτῇ γεγραμμένα	(PC functions substantively as a predicate nominative to Μακάριος)[41]
ὁ γὰρ καιρὸς ἐγγύς	(SC functions adverbally modifying the preceding three participles and is the apodosis part of the enthymeme of v. 3)

The Syntactical Function of Words

Numerous syntactical decisions await the reader of Revelation 1:1–3. To begin, what is the nature of the genitives in the phrase, Ἀποκάλυψις Ἰησοῦ Χριστοῦ? Three options present themselves: (1) Ἰησοῦ Χριστοῦ are objective genitives thus rendering the following translation, "The revelation of/about Jesus Christ." (2) Ἰησοῦ Χριστοῦ are subjective genitives thus rendering the following translation, "The revelation from Jesus Christ."[42] (3) More likely the genitives are plenary genitives, meaning both objective and subjective genitives are in view. Thus, the divine revelation is both about Jesus Christ in the sense that the whole book unveils the theme that Jesus is Lord and also from Jesus Christ.[43]

Next, the subject of ἐσήμανεν is unclear, but it most likely alludes to God and is thus coordinate with ἔδωκεν. Others would say that "Jesus Christ" is the subject, who is referred to by the indirect object αὐτῷ. Indeed, there are instances in Revelation in which the indirect object is the subject of the verb (2:21; 12:14; 14:4). These references, however, are all subordinate clauses.[44] On balance, then, it seems that God is the subject of ἐσήμανεν.

Since ἐμαρτύρησεν is an epistolary aorist, what the author writes in the present will be a past event from the perspective of the readers. Consequently, it must be translated as a past tense, "who bore witness." Aune takes ὅσα εἶδεν to be a subordinate clause that stands in apposition to τὸν λόγον τοῦ θεοῦ καὶ τὴν μαρτυρίαν Ἰησοῦ Χριστοῦ and

---

41. The three preceding participial clauses function as the protasis in the enthymeme that comprises verse 3.

42. Aune supports this view noting that ἣν ἔδωκεν αὐτῷ ὁ θεὸς suggests that God gave the revelation to Jesus Christ who then as the subject passed it on (*Revelation 1–5*, 6).

43. See, for example, Revelation 1:9–3:22.

44. Aune, *Revelation 1–5*, 6.

serves as the object of ἐμαρτύρησεν.[45] I rather think ὅσα εἶδεν is a relative clause functioning adjectivally by modifying the noun Ἰωάννῃ. In the phrase τὸν λόγον τοῦ θεοῦ, τοῦ θεοῦ most likely is a subjective genitive due to the context of the revelation.

It is difficult to decide whether the καὶ that connects τὸν λόγον τοῦ θεοῦ and τὴν μαρτυρίαν Ἰησοῦ Χριστοῦ is a relative pronoun or an appositional term. I see a nuance between the two phrases that is indicative of the nuance between God and Jesus in Revelation 1:1–3. In the phrase τὴν μαρτυρίαν Ἰησοῦ Χριστοῦ, Ἰησοῦ Χριστοῦ like τοῦ θεοῦ is more likely a subjective genitive. The definite article (οἱ) that governs the two substantival participles, ἀκούοντες τοὺς λόγους τῆς προφητείας and τηροῦντες τὰ ἐν αὐτῇ γεγραμμένα indicates that the two groups are one and the same. In the phrase, τοὺς λόγους τῆς προφητείας, τῆς προφητείας could be a qualitative genitive used as an adjective resulting in the translation, "prophetic words." Aune's suggestion seems more accurate, however, when he takes the genitive as appositional resulting in the translation, "the words, that is the prophecy." The prepositional phrase ἐν αὐτῇ modifies τῆς προφητείας.

The Style of Revelation 1:1–3

Two stylistic matters in Revelation 1:1–3 deserve attention: the title (vv. 1–2) and the beatitude (v. 3).[46] The title (as well as the Beatitude) identifies the writing as an apocalypse and includes a number of features that comprise the medium component of apocalyptic literature:

1.0	Medium		
1.1	Visual		
1.1.	Visions		
1.1.2	Epiphanies	1:1	Jesus Christ and angels
1.2	Auditions		
1.2.1	Discourse	1:1	God showed to John the revelation of/from Jesus Christ
1.3	Otherworldly journey	1:1	Jesus Christ and angels
1.4	Writing	1:3	prophetic words
2.0	Otherworldly mediator	1:1–2	Jesus Christ and angels
3.0	Human recipient	1:1	John

45. Ibid., 6.

46. The Title of the Apocalypse of Weeks in 1 Enoch 93:1–3 is similar to the title of Revelation 1:1–3.

The Beatitude in Revelation 1:3 is one of seven in the book (cf. 14:13; 16:15; 19:9; 20:6; 22:7, 14). As Aune observes, the Beatitude that comprises Revelation 1:3 is an enthymeme, a two-part statement consisting of a protasis and an apodosis. The apodosis introduced by γὰρ provides the reason for the makarism.[47] We may say, then, that the one who reads aloud and the ones who hear and obey the content of the revelation are blessed, because the time of consummation is near. These words are reminiscent of Deuteronomy 33:1 for good reason, as we will see under the theological section.

Semantics

"Semantics" has to do with the meaning of words. In interpreting the Bible, semantics involve doing word studies. There is no more fitting word in Revelation 1:1–3 requiring a word study than the first word. Ἀποκάλυψις and its cognate verb ἀποκαλύπτω make for an interesting analysis. In Classical Greek, neither term occurs with theological reference to the deity disclosing truth to human beings. Interestingly enough, the term used in Classical Greek for the deity unveiling truth to the devotee is σημαίνω, the noun form of ἐσήμανεν, which occurs in Revelation 1:1. The noun form is found in texts associated with the Delphic oracle. Surprisingly, although both forms do occur in the LXX, neither of them convey the theological meaning of God disclosing truth to his people. Ironically, neither ἀποκάλυψις nor ἀποκαλύπτω occurs in the numerous documents of apocalyptic literature we have studied thus far.

When we turn to the New Testament, however, the infinitive of ἀποκαλύπτω occurs three times, the past tense of the verb occurs twenty-six times, while the noun occurs ten times, largely in connection with the gospel of Jesus Christ. It seems fitting that the verb and noun forms explode in occurrence with Jesus Christ, the ultimate revelation of God to humans. We can cluster the preceding occurrences into some five categories that connect Jesus Christ with divine revelation: (1) The Son reveals the Father (Matt. 11:27/Luke 10:22). In other words, one can only know God as Father through the revelation of Christ. (2) Conversely, God reveals the Son. He does so to Paul on the Damascus Road (Gal. 1:12, 16); to his spiritual children (Matt. 11:25; Luke 10:21); to Peter that Jesus is the Christ (Matt. 16:17); in the righteousness of the gospel of Jesus Christ (Rom. 1:17); in the meaning of the cross of Christ, which is foolishness to the lost but the power of God to the saved (1 Cor. 2:10); to the prophets about the coming of Christ (1 Peter 1:12); God revealed the Law to prepare the world for the gospel by convicting the world of its sin and thereby driving the world to

---

47. Aune, *Revelation 1–5*, 10.

the gospel of grace (Gal. 3:23). (3) The gospel of Christ is revealed to the Gentiles so that they can become a part of the people of God (Luke 2:35; Rom. 16:25; Eph. 3:3, 5). (4) The Second Coming of Christ will be a revelation of his splendor and power, and will deliver his followers (Luke 17:30; Rom. 8:18–19; 1 Cor. 1:7; 3:13; 2 Thess. 1:7; 2:3, 6, 8; 1 Peter 1:13; 4:13; 5:1; Rev. 1:1). (5) God's revelation aids worshipping Christ (1 Cor. 14:6, 26, 30) and spiritual growth in Christ (Eph. 1:17).

Helpful resources for word studies include concordances, lexicons, and theological dictionaries:[48]

Concordances

- J. R. Kohlenberger, E. W. Goodrick, and J. A. Swanson. *The Exhaustive Concordance to the Greek New Testament* (Grand Rapids: Zondervan, 1995).

- G. V. Wigram, *The Englishman's Greek Concordance of the New Testament* (Peabody, MA: Hendrickson, 1996).

Lexicons

- W. Bauer, W. F. Arndt, F. W. Gingrich, and F. W. Danker, *A Greek-English Lexicon of the New Testament and Other Early Christian Literature,* third edition (Chicago: University of Chicago Press, 2000).

- J. P. Louw and E. Nida, *A Greek-English Lexicon of the New Testament Based on Semantic Domains,* 2nd edition, 2 volumes (New York: United Bible Societies, 1989).

Theological Dictionaries

- C. Brown, ed., *The New International Dictionary of New Testament Theology,* 4 volumes (Grand Rapids: Zondervan, 1986).

- G. Kittel and G. Friedrich, eds., *Theological Dictionary of the New Testament,* 10 volumes (Grand Rapids: Eerdmans, 1964–73).

In conclusion, the literary step of interpreting the Scripture is comprised of four components, as we have seen: structure, syntax, style, and semantics. We analyzed Revelation 1:1–3 in light of those components.

---

48. This list of resources comes from John D. Harvey, *Interpreting the Pauline Letters: An Exegetical Handbook* (Grand Rapids: Kregel, 2012), 139.

THEOLOGICAL ANALYSIS

One would expect from what has been written in this work so far that Revelation 1:1–3 should in some way be affected by the story of Israel, and the passage does not disappoint. Indeed, Revelation 1:1–3 is heavily indebted to the story of Israel in two ways. First, six themes in Revelation 1:1–3 are better understood by the story of Israel. Second, Revelation 1:1–3 also gives evidence of being framed after the components of the covenant format of Deuteronomy. To these two considerations we now turn as we uncover the theological message of Revelation 1:1–3, which itself deeply governs the entire book of Revelation (recall our chapter 2 on this last point).

Six Themes in Revelation 1:1–3 That Are Affected by the Story of Israel

First, the term "Ἀποκάλυψις," as we discovered in chapters 1–3, is rooted in the story of Israel. In chapter 1, we saw that the function component of the genre of apocalyptic literature located such literature in the covenant curses of the messianic woes while holding out the hope of the covenant blessings of the kingdom of God/messianic kingdom. In chapters 2 and 3 we learned that the story of Israel influenced more than just the function component of apocalyptic literature, it impacts the form and content components as well. The Apocalypse fits into that pattern.

Second, the apocalypse is all about Jesus the Messiah. We must not overlook the obvious fact that Jesus is understood by the author of Revelation to be the long-awaited Messiah, the inaugurator of the restoration of Israel and the new covenant. We saw in chapters 1–3 that both of these themes permeate Revelation.

Third, the mention of prophecy in Revelation 1:3 and its development throughout the book of Revelation is patently connected with the story of Israel, because the message of sin, exile, and restoration was the main focus of the Old Testament prophets. Recall from our analysis of biblical prophetic-apocalyptic texts and apocalyptic literature in Second Temple Judaism that angels played a significant role in the passing on of the divine message to humans related to the story of Israel; Revelation 1:1 is informed by that theme.

Fourth, the two clauses, ἃ δεῖ γενέσθαι ἐν τάχει (1:1) and ὁ γὰρ καιρὸς ἐγγύς (1:3), distinctly remind one of Daniel 7:22 (ὁ καιρὸς ἔφθασεν; cf. 2:28–29) and Mark 1:15 (πεπλήρωται ὁ καιρὸς καὶ ἤγγικεν) in that they depict an already/not-yet-fulfilled perspective. Thus Daniel 7:22 seems to imply that the restoration of Israel/kingdom of God already would begin with the victory of the Maccabean revolt, and yet the kingdom of

God was not completely established by the freedom fighters. Mark 1:15 similarly relates that the restoration of Israel/kingdom of God already dawned in Jesus's ministry, but its consummation awaited a later time. So also the two clauses in Revelation 1:1–3 suggest that the restoration of Israel/kingdom of God has been inaugurated but not yet completed.

In the words, "soon" (*én táchei,* [v. 1b]) and "the time is near" (*hó kairòs éggús* [v. 3]) we meet an interpretive difficulty that has generated conflicting views. First, preterists argue that the prophecies were *immediately* fulfilled in Christ's judgment upon Jerusalem in A.D. 70. Second, dispensationalists argue that "soon" and "the time is near" mean *imminent,* not immediate. In other words, there might be an interval between John's day and the fulfillment of his prophecies, but when those prophecies begin to be fulfilled—whenever that may be—they will unfold rapidly. Third, historical premillennialists and amillennialists appeal to the already/not-yet eschatological tension in order to interpret the two preceding phrases. This view can be stated as follows: (a) "soon" and "the time is near" meant *immediate,* but in reality, the return of Christ was delayed (for at least two thousand years). (b) This delay, however, was not terribly unsettling to the early church, for it viewed the First Coming of Christ as the most climactic event in history. And the eschatological significance of it prevented the church from worrying about when the Parousia would occur. We concur with this last view.

Indeed, a good case can be made that the already/not-yet eschatological dynamic is the key to interpreting Revelation 1:19 in a similar light. The threefold clause, "what you have seen, what is now and what will take place later" is correctly understood as significant for grasping the chronological outline of the Apocalypse. Futurists usually take the three clauses as referring to the past (the vision of the risen Christ, chapter 1), the present (the seven churches, chapters 2–3), and the future (the great tribulation, the Parousia, the temporary messianic kingdom, and the eternal state (chapters 4–22). Preterists understand the clauses as being on the verge of fulfillment, accomplished at the fall of Jerusalem in A.D. 70. Many amillennialists and historic premillennialists, however, understand the verse in the following manner: "what you have seen" refers to the whole of the vision given to John—that is, the book of Revelation (cf. 1:11)—which consists of two time frames: "the things that are"—the already (the kingdom of God in heaven)—and "the things that will be"—the not-yet (the kingdom of God descended to earth). Our reading of Revelation follows this last viewpoint.

Fifth, the word, ἐσήμανεν, in Revelation 1:1 should be translated "signified." Interestingly enough, the same word is used in Daniel 2:23, 45 (σημαίνω) with reference to God revealing His plans via symbols. Apocalyptic literature followed suit in conveying the divine message through symbolic language. Revelation's symbolic language

constituted coded language that the Roman Empire could not understand. When such language is decoded, the message of Revelation
is clear: did Rome destroy Jerusalem? Then God will shortly destroy
Rome and thereby bring about the restoration of Israel/kingdom of
God/messianic kingdom that the Old Testament prophets forecasted.

Sixth, the pronouncement of blessings on the obedient hearers of
the message of Revelation (Rev. 1:3) amounted to the realization of
the new covenant blessings. These hearers will be spared the covenant
curses on Rome that the three sets of judgments conveyed (seals, trumpets, bowls).

Revelation 1:1–3 and the Components of the Covenant Format

I would suggest that we can go further than just identifying the aforementioned six themes of the story of Israel in Revelation 1:1–3. We can
actually detect the components of the covenant format therein. The
reader will recall from an earlier chapter that the covenant structure
shapes the outline of the book of Deuteronomy. Those same elements
occur in Revelation 1:1–3 as the following chart.[49]

The Covenant Format of Deuteronomy	The Covenant Format and Revelation 1:1–3
Deuteronomy 1:1–5 Preamble – God identifies his name.	Revelation 1:1 The title introduces the revelation of Jesus Christ; that is to say, Jesus is the Messiah who is equal to God (see Rev. 1:10–20; Chapters 4–5 where John equates Jesus with God).
Deuteronomy 1:6–3:29 Historical Prologue – God rehearses His salvation acts on behalf of Israel.	Revelation 1:1 "Revelation of Jesus Christ" serves not only as the title of the book but also anticipates the saving acts of Jesus Christ on behalf of his people: his sacrificial death, victorious resurrection, his heavenly reign, and his triumphant return.
Deuteronomy 4–26 Stipulations – God provides the stipulations/law that Israel must obey if it wants to remain in covenant with God.	Revelation 1:3 The ones who obey the call of Revelation to worship Christ not Caesar constitute the stipulations component of the covenant format.

---

49. I am not suggesting that Revelation 1:1–3 follows the precise order of the covenant format of
     Deuteronomy but, rather, that all of the components are present.

The Covenant Format of Deuteronomy	The Covenant Format and Revelation 1:1–3
Deuteronomy 27–30 Curses and Blessings – Curses and Blessings are pronounced on Israel if it disobeys or follows the divine stipulations, respectively.	Revelation 1:3 The covenant blessings are pronounced on those who obey Christ but the covenant curses are pronounced on those who do not, as detailed in the three sets of divine judgments on Caesar and those who worship him (see Rev. 6–19).
Deuteronomy 31:9, 24–26 Document Clause – God commands that the covenant be placed for the public to see (in the Temple or on stone).	Revelation 1:1–3 The words, "Revelation," "word of God," testimony of Jesus Christ," and "prophecy" remind one of the document clause or the making public of the divine covenant. Indeed, we noted earlier that the scroll of Revelation that only Christ can open is the Book of the covenant with its three sets of judgments that God pours out on the followers of the beast (Rev. 5–19).
Deuteronomy 31:26–32:47 Witnesses – God appeals to witnesses to confirm the covenant.	Revelation 1:1–3 The emphasis on testimony or witness in these verses reminds one of the witnesses of the covenant format. Thus the chain of witnesses to the new covenant passes from God to Jesus to his angel to John to his prophetic community. At the end of Revelation, in 22:6–8, John testifies to the trustworthiness of what he has seen in the divine revelation. Interestingly enough, Revelation 22:18–19 warn against adding or subtracting from the message of Revelation. This warning is rooted in Deuteronomy 4:2; 12:32 which warns ancient Israel to neither add or subtract from the stipulations of the covenant.

Chapter in Review

This chapter sought to accomplish three tasks relative to interpreting the text, in this case Revelation 1:1–3. First, it examined the historical setting of Revelation. Such a background informs the genre of Revelation, its authorship, the date and historical setting of its writing, the major schools of interpretation of the book, and the relationship among Revelation, the Epistles of John, and the Gospel of John. More specifically, we argued that the historical background informing Revelation 4–19 is the Arch of Titus. Second, we analyzed the literary aspects of Revelation 1:1–3, its structure, syntax, style, and semantics. Third, we argued that the theological theme informing Revelation 1:1–3 is the story of Israel.

6

COMMUNICATING A PASSAGE IN REVELATION

The Chapter at a Glance

Having accomplished the step of interpreting Revelation 1:1–3, we now move to the task of exposition; that is, communicating Revelation 1:1–3 to today's world. Three steps are necessary for this task.

- Putting together a first-century synthesis of the text

- Taking that step further to its twenty-first-century appropriation

- Delivering that message to today's audience by packaging it homiletically.

FIRST-CENTURY SYNTHESIS

OUR STUDY OF REVELATION 1:1–3 NOW REQUIRES that we apply the truth(s) of this unit to modern living. To do so we need to negotiate two considerations: what this text meant to the first century (interpretation), that is, to the apostle John's audience; and then what this passage says to us in the twenty-first century (application). Not starting with the first consideration has generated many sincere but bizarre readings of Revelation 1:1–3, if not of the entire book of Revelation.[1] In other words, beginning with the application of a biblical text before first ascertaining its original meaning is eisegesis, reading something into the text that was not originally intended, but not exegesis, letting the meaning flow out of the text.

To establish the first-century synthesis involves answering two questions. First, what did John say? This question will lead us to the central point of the passage. The second question is: What is the shared need(s) of the passage? This question leads us to the particular need John is addressing in his day, and—because the Bible is divinely inspired and applicable to all times—what the corresponding needs are in the twenty-first century.

What Did John Say?

To answer this first question, four steps are needed: Identify the general topic of Revelation 1:1–3; discover the narrower topic addressed therein; see how that subject informs the text; and summarize the findings in one sentence.

The General Topic

Our passage introduces us to the book of Revelation. That book is about the true restoration of Israel that is coming soon through Jesus Christ. The word "apocalypse," as we have repeatedly seen in prophetic-apocalyptic passages in the Bible and in Second Temple Judaism, is rooted in the imminent restoration of Israel. For Revelation, those who obey Jesus Christ will experience the blessings of that restoration, the new covenant.

The Narrower Topic

Here we can do no better than to recall the components of the Old Testament (actually Deuteronomy) covenant format that we discovered in Revelation in our last chapter, components that find their ultimate fulfillment in following Jesus Christ:

The Covenant Format of Deuteronomy	The Covenant Format and Revelation: 1:1–3
Deuteronomy 1:1–4: Preamble – God identifies his name.	Revelation 1:1: The title introduces the revelation of Jesus Christ; that is to say, Jesus is the Messiah who is equal to God (see Rev. 1:10–20; Chapters 4–5 where John equates Jesus with God).

---

1. I have tried to offer healthy corrections to some of these outlandish readings of Revelation in several books, especially *Doomsday Delusions: What's Wrong with Predictions about the End of the World* and *The Writings of John*, especially my exposition of Revelation in *The Writings of John*.

The Covenant Format of Deuteronomy	The Covenant Format and Revelation: 1:1–3
Deuteronomy 1:6–3:29: Historical Prologue – God rehearses His salvific acts on behalf of Israel.	Revelation 1:1: "Revelation of Jesus Christ" serves not only as the title of the book but also anticipates the saving acts of Jesus Christ on behalf of his people: his sacrificial death, victorious resurrection, his heavenly reign, and his triumphant return.
Deuteronomy 4–26: Stipulations – God provides the stipulations/laws that Israel must obey if it wants to remain in covenant with God.	Revelation 1:3: The ones who obey the call of Revelation to worship Christ not Caesar constitutes the stipulation component of the covenant format.
Deuteronomy 27–30: Curses and Blessings – Curses and blessings are pronounced on Israel if it disobeys or follows the divine stipulations, respectively.	Revelation 1:3 The covenant blessings are pronounced on those who obey Christ but the covenant curses are pronounced on those who do not, as detailed in the three sets of divine judgments on Caesar and those who worship him (see Rev. 6–19).
Deuteronomy 31:9, 24–26: Document Clause – God commands that the covenant be placed for the public to see (in the temple or on stone).	Revelation 1:1–3: The words, "Revelation," "word of God," "testimony of Jesus Christ," "prophecy" remind one of the document clause or the making public of the divine covenant; indeed, we noted earlier that the scroll of Revelation that only Christ can open is itself the Book of the Covenant with its three sets of judgments that God pours out on the followers of the beast (Rev. 5–19).
Deuteronomy 31:26–32:47: Witnesses – God appeals to witnesses to confirm the covenant.	Revelation 1:1–3: The emphasis on testimony or witness in these verses reminds one of the witnesses of the covenant format. Thus the chain of witnesses to the new covenant passes from God to Jesus to his angel to John to his prophetic community. At the end of Revelation (22:6–8), John testifies to the trustworthiness of what he has seen in the divine revelation. Interestingly enough, Revelation 22:18–19 warns against adding or subtracting from the message of Revelation. This warning is rooted in Deuteronomy 4:2; 12:32, which warns ancient Israel to neither add nor subtract from the stipulations of the covenant.

How the Subject Informs the Text

We recall that our unit consists of two sentences, which we now re-examine in light of the narrowed subject:

Verses 1–2: The revelation/restoration of the new covenant in Christ is imminent.

Verse 1a   Jesus Christ is the means of the revelation/restoration of true Israel.

Verses 1b–2   Jesus Christ, his servants, an angel, John, and his community are the messengers of the revelation/restoration of true Israel.

Verse 3:   The imminent coming of the new covenant in Christ to true Israel brings blessing.

Verse 3a   Christ promises covenant blessings to the readers of Revelation.

Verse 3b   Christ promises covenant blessings to the obedient hearers of Revelation.

One-Sentence Summary of the Findings

Those who obey God will experience the covenant blessings of the revelation (apocalypse) of Jesus Christ, which is the true restoration of Israel.

What Is the Shared Need of the Passage?

This question can be answered in two steps: isolate the need(s) addressed in the historical and literary context of the passage; determine the need(s) contemporary listeners share with the original audience.

The Original Needs Addressed in the Passage

There are two needs to which John spoke in his day relative to the temptation for Christians to deny Christ by worshipping Caesar. First, those who resist the temptation to sell out to Caesar and not to remain faithful to Christ should realize that they will receive the blessings of the new covenant. Second, such faithful followers of Jesus should remember that the return of Christ is imminent (that is, it can happen at any time, though imminent should not be confused with "immediate").

Contemporary Needs Addressed by the Passage

The above two principles powerfully apply to modern Christians (and to Christians of all time, for that matter) in the same twofold way. First, the harsh reality of the Christian life is that those who live godly will suffer for their faith (cf. 2 Tim. 3:12; Matt. 5:10–12). That suffering may take various forms. Outside the Western world and its protection of freedom of religion, countless thousands of believers literally suffer persecution for their Christian faith—everything from isolation to imprisonment to death. Christians who have the precious privilege of religious freedom, however, also suffer for their faith in more subtle ways: they can be snubbed, ridiculed, even ostracized. The truth remains, however—whoever is obedient to Jesus Christ will receive the blessings of the new covenant, namely, salvation, forgiveness, and the hope of heaven; blessings the book of Revelation details. Second, even though some two thousand years have elapsed with no sight of Christ's return, the hope of his imminent appearing will continue to sustain believers until that day, which is the message of Revelation as a whole.

TWENTY-FIRST-CENTURY APPROPRIATION

Here we get more specific about how to apply Revelation 1:1–3 and indeed the whole book of Revelation to today's world. We do so by attempting to answer three questions:

1. What are the connections between our passage and the twenty-first century?
2. What are the corrections our text offers to the twenty-first century?
3. What are the commendations Revelation 1:1–3 provides for the twenty-first century?

The answers to these three questions might just remove some of the fear often attached to the book of Revelation as a whole.

What Are the Connections between Revelation 1:1–3 and the Twenty-First Century?

In 2014 and 2015, we have witnessed the reprisal of the phenomenally best-selling series, *Left Behind*,[2] with its second rendition of the first movie, *Left Behind*, starring the likes of Nicolas Cage. Long before the *Left Behind* series, Hal Lindsey had already capitalized on the deeply inquisitive interest in humans regarding the return of Christ and the end of the world with his *The Late Great Planet Earth*.[3] Indeed, Lindsey's books spawned a plethora of works devoted to explaining the fast appearing of the Second Coming of Christ and the end of the

---

2. Tim F. LaHaye and Jerry B. Jenkins, *Left Behind: A Novel of the Earth's Last Days* (Carol Stream, IL: Tyndale, 1995) was the first book in the series, which sold more than 40 million copies.

3. Hal Lindsey, with C. C. Carlson, *The Late Great Planet Earth* (Grand Rapids: Zondervan, 1970). This book and others written by Lindsey have also sold millions of copies.

world as we now know it. Actually, as I and other authors have demonstrated, almost every generation of Christians since the first generation of the Christian movement in the first century was convinced that they lived in the last generation before the end of the world.[4] So, it is not surprising that vital questions continue to loom large among believers and nonbelievers alike regarding the return of Christ and the end of the world.

In fact, there are at least three connections between Revelation 1:1–3 and the book as a whole with today: (1) Will Christ really return, since almost two thousand years have elapsed without his promised Second Coming having occurred? (2) Did Israel's return to her land and her reconstitution as a nation in 1948 begin the last generation before the return of Christ? (3) Does Israel, or the Jewish race, have a future in the plan of God, or has the church replaced Israel for good? We now seek to answer these questions that connect so profoundly especially with our world today. To do so, we must first move to our overall second point, namely, the corrections our text provides regarding these questions.

What Are the Corrections Revelation 1:1–3 Offers to the Twenty-First Century?

Here we hope to dissipate some of the confusion Revelation 1:1–3 often causes for modern day readers of the Apocalypse.

Will Christ Really Return, Since Almost Two Thousand Years Have Elapsed without His Promised Second Coming Having Occurred?

The reader might remember that we touched upon this subject in the last chapter in some detail when we discussed the various views of how to interpret Revelation. Here we simplify the issue by mentioning three major views of the interpretation of Revelation, including 1:1–3. The question of when Christ will return centers on the words in Revelation 1:1–3, "what must soon take place" (1:1) and "the time is near" (1:3).

The preterist (past) view believes that *all* of the prophecies of Revelation along with the Olivet Discourse occurred in their entirety in the first generation after Jesus died, at the fall of Jerusalem to the Romans in A.D. 70. In other words, the coming again of Jesus took place when he poured out judgment upon Jerusalem via the Romans. In other words, "soon" and "near" mean exactly that—immediately, within the first generation! As I have argued elsewhere, however, the descriptions of the return of Christ in Revelation and in the Olivet

---

4.   Pate and Haines, *Doomsday Delusions,* 18–22, and the other authors we mention.

Discourse much better fit the traditional understanding of Christ's second coming at the end of history, not at the fall of Jerusalem in A.D. 70.[5]

The futurist view of Revelation 1:1–3 and the timing of the return of Christ, especially the dispensational pretribulation rapture school of thought, also takes the words "soon" and "near" as immediate because this approach separates the rapture from the Second Coming of Christ. The former can happen anytime because there are no signs of the times to be accomplished before the secret rapture of the church to heaven which initiates the beginning of the signs of the times or great tribulation/messianic woes. The latter occurs simultaneously with the Second Coming of Christ. The following chart, however, demolishes such a view by showing that Paul's talk of a rapture (1 Thess. 4:13–18) matches the Second Coming described in the Olivet Discourse, thereby equating the two events:[6]

Olivet Discourse (Matthew)	Event	Paul
24:5	Warning about deception	2 Thessalonians 2:2
24:5, 11, 24	Lawlessness, delusion of the nonelect, signs and wonders	2 Thessalonians 2:6–11
24:12	Apostasy	2 Thessalonians 2:3
24:15	Antichrist in the temple	2 Thessalonians 2:4
24:21–22	Tribulation preceding the end	2 Thessalonians 1:6–10
24:30–31	Parousia of Christ, on clouds, at the time of a trumpet blast, with angelic accompaniment	1 Thessalonians 4:14–16
24:30–31	In power	2 Thessalonians 2:8
24:31	Gathering of believers	1 Thessalonians 4:16 2 Thessalonians 2:1
24:36, 42, 44, 50; 25:13	Unexpected and uncertain	1 Thessalonians 5:1–4
24:42–25:13	Exhortation to watch!	1 Thessalonians 5:6–8

5. See ed. C. Marvin Pate, *Four Views on the Book of Revelation*, especially the separation of the return of Christ from the fall of Jerusalem in Luke 21 (166–68).

6. The chart comes from *The Rapture: Pre-, Mid-, or Post-Tribulational* by Gleason L. Archer Jr., Paul D. Feinberg, Douglas J. Moo, and Richard R. Reiter (Grand Rapids: Zondervan, 1984), 194.

In other words, the key passage supposedly supporting a secret rapture—1 Thessalonians 4:13–18—turns out to be describing the Second Coming of Christ.

The already/not-yet view actually encompasses a number of views of eschatology (from amillennial to postmillennial to historic premillennial to progressive dispensational). The common denominator of these views—already/not-yet—says that the kingdom of God and the signs of the times actually began with the first coming of Jesus (the "already" aspect) but that they were not completely fulfilled then (the "not-yet" aspect). The latter will only happen at the Second Coming of Christ. One way to demonstrate this view would be to see how the already/not-yet eschatological tension characterizes the Olivet Discourse as it occurs in Matthew 24.[7]

The Already: The Fall of Jerusalem	The Not-Yet: The Parousia
Partial fulfillment (Matthew 24:4–20)	**Final fulfillment (Matthew 24:21–31)**
A. Tribulation (Matthew 24:8) B. Messianic pretenders (Matthew 24:4–5) C. Wars (Matthew 24:6–7) D. Persecution (Matthew 24:9–10) E. Apostasy (Matthew 24:11–13) F. Fall of Jerusalem (Matthew 24:15–20)	A. Great Tribulation (Matthew 24:21, 29) B. Messianic pretenders (Matthew 24:23–26) C. Wars (Matthew 24:22) D. Persecution (Matthew 24:22) E. Apostasy (Matthew 24:24) F. Parousia (Matthew 24:30–31)

The upshot of this view is that Jesus and his followers entered into both the signs of the times/great tribulation/messianic woes (all the same) during the first coming of Christ and the arrival of the kingdom of God. Thus, both the signs of the times (the opposition to the kingdom of God) and the kingdom of God have already begun and will continue, even intensify in their opposition to one another, but the conclusion of both—the not-yet aspect—awaits the Second Coming of Christ. In other words, the church will not be raptured to heaven before the arrival of the eschatological tribulation but, rather, the church will have to endure it by being faithful followers of Jesus Christ, which is what it has been doing for some two thousand years. On this reading of Revelation 1:1–3, "soon" and "near" mean "imminent" (not "immediate"; *contra* the preterist and

---

7. The chart comes from C. Marvin Pate, *40 Questions About the Historical Jesus* (Grand Rapids: Kregel, 2015), 303.

futurist rapture views). Because the signs of the times and the kingdom of God already began with Jesus and the first generation of Christians/church, the second coming could happen today or not for many years to come. "Imminent" means anytime, not "immediate."

Did Israel's Return to Her Land and Her Reconstitution as a Nation in 1948 Begin the Last Generation before the Return of Christ?

The issue here centers on Jesus's statement in the Olivet Discourse where he promised that "this generation will not pass away until all of these things come to pass" (Matt. 24:34//Mark 13:30//Luke 21:32). To which generation did he refer? The most popular answer to this famous question is the generation that witnessed the return of Israel to her land in 1948; in other words the modern generation. Actually, there are five possible answers to the question of which generation Jesus referred to as the one that would witness his Second Coming, with 1948 as only one of those possibilities. We now mention those five possibilities. Two of them refer to the past. Two of them refer to the future, while one of them translates *geneia* in a different way than the other four alternatives.

The first alternative (past) suggests that Jesus's promise was completely fulfilled at the fall of Jerusalem to the Romans in A.D. 70, the first generation of Christians. Since we already examined this possibility as well as provided our rebuttal to it, we need not linger on this perspective except to recall that the "already" aspect of Jesus's prophecy occurred at the fall of Jerusalem, but the "not-yet" aspect did not. The latter awaits the return of Christ, which will probably be preceded by an increased intensity of the signs of the times that the fall of Jerusalem in A.D. 70 did not witness. Recall our chart above regarding Matthew.

The second alternative (past) suggests that by his promise that "this generation will not pass away before all these things (the signs of the times) will pass away," Jesus meant his generation, but Jesus was wrong because he did not return in that first generation. This view is the predominant view of the liberal approach to the Bible, not believing it is God's inspired word. Ironically, this interpretation suffers from the same mistake of the first view above, namely, that it does not recognize the eschatological tension of the "already/not-yet" aspects of Jesus's promise. In other words, part of Jesus's promise was most assuredly fulfilled at the fall of Jerusalem to the Romans in Jesus's generation (the first half of the Olivet Discourse), with the second half of the Olivet Discourse still awaiting the full and final accomplishment of Jesus's prophecy in the future.

The third alternative (future) suggests that the reconstitution of Israel as a nation again in 1948 began the last generation before the return of Christ. As we mentioned above, this view is the most cherished popular interpretation of Jesus's promise that the coming generation would witness the fulfillment of the signs of the times before his return. Moreover, this view also believes that the rapture of the church will happen before the signs of the times begin; in other words, the church will be caught up to heaven before all hell breaks loose on earth. To put it yet another way, there are no signs of the times to be fulfilled before the rapture of the church occurs. Since, therefore, 1948 began the last generation, the last seven years of which will see the unfolding events of the Olivet Discourse and Revelation, we are living in the last days and the rapture can occur at any time.

What are we to say to this view so successfully presented since Hal Lindsey's works? Since whole books have been devoted to this subject,[8] we need not go into great detail to refute this particular futuristic view of Jesus's prophecy. Instead, we will simply state three pieces of evidence that make it most difficult to sustain this view. First, the New Testament is clear that the last days (signs of the times/great tribulation/messianic woes) began in the first century with the first advent of Christ (Acts 2:16–17; Heb. 1:2; 1 Tim. 4:1; 2 Tim. 3:1; 1 John 2:18), not in the generation begun in 1948 with Israel's return to her land. Second, as we noted above, the major passage to which pretribulation rapturists appeal is 1 Thessalonians 4:13–18, but that passage, along with 1 Thessalonians 5, matches the Olivet Discourse, the subject of which almost all agree is the great tribulation or signs of the times before the Second Coming of Christ. Third, experts agree that a generation is about forty years. So 1948 plus forty is 1988, a year at least one prophecy buff predicted would see the return of Christ.[9] Jesus did not return in 1988, nor at any other readjustment of the years of a generation that prophecy buffs projected. Yet, rather than admit that 1948 and the return of Israel was not what Jesus had in mind when he made his famous prophecy about the last generation, sincere advocates of this view keep changing the date of this, the last generation.

The fourth alternative (future) suggests that the generation that will observe the Second Coming of Jesus is simply the last generation when he comes, which only God knows. According to the Olivet Discourse (Matt. 24:36//Mark 13:32), not even Jesus knows when the last generation will be and thus when he will return; only God the Father knows that. So the last generation could be the one we are in now (but not to be equated with 1948 for reasons we already noted) or it could be many years from now. Since the Christian does not know, we are to live as if this generation is the last one, whenever that may be. I suspect that this view is the best answer to our question above.

---

8. See again *Doomsday Delusions*.

9. Edgar C. Whisenant, *88 Reasons Why the Rapture Will Be in 1988* (Nashville: World Bible Society, 1988).

The fifth alternative suggests that *geneia* does not mean "genera-tion" but "race." On this reading, Jesus's promise was that Israel as a race will not pass away before the Second Coming of Christ. As a matter of public record, twenty years ago when I wrote my Luke commentary, I chose this view.[10] I still believe that Israel as a race will not pass away (despite the horrendous attempts to destroy the Jews) before the Second Coming. Furthermore, I continue to believe that God has not finished with Israel, but will bring her to accept Jesus as her rightful Messiah (see the next point). Today, however, I question whether that neces-sitates translating *geneia* as "race." I suspect rather that the term means "generation."

Has the Church Replaced Israel in God's Plan?

Many in the past have answered that question with an emphatic "yes!"[11] Their logic is as follows: since Israel rejected Jesus as its rightful Messiah, God cast away the nation and replaced it with the Church. According to this approach, there is no future for Israel in the ultimate plan of God. Such an approach is called "replacement theology." Besides running the risk of being anti-Semitic, this approach also fails to grasp the "already/not-yet" eschatological tension that pertains to both Israel and the Church in the book of Revelation (cf. also Romans 9–11 and Luke-Acts). In Revelation, there are two key passages in this regard: chapter 7 (cf. Revelation 14) and chapters 21–22. Concerning the first passage, if only one group is intended, then the group is the church, which has replaced Israel. If two, the passage refers to two groups—the Jewish remnant that converts the great multitude of Gentiles—then Israel still has a place in the plan of God even after rejecting its Messiah. Concerning Revelation 21–22, it is often said that the New Jerusalem so beautifully described there is the Church, not Israel. We now pro-ceed to look at these two Revelation texts relative to whether or not the church has replaced Israel.

Revelation 7 (compare chapter 14)
Those claiming that only one group—the Church—is being de-scribed in Revelation 7 set forth three key reasons in defense of the view that the 144,000 is the innumerable multitude in Revelation 7. First, there was no record of the twelve tribes of Israel during John's day and therefore his order of tribes symbolically replaces Israel with the church. So, the twelve tribes are to be interpreted figuratively, not ethnically. Second, in the rest of the New Testament, the church is por-

---

10.   C. Marvin Pate, *Luke*, Moody Gospel Commentary (Chicago: Moody, 1995), 410–11.

11.   Reformed or Covenant Theology has championed this view.

trayed as the replacement of Israel (Rom. 2:29; 9:6–8; Gal. 3:29; 6:16; Phil. 3:3; Jas. 1:1; 1 Pet. 1:1; 2:4, 9). Third, the sealing of the 144,000 is a symbol of Christian baptism, to which all New Testament Christians submitted. The sealing of the 144,000, therefore, is to be understood as the church's identification with Christ through baptism, not the setting a part of a Jewish Christian remnant in the great tribulation.

There are significant problems with the preceding three arguments. Against the first argument, Josephus (A.D. 90) reckoned with the existence of the twelve tribes of Israel in his day (*Ant.* 11.133). Moreover, there was a widespread Jewish eschatological hope of the regathering of the twelve tribes of Israel which was based on the assumption of their actual existence in the world (Isa. 49:6; 63:17; Ezek. 47:13, 21–23; 48:30–31; Zech. 9:1; *4 Ezra* 13:12–13, 39–49; *Sirach* 36:10; *Pss. Sol.* 17:26–28, 43–44; 1 QM 2:2–3; 3:13–23; 1 QSa 1:15, 29; *Shemoneh Esreh* [Eighteen Benedictions]; Josephus, *Ant.* 11.133; etc.).

The above New Testament references to the supposed replacement of Israel by the Church need to be seen alongside another line of witness in the New Testament, namely, that God will one day restore ethnic Israel to himself (see Matt. 10:23 and especially Romans 11). To put it another way, although the Church is often described in the New Testament in terms of Old Testament Israel, that fact does not mean that the Church has permanently replaced Israel in the plan of God. Furthermore, there is no clear-cut example of the church being called "Israel" in the New Testament or in the church fathers before A.D. 160.[12]

Sealing[13] in the ancient world could mean various things: a barbarian custom; a mark of disgrace; a sign of ownership/protection; a sacral rite in some cults; circumcision; a term for Christian baptism.[14] In our estimation, sealing as a mark of ownership/protection is the best meaning of Revelation 7:4, because it is based on Ezekiel 9:4. That passage describes the Hebrew letter *Taw* as being placed on the foreheads of the Jewish remnant so that they would not be destroyed with the rest of Israel during God's judgment on the nation. This background precisely fits the sealing of the Jewish Christian remnant during the great tribulation period, as we will see below.

Several reasons convince us that Revelation 7:1–8 is not to be equated with Revelation 7:9–17. First, the numbers are different: 144,000

---

12. See Peter Richardson, *Israel in the Apostolic Church*. SNTSMS (Cambridge: Cambridge University Press, 1969), 74–84, 206.

13. The seal, *σφραγις*, was the impression of a seal in clay or wax. Seals could be worn suspended from a chain or cord around the neck or the seal could form the ring on the monarch's finger.

14. See Aune, *Revelation 6–16* 52B (Nashville: Nelson, 1998), 456–59. The seal on the foreheads of the 144,000 is the righteous counterpart to the mark of the beast (Rev. 13:16–18). The seal also reminds one of Jewish phylacteries on the male's forearm and forehead.

and an uncountable number. Second, the twelve tribes of Israel are best taken as ethnic Jews (the remnant), while the innumerable host is best seen as the fulfillment of God's promise to Abraham that his seed would consist of all nations, not just Jews (Gen. 17:4–6; Rom. 4:16–18; 9:6–13; Gal. 3:16). Third, the 144,000 are on earth, but the uncountable host is in heaven. Fourth, the 144,000 face the imminent danger of the great tribulation while the innumerable host of martyred Gentile Christians are now safely home in heaven.

Fifth, the idea that a Jewish remnant could be protected in the land of Israel while enduring the great tribulation is amply attested in ancient Judaism (Dan. 12:12; 1QH 3; *4 Ezra* 9:7–8; 12:34; 13:26, 48–49; *2 Apoc. Bar.* 29:1–2; 40:2; 71:1; Mark 13:13; 1 Thess. 4:15–17).[15] Such protection undoubtedly recalls God's preservation of the Hebrews during the Egyptian plagues (cf. Rev. 7:1–8; 14:1–5; 17:14 with Rev. 8:1–9:21; 15:1–18:21; Exod. 7:8–12:36). Some would label this aspect of John's eschatology "midtribulationist." It seems more accurate to say, however, that the divine seal upon the 144,000 reflects John's belief that the kingdom of God (which is advanced by the activity of that group) has dawned. This "already" perspective is tempered by the grim reality that these saints will, though protected, still have to endure the entirety of the great tribulation. In actuality, it is they who most likely form part of the righteous warriors in the end-time holy war (cf. Rev. 14:1–5 with Rev. 19).[16]

Further support for not equating the 144,000 (Jewish Christians) with the innumerable host (Gentile Christians) comes from those Old Testament passages that speak prophetically of Gentiles joining Israel in worshiping God at the temple in Jerusalem during the end times (e.g., Isa. 2:2; 49:6; 56:6–8; Zech. 14:16). Such a perspective continues in the New Testament with Paul, who may well have understood his collection from the Gentiles for the poor in Jerusalem as the beginning fulfillment of those Old Testament prophecies (see Rom. 15:23–33; 1 Cor. 16; 2 Corinthians 8–9). This notion seems to also inform Revelation 7.[17]

If the 144,000 is the same group as Revelation 14:1–5 (which it undoubtedly is), then the combined passages should be seen as presenting the Jewish Christian remnant as God's soldiers who engage in the

15. W. D. Davies makes this point in *The Gospel and the Land* (Berkeley/Los Angeles: University of California Press, 1974), 49–52; see also Aune, *Revelation 6–16*, 443–45.

16. Some might want to label this interpretation as "mid-tribulational" (so Gleason L Archer, *The Rapture*. 139–44), but there are two problems with that assumption: (1) the 144,000 are on earth, not raptured to heaven; and (2) according to Revelation 6:19, the first three and a half years is also included in the wrath of God, something midtribulationists and pretribulationists want to avoid saying the church will endure.

17. This view would be enhanced if an eschatological reading of the Feast of Booths behind Zechariah 14 is operative in Revelation 7; especially since the Jewish remnant win the nations to God in the end times; see Aune, *Revelation 6–16*, 448–50.

eschatological holy war which results in the restoration of Israel (cf. the following passages: 1 QM; *Pss. Sol* 17:26–28, 43–44; Revelation 19).[18]

We conclude this interpretive issue of Revelation 7 by stating our opinion in the matter: the 144,000 is not the innumerable host (so the pretribulationist view), but, nevertheless, *both* undergo the great tribulation (so the posttribulationist view). I have argued elsewhere that the 144,000 (the twelve tribes of Israel squared plus one thousand) is none other than the symbolic number for the Jewish remnant that escaped the fall of Jerusalem to the Romans by sneaking out of the doomed city in between General Vespasian leaving the siege of the city to his son, Titus, before going to Rome to be declared emperor.[19] The multitude of Gentiles constitutes the church, which was ferociously targeted by Emperor Nero in A.D. 64.

How does the already/not-yet perspective explain Revelation 7? In my opinion the 144,000, the Jewish remnant which accepted Jesus as their Messiah in the first century, is the already aspect, which foreshadows the coming conversion of the Jewish race at the return of Christ, the not-yet aspect (cf. Romans 11). The great multitude of Gentiles were those Gentiles who accepted Jesus Christ but paid the ultimate price at the hands of Nero from A.D. 64–68 and others, like Emperor Domitian in the 90s, the ruler at the time of the writing of the Apocalypse. This "already" aspect of the conversion of the Gentiles is mentioned often in Jewish Scripture and Second Temple writings (as we saw earlier in this study). The "not-yet" aspect will be the final conversion of the Gentiles to Christ who will live in the New Jerusalem, much like Judaism envisioned would happen as Gentiles streamed into Jerusalem at her restoration to worship the true God.

Revelation 21–22

Now that we have sorted through Revelation 7, our discussion of Revelation 21–22 will be brief. The beatific vision of the New Jerusalem

---

18. Daniel Reid identifies three militaristic aspects of the description of the 144,000 in Revelation 7:1–8, "(1) In Rev. 7:1–8 we learn that the number is derived by multiplying twelve tribes by 12,000 from each tribe. The Hebrew…for "thousand [*aleph*]" may have served as a technical term for a military unit in Israel (Num. 1; 26; Jdgs. 5:8; I Sam. 17:18; 1 Chron. 13:1) and may have been so intended in Revelation. (2) The census list of the 144,000 recalls in some aspects the listing in Num. 1:20–46 of able-bodied male Israelites prepared for war (Rev. 14:4 also implies males). (3) The seer's list is headed by Judah, from which the lion of 5:5 comes, an image associated with the son of David's prowess in war."), Tremper Longman III and Daniel G. Reid, *God is a Warrior*. (Grand Rapids: Zondervan, 1995), 185. To these military features, Aune adds a fourth possible military characteristic: the chastity of the 144,000 as depicted in Revelation 14:4 may reflect the purity regulations required of participants in a holy war (Lev. 15:16; Deut. 23:9–10; 1 Sam. 11:11; 1QM 7:3–7), Revelation 6–16, 812.

19. See Pate, *The Writings of John*, 416–18.

combines both the twelve tribes of Israel and the twelve apostles. Put another way, this passage describes the not-yet aspect we referred to above coming to its fruition: Jews are restored to God in the New (restored) Jerusalem by believing in their Messiah, Jesus Christ, while Christian Gentiles pour into the holy city to pay their homage to Jesus their King. The three judgments that we discussed in Revelation earlier support our reading of Revelation 21–22. Rome destroyed Jerusalem; God will destroy Rome after which comes the divine restoration of Israel in the holy city.

What Are the Commendations Revelation 1:1–3 Offers to the Twenty-First Century?

Here we may be brief as we suggest three commendations our passage offers to Christians today. First, blessed are those who are obedient to Jesus Christ in the face of persecution, thereby demonstrating their genuine faith. We might label this notion "the perseverance of the saints." Second, blessed are those who pass on the testimony of Jesus Christ. Verses 1–2 are filled with the importance of passing on the witness of Christ—from God to Christ to his servants to an angel to John to the seven churches in Asia Minor of that day. Believers today need to continue to be links in the chain of the testimony of Jesus Christ. Third, blessed are those believers who continue to expect the return of Christ, even if it has been almost two thousand years since Jesus first uttered the promise of his return. So we see that the message of Revelation 1:1–3 is highly significant. "Soon" and "near" have not lost their sense of emergency for the church.

HOMILETICAL PACKAGING

This third point moves from the first-century synthesis and twenty-first-century appropriation to communicating or preaching Revelation 1:1–3. The older term for this procedure is called "homiletics." Such a process involves explaining how the main point of our text is developed in the verses that comprise it. Before unfolding this overall point, we make three observations.

First, there is a bit of a debate concerning whether a biblical text should be handled deductively or inductively. The former term approaches the homiletical procedure by starting with the main idea and then seeing how it unfolds in the verses of the passage. The latter term, approaches the passage by developing each verse first and then arriving at the main point of the passage. We might say that the deductive technique provides clarity for the audience while the inductive technique sustains the suspense of the audience. In my opinion, there is really no need to pit the two approaches against each other. The exegesis of the passage prior to the homiletical packaging is inductive in nature while the preparation to communicate the text is deductive in nature. In our mind, then, the exegesis of Revelation 1:1–3 has already prepared us to state the main point of the passage, which I suggest is that God is faithful to His covenant with Israel through Jesus Christ. This conclusion leads us to our next introductory comment.

Second, we must allow the covenant theme we have discovered in our exegesis to have pride of place in preaching Revelation 1:1–3. Recall the covenant components informing our passage: the whole book of Revelation is the book of the covenant or the *document clause* (cf. 1:1a with our earlier discussion of Revelation 6 and following); the *preamble* is Jesus Christ who is none other than God (1:1a); (recall that Revelation 4–5 equate God and Christ); *the historical prologue* is that God has kept His covenant with Israel through the work of Jesus Christ (1:1a); the *witnesses* of the covenant are clearly referred to in Revelation 1:1–2; the *stipulation* of the covenant is to be obedient to Christ/God 1:3); the *blessings* of the covenant come from following the stipulation of obedience to God 1:1–3.

Third, before the message is over the three connections/corrections we identified above will need to be addressed. We discovered earlier that the connections between Revelation 1:1–3 and our day also constitute the three corrections our passage offers to modern audiences. (1) Does the fact that almost two thousand years have elapsed since Jesus promised he would return cancel out that prophecy? (2) Did Israel's return to her land and her reconstitution as a nation in 1948 begin the last generation before Christ returns? (3) Has Israel's disobedience to God regarding the Old Covenant disqualified her before God and the new covenant? Moreover, the commendations noted earlier in this chapter should surface in our treatment of Revelation 1:1–3: blessings for being obedient to Christ; blessings for testifying of Christ; and blessings for being alert for the return of Christ.

We now move to stating the overall point communicated through Revelation 1:1–3, after which we see how that big idea unfolds in the passage.

Proposition, or the Main Idea of Revelation 1:1–3: God Is Faithful to His Covenant with Israel through Jesus Christ (v. 1a).

The opening clause, "The revelation of Jesus Christ which God gave to him . . ." is the basis of the proposition statement. A number of considerations show this opening clause is undergirded by theme of the of the covenant. First, probably the dominant truth that we have learned in the previous chapters of this handbook is that "apocalypse" equals the story of the restoration of Israel. Thus the technical term "revelation" taps into the theme of the restoration of Israel. Second, the restoration of Israel is being accomplished through Jesus Christ, who is God. In other words, God is keeping His covenant with Israel through the work of Jesus Christ. The book of Revelation tells us how: Jesus's obedient death on behalf of the sins of the world and his resurrection from death have made his followers (Jew and Gentile) alike, priests before God (1:6), a term distinctly applied to Israel in the Old Testament (Exod. 19:6). In other words, Jesus's obedience to God to the point of death itself constitutes the obedience to the covenant that Israel never accomplished. Third, the resurrection of Jesus amounts to the blessings associated with the restoration of Israel longed for by the prophets. Recall how Ezekiel 37 compares Israel's future restoration to the resurrection.[20] Thus Jesus's obedience to God even until death met the stipulation of the new covenant and Jesus's resurrection constitutes the blessings of the new covenant, namely, forgiveness, fellowship with God, and the promise of ultimate victory.

We have justified our interpretation that Revelation 1:1a is the propositional statement that governs verses 1–3: God is faithful to his covenant through Christ. We now outline our text by delineating the four points that develop that big idea.

Verses 1:1b–2: The Witnesses to God's Faithfulness to His Covenant with Israel through Christ

The reader will recall that in Israel's covenant with God, witnesses were appealed to for the purpose of testifying to the fact that God would keep his part of the covenant with Israel and to witness if Israel kept her part of the covenant with God. In the Old Testament these witnesses centered on long-lasting realities like mountains, history, or heaven itself (see Deut. 31–31). The witnesses to God's new covenant with Israel in Revelation 1:1–2 are: God himself, Jesus Christ, Christ's servants (the prophetic Johannine community (Rev. 22:9), an angel, and John and his audience. These witnesses form "the word of God" and "the testimony of Jesus Christ" (v. 2). That is to say, these witnesses are as trustworthy as God himself. Moreover, we remember from our earlier discussion that the already/not-yet eschatological tension is operative in the new covenant: the Jewish remnant who received Jesus as their Messiah corresponds to the already aspect of the New Covenant while the full conversion of Jews at the parousia is the not-yet aspect.

Regarding the Gentiles and the new covenant, the already aspect corresponds to the many Gentiles who accepted Christ while the not-

---

20. See my *Teach the Text Series: Romans* (Grand Rapids: Baker, 2013), 19.

yet aspect points to the full number of Gentiles coming to Christ as determined by God (Luke 21:24; Rom. 11:25) and streaming into the New Jerusalem (cf. Revelation 21–22). These remarks demonstrate that the connection/correction concerning whether Israel has a place in God's future plan is answered: yes, through the Jewish remnant believers in Jesus we have the already aspect of God's promise to restore Israel and in the divine schedule, all of Israel will be converted to their Messiah—Jesus Christ. In other words, in Revelation there is no replacement theology to be found.

Verse 3a: The Blessings of God's Faithfulness to His Covenant with Israel through Christ

The two blessings mentioned in verse 3a belong to the reader of the scroll of Revelation and the obedient hearers of that message. These blessings are indicative of all those who believe in Jesus Christ and demonstrate that belief by being faithful to God in Christ during great persecution for that very faith. In other words, the blessings of the new covenant belong to the overcomers (see Rev. 5:5–6; 11:7; 12:11; 13:7; 15:2; 17:14; 21:7). We learn from Revelation that the blessings of the new covenant include acceptance before God (Rev. 1:5–6), the sense of the presence of Jesus Christ with them during such tribulation (2:8–11), the hope of heaven (Revelation 21–22), and vindication before those who oppressed them at the return of Christ (Rev. 6:9–10; 19).

Verse 3b: The Stipulations of God's Faithfulness to His Covenant with Israel through Christ

The stipulations of God's covenant are to hear the message of Revelation and to take it to heart. Taking God's covenant to heart was the major problem with Israel in the Old Testament and ultimately ended in her judgment and exile. Here in Revelation 1:3b, the stipulation desired is obedience to Christ despite being persecuted for continuing to follow him. This obedience is in opposition to those in Revelation who called themselves Jews and followers of God but are not because they fell away from God's grace by capitulating to Caesar worship (see Rev. 2–3). Our remarks thus far in developing the big idea of Revelation 1:1–3 also provide three commendations to the Christian. They will be blessed if they are obedient to Christ despite fierce opposition to their faith. They will be blessed for testifying to the gospel of Jesus Christ. They will be blessed if they do not give up on God's promise but remain alert and vigilant in expecting Christ's return.

Verse 1c; 3c: The Timing of God's Faithfulness to His Covenant with Israel through Christ

Here we remember our earlier discussion of the timing of Christ's return as being "soon" (v.1c) and "near" (v.3c). These words allude to the already/not-yet eschatological tension that characterizes Christian existence. With the first coming of Christ both the kingdom of God and the messianic woes entered into history (the already aspect), but both will intensify until Christ returns (the not-yet aspect). In other words, the Christian both participates in the kingdom of God and Christ and endures the great tribulation that opposes such a kingdom; but at God's appointed time, the kingdom of God will finally defeat its satanic opposition and believers will enter into eternal bliss. Consequently, believers must be obedient to Christ no matter what they endure as they await his blessed return. These remarks answer the connections/corrections about the return of Christ. The already aspect relates to the first coming of Christ and his generation while the not-yet aspect of his return is not dependent on the regathering of Israel to her land in 1948, but will be the last generation alive when Jesus comes. The suggestion that 1948 is the last generation before Christ's return has already proved erroneous numerous times. Since the signs of the times began with Jesus's first coming and have no doubt intensified through the centuries, Jesus could come today or not for another millennium. I might put it this way: Israel's restoration to her rightful land in 1948 was providential but not necessarily eschatological.

Chapter in Review

We have discovered in this chapter that there are three steps that are necessary in communicating a biblical passage to today's world, in this case Revelation 1:1–3: putting together a first-century synthesis of the text; taking that step further to its twenty-first-century appropriation; and then delivering that message to today's audience by packaging it homiletically.

When speakers have taken these three steps, they will no doubt feel confident that what they say is an accurate reading of the Bible and that it has divine power to change the lives of the audience.

7

FROM TEXT TO SERMON: TWO EXAMPLES

The Chapter at a Glance

Chapters 4–6 set out a process for interpreting and communicating passages relative to biblical prophetic-apocalyptic passages in the New Testament. The process put forth in chapters 4–6 can be reduced to three major steps: textual criticism, exegesis, and exposition.

- Text criticism establishes the text, along with providing a translation of the passage.

- Exegesis (historical and literary analysis) examines the message the first-century author communicated to his original audience.

- Exposition (theological analysis and homiletical packaging) then builds a bridge to twenty-first-century listeners and packages the message in a way that makes it both striking and practical.

- This chapter applies the entire process to Romans 11:25–27 and 2 Thessalonians 2:6–7.

ROMANS 11:25–27

25 Οὐ γὰρ θέλω ὑμᾶς ἀγνοεῖν, ἀδελφοί, τὸ μυστήριον τοῦτο, ἵνα μὴ ἦτε [παρ'] ἑαυτοῖς φρόνιμοι, ὅτι πώρωσις ἀπὸ μέρους τῷ Ἰσραὴλ γέγονεν ἄχρι οὗ τὸ πλήρωμα τῶν ἐθνῶν εἰσέλθη **26** καὶ οὕτως πᾶς Ἰσραὴλ σωθήσεται, καθὼς γέγραπται·

ἥξει ἐκ Σιὼν ὁ ῥυόμενος,
  ἀποστρέψει ἀσεβείας ἀπὸ Ἰακώβ.
27 καὶ αὕτη αὐτοῖς ἡ παρ' ἐμοῦ διαθήκη,
  ὅταν ἀφέλωμαι τὰς ἁμαρτίας αὐτῶν.[1]

Textual Criticism and Translation

The UBS4 includes a textual variant in verse 25: should it be παρ' or ἐν or no preposition but the simple dative (ἑαυτοῖς)? The former with the dative would be rendered "beside" or "in the presence of," while the latter is rendered "in." Omitting either preposition speaks for itself. The NRSV opts for including παρ' and treating it as a comparative, "wiser *than* you are." The NASB goes with ἐν, translating the preposition thusly, "wise *in* your own estimation." The NIV seems to eliminate either of the prepositions, producing the following wording, "so that you may not be conceited."

Let us quote Bruce M. Metzger at this point and then assess the data accordingly:

> Although it can be argued that the simple dative, without out a preposition, may be the original reading (supported, as it is, by P[46] F G Ψ 1739 *al*) and that the difficulty of construing the sense prompted scribes to insert ἐν or παρ', the Committee decided that it would be safest to adopt παρ', which is strongly supported by ℵ C D *al*, but to enclose it within square brackets in order to indicate considerable doubt whether it belongs in the text.[2]

Extrinsic Probabilities

We really have three possibilities here: there was not a preposition in the original text; παρ' was the original reading; or ἐν was the original reading. Here is the breakdown of manuscript evidence respective to

---

1. K. Aland, B. Aland, J. C. Martini, and B. M. Metzger, *Novum Testamentum Graece,* 28th Edition (Stuttgart: Deutsche Bibelgesellschaft, 2012).

2. B. M. Metzger, *A Textual Commentary on the Greek New Testament, Second Edition: A Companion Volume to the United Bible Societies' Greek New Testament,* 4th rev. ed. (London/New York: United Bible Societies, 1994), 465.

each reading. First, no original preposition is supported by P⁴⁶ F G Ψ 1739 *al*. Second, παρ' is supported by ℵ C D *al*. Third, ἐν is supported by A and B. Now we can assess the extrinsic probabilities in terms of geographical distribution and the age of the manuscripts.

Regarding the geographical distribution, in general we have the best chance of identifying the original if that reading is widely spread, thus demonstrating its preference by ancient Christianity. The basic geographical locations are: Egypt/Alexandrian, Northeast Turkey/Byzantine, and Rome/Western. One can deduce from this data that if one reading has only one location supporting it while another reading has two locations supporting it, all things considered (for example the date of the reading), the reading with the two locations supporting it is probably the original text. In the order listed above, here are the geographical distributions. First, that there was no preposition is attested by two geographical areas: Alexandrian (P⁴⁶) and Byzantine (F G Ψ 1739). Second, that there was παρ' is also supported by two locations: Alexandrian (ℵ C) and Western (D). Third, ἐν is only found in one location, Alexandrian (A and B). So thus far we begin to suspect that ἐν is not the original reading.

The date of the readings does not help us much. That is so because all three possibilities have Alexandrian support, the oldest manuscripts. P⁴⁶ (second century) is an Alexandrian text, while παρ' is found in ℵ, the oldest Alexandrian uncial, and ἐν is recorded in A (Alexandrinus, fifth century) and B (Vaticanus, fourth century).

What we may say thus far is that most probably ἐν is not original owing to the fact that it is only supported by one geographical area—Alexandrian. We shall see why in the transcriptional probabilities to follow. We are left, then, with either no preposition in Romans 11:25 or παρ'.

Transcriptional Probabilities

Here we apply the four questions that text critics follow in deciding between variant readings to our situation. The first question regarding the shortest reading does not pertain since the decision is between no reading and a preposition. Neither does the second question regarding the oldest reading apply because both readings are supported by the Alexandrian family type. The third question regarding the most difficult reading, however, applies since no preposition seems to have created difficulty in translating the text. That consideration plays into the fourth and deciding question in this case: Which reading bests accounts for the appearance of the other readings? This question aptly applies to the reading without a preposition because without it the sense of ἵνα μὴ ἦτε ἑαυτοῖς φρόνιμοι, (in order that you might not among yourselves be wise) is incomplete. The nuance of the dative plural ἑαυτοῖς is ambiguous. We therefore conclude from the third and fourth questions that first παρ' was added to the original text after which a scribe added ἐν to further clarify the nuance of παρ'.

Intrinsic Probabilities

Comparing Romans 11:25 with Romans 12:16 is illuminating regarding our text critical discussion, τὸ αὐτὸ εἰς ἀλλήλους φρονοῦντες. This phrase is similar to Romans 11:25 in that both verses use a form of φρονεῖν, preceded by a plural pronoun: ἀλλήλους (12:16) and ἑαυτοῖς (11:25). Romans 12:16 supplies an accusative preposition that governs the accusative plural pronoun, εἰς ἀλλήλους φρονοῦντες. It is reasonable that the scribe added παρ' to ἑαυτοῖς φρόνιμοι in Romans 11:25, thus creating harmony between a dative and a preposition that would govern the dative plural pronoun, in keeping with Romans 12:16.

Conclusion

The extrinsic probabilities seem to eliminate ἐν as the original since it only is supported by one family type whereas no preposition and παρ' readings are supported by two geographical locations. The transcriptional probabilities seem to point to no preposition in the original text because it better answers the questions of difficulty and which reading gave rise to the other readings. The intrinsic probabilities appear to confirm that a later scribe wanted to clarify the meaning of Romans 11:25 by adding παρ' to it, which would then match the syntax of Romans 12:16. One has to think long and hard about disagreeing with the eminent textual critic Bruce M. Metzger, whose committee inserted the παρ' into Romans 11:25. Even Metzger, however, puts the preposition in brackets, [παρ'], disclosing his doubt about that reading. Therefore, when all is said and done I think there was no original preposition in Romans 11:25, to which first was added παρ' and then was later replaced with ἐν by a scribe for the purpose of clarifying the ambiguity of παρ'.

Translation

Except for the quotation of Isaiah 59:20–21, Romans 11:25–27 is one long sentence that consists of several clauses:

1. An infinitive clause: **25** Οὐ γὰρ θέλω ὑμᾶς ἀγνοεῖν, ἀδελφοί, τὸ μυστήριον τοῦτο,

2. A subordinate clause: ἵνα μὴ ἦτε [παρ'] ἑαυτοῖς φρόνιμοι

3. A relative clause, comprised of three points: (a) ὅτι πώρωσις ἀπὸ μέρους τῷ Ἰσραὴλ γέγονεν (b) ἄχρι οὗ τὸ πλήρωμα τῶν ἐθνῶν εἰσέλθη **26** (c) καὶ οὕτως πᾶς Ἰσραὴλ σωθήσεται, καθὼς γέγραπται

4. A quotation of Isaiah 59:20–21:
ἥξει ἐκ Σιὼν ὁ ῥυόμενος,
   ἀποστρέψει ἀσεβείας ἀπὸ Ἰακώβ.
27 καὶ αὕτη αὐτοῖς ἡ παρ᾽ ἐμοῦ διαθήκη,
   ὅταν ἀφέλωμαι τὰς ἁμαρτίας αὐτῶν.

I offer the following translation of Romans 11:25–27:

> For I do not want you to be ignorant, brethren, con-
> cerning this mystery, in order that you might not be
> arrogant among yourselves, that a hardening in part
> has come upon Israel, until the fullness of the Gentiles
> comes in, and so all Israel will be saved, just as it is writ-
> ten, "the deliverer will come from Zion, who will turn
> Jacob from ungodliness. And this is my covenant with
> them, when I take away their sins."

For the moment I simply observe that the NIV, NASB, and the NRSV
all render the most controversial words in our passage—καὶ οὕτως—as
comparative ("and thus" or "and so), not as temporal ("and then").

Historical Analysis

Purpose of Romans

The historical background of Romans requires that we discuss the
purpose for the book of Romans. Although there continues to be much
debate as to why Paul penned his letter to the Romans, the apostle himself leaves the reader in no doubt as to his purpose. Paul was divinely
called to lead the way in bringing about the end-time conversion of the
nations, a mission in which the church at Rome was to play a critical
role (see Rom. 1:1–15; 15:14–33; 16:25–27). Rome, therefore, was to
be the last major stopping point before the apostle launched the final
leg of his eschatological mission to Spain, the end of the then-known
world (see again Rom. 15:14–33).[3] In order to garner the support of the
Christians in Rome, the capital city of the Roman Empire, Paul had to
accomplish two tasks. First, Paul had to motivate the Jewish and Gentile
Christians in Rome to start getting along again (see especially Romans
9–11; 14–15); otherwise the church would not be unified enough to
support him financially and spiritually in his Spanish mission. Second,

---

3. Robert Jewett has shown convincingly that Paul's mission to Spain was uppermost in Paul's
   mind when he wrote Romans (*Romans* [Minneapolis: Fortress, 2007]). We agree with
   Jewett for the most part, except that we do not think that author has focused enough on the
   eschatological status of Paul's mission to Spain via Rome; see our pertinent remarks below.

even before that, Paul had to convince the Roman Christians that he was a legitimate apostle and therefore worthy of their support. Douglas Moo pinpoints this aspect of Romans very well:

> Paul's ultimate destination is Spain. As he clearly hints in 15:24, he is coming to Rome, among other things, to get the Romans to help him with that mission. But Paul has never been to Rome. Moreover, he is a controversial figure in the early church. As both a faithful Jew and God's "point man" in opening the Gentile mission, he has been constantly under suspicion. Jewish Christians thought he was giving too much of the old tradition away, whereas Gentile Christians thought he was still too Jewish. A lot of false rumors about what he teaches and does swirl around him (cf. 3:8). Paul therefore probably knows he is going to have to clear the air if he expects the Romans to support him. Thus . . . he writes Romans to clarify just what he believes.[4]

Paul writes Romans, then, to defend his gospel of the grace of God through Christ by arguing that it is rooted in the Old Testament (Romans 2–5), providing the disclaimer that it is not antinomian in ethic (God's grace is *not* a license to sin; so Romans 6–8), and holding out a future for Israel (Romans 9–11). All of these concerns would have helped to allay the fears of Jewish Christians in Rome that Paul was anti-Jewish. From the same chapters, however, the Gentile Christians in Rome would have welcomed Paul's teaching that Gentiles are saved by faith in Christ apart from the law and that the conversion of the nations is a significant part of God's plan. In other words, viewing Romans as Paul's official doctrinal statement designed to introduce himself to the congregations at Rome for the purpose of gathering their support for the end-time conversion of the nations, seems to nicely explain the historical background of the book.

General Context of Romans 11:25–27

Romans 11:25–27 speaks of the future salvation of Israel. Such a conviction on Paul's part is rooted in the Old Testament covenant. In particular, our passage quotes Isaiah 59:20–21 (LXX), which envisions the day when God will restore Israel to himself, thereby keeping his promise to make a new covenant with his people (see also Jer. 31:33; Ezek. 36:27). I have argued elsewhere that the theme of the new covenant governs the

---

4. Douglas J. Moo, *Romans*, The NIV Application Commentary (Grand Rapids: Zondervan, 2000), 22; though it should be noted that Moo does not make Paul's mission to Spain the all-encompassing purpose for writing Romans as we are arguing here.

entire book of Romans. In particular, I claimed that the covenant format
that comprises the book of Deuteronomy is also the outline of Romans.
These components can be seen in chart form:

Old Covenant of Israel in Deuteronomy	New Covenant in Romans
1. Preamble: Deuteronomy 1:1–5	1. Romans 1:1–5 (Christ , the Son of God and the conversion of Gentiles before the restoration of Israel)
2. Historical Prologue: Deuteronomy 1:6–3:29	2. Romans 1:16–17 (spiritual, not physical or geographical, restoration in Christ)
3. Stipulations: Chaps. 4–26	3. Romans 1:18–4:25 (by faith in Christ not the law of Moses)
4. Blessings: Chaps. 27–30	4. Romans 5–8 (blessings on believing Gentiles)
5. Curses: Chaps. 27–30	5. Romans 9–11 (curses on unbelieving Israel)
6. Appeal to Witnesses: Deuteronomy 31:26–32:47	6. Romans 12:1–15:33 (renewal of the covenant ceremony)
7. Document Clause: Deuteronomy 31:9, 24–2	7. Romans 16 (on a letter not on stone)

Romans 11:25–27 corresponds to the covenant curses on Israel
spelled out in Romans 9–11, but it also envisions the new-covenant
blessings being poured out on Israel in the end-times as she embraces
Jesus as her Messiah. The reader is by now familiar with the hope of
the restoration of Israel, and this promise is the backdrop of Romans
11:25–27.

Immediate Context

Romans 11:25–27 occurs in the most famous Pauline section regarding the problem of Israel—Romans 9–11. Simply put, Romans
9–11 corresponds to the covenant curses spelled out in Deuteronomy
27–30. We may outline Romans 9–11 in the following way:

Romans 9	Israel's past blessings
Romans 10	Israel's present rejection of the Messiah and the subsequent covenant curses that rest upon her
Romans 11	the present salvation of the Gentiles and the future salvation of the Jews

In Romans 11, Paul makes three points. First, Israel's rejection of Jesus Messiah is partial, not total (vv. 1–10). Some Jews have in fact responded in faith to Christ (the "remnant"), Paul included. Second, Israel's rejection of Jesus Messiah actually serves a merciful purpose, namely, it paved the way for Gentiles to come to Christ (vv. 11–24). Such a rejection, however, is not the end of the story for Israel because God will use the Gentiles' conversion to stir the Jews to jealously to receive Jesus as their Messiah. Gentile Christians should not become arrogant, then, as if they are the only ones God will save. Third, Israel's rejection of their Messiah is temporary, not permanent (vv. 25–27). A day is coming when all Israel will be saved under the new covenant. One can see from this context that Romans 11:25–27 is the key to the third point.

Literary Analysis

Structure

We presented the grammatical structure of Romans 11:25–27 above in the translation section. Now we provide the outline that flows from that structure. The key concept that governs Romans 11:25–27 is "mystery" (v. 25), which is presented in three points:

A. The Meaning of the Mystery (v. 25)
B. The Warning Attached to the Mystery (v. 25a)
C. The Components of the Mystery (vv. 25b–27):
    1. The hardening in part on Israel (v. 25b)
    2. The fullness of the Gentiles (v. 25c)
    3. The salvation of all Israel (v. 26a–27):
        a.   The meaning of καὶ οὕτως (v. 26a)
        b.   The meaning of "all Israel will be saved" (v. 26b)
        c.   The Old Testament basis of the salvation of Israel (vv. 26c–27)

Syntax and Semantics

The most debated part of Romans 11:25–27 is the third part of the relative clause in v. 26. There we meet with a syntax issue (how are the words, καὶ οὕτως, related?), and then two semantical issues (what does Ἰσραὴλ mean? what does πᾶς Ἰσραὴλ mean?). We now address these three issues in order.

First, what do the words καὶ οὕτως "all Israel will be saved" mean? Some take the phrase as temporal, "and then," meaning that after the spiritual hardening of Israel and the fullness of the Gentiles, *then* all Israel will be saved. A temporal rendering of καὶ οὕτως, however, is rare in Paul. Most, therefore, take the phrase comparatively—"and so" or "and in this manner"—referring to the immediate context of verse 25. Some commentators go on to suggest that verse 26 refers to the remnant (including both Jew and Gentile; i.e., the church), thereby ruling out any future conversion of national Israel. It is preferable, however, to take the ante-cedent of verse 26 as the Gentiles coming into the community of faith, which, when completed, turns Israel to Jesus the Messiah. The future tense in "will . . . be grafted" (v. 24) and "will be saved" (v. 26) supports this conclusion. On this reading, verse 26 refers to an event that will wit-ness a national turning of Israel to Christ. It should be pointed out that this view depends on the meaning of "Israel," our next point.

Second, what does "Israel" mean? If it means *spiritual* Israel, then the referent would include Gentiles as well as Jews, and Paul is not then necessarily saying that *national* Israel will be restored to God. The "spir-itual" Israel view is unlikely, however, seeing that the other ten times "Israel" is used in Romans 9–11 (9:6 [twice]; 27 [twice], 31; 10:19, 21; 11:2, 7, 25) refer to ethnic Israel. For verse 26 to posit a different mean-ing is unlikely.

Third, what does "all Israel" mean? Three main possibilities have been suggested. (1) Covenantal/Reformed theologians take the phrase to mean *spiritual* Israel, the elect of God including both Jew and Gentile Christians (i.e., the church). To say, however, that the church will be saved is redundant. (2) Dispensationalists take the words to refer to *na-tional* Israel, Israel as a whole, though not necessarily every individual Israelite. The phrase "all Israel" is used elsewhere to refer to the nation but without necessarily including every Jew (cf. 1 Sam. 7:2–5; 25:1; 1 Kings 12:1; 2 Chron. 12:1–5; Dan. 9:11; cf. *bSan* 10:1). (3) The most recent theory is the *unified* Israel interpretation proposed by Bruce Longenecker, which builds on the second possibility. He writes:

> Instead, in 11:26 Paul is thinking exclusively of an ethnic entity, and moreover, of that entity as a whole. Throughout 9–11, Paul draws out the disparate courses of two groups—believing and unbelieving—within ethnic Israel. By the inclusive "all" in 11:26, he joins both groups together. Thus Paul looks forward to the time when not only the remnant of Israel who have be-lieved but also those of Israel who have strayed from the course of their unbelief will be saved. When Paul speaks of "all Israel" in 11:26, what he has in mind is an ethnic group whose members at present are schismati-cally divided. In this sense, his point is not so much that all *Israel* will be saved, but that *all* Israel will be saved.[5]

---

5. Bruce W. Longenecker, "Different Answers to Different Issues: Israel, the Gentiles and Salvation History in Romans 9–11," *Journal for the Study of the New Testament* 36 (1989): 97.

In other words, "all Israel will be saved" refers to the future event of the nation of Israel's conversion to Jesus as Messiah, which will unite it with those Jewish Christians (spiritual Israel) throughout the period of the church. Truly, all Israel, united Israel, will for the first time be saved.

Style

The style of Romans 11:25–27 is best explained by its genre, which is prophetic-apocalyptic in nature. Having reached that conclusion, however, this passage is not thorough-going prophetic-apocalyptic such as we meet in 1 Thessalonians 4–5 and in 2 Thessalonians 2. Still, Romans 11:25–27 is a prophetic-apocalyptic piece rounding out Paul's explanation of the problem of Israel in salvation history.

Theological Analysis

Here we attempt to identify the central point of Romans 11:25–27, after which we pinpoint the shared need of the text which bridges Paul's day with our own.

Central Point

The structural outline of Romans 11:25–27 makes it clear that Paul's central concern is the mystery Paul reveals to his audience. We must examine three points connected with that mystery.

The meaning of the mystery (v. 25) requires extensive discussion since it is the key to the passage. The background of Paul's usage of μυστήριον is not to be found in the mystery religions as once was thought,[6] but rather in Jewish prophetic-apocalyptic circles as found in Daniel (see, for example, 2:18–19, 27–30) and in Second Temple Judaism (*1 Enoch* 41:1; 46:2; 103:2; 104:10, 12; 106:19; *4 Ezra* 10:38; 12:36–38; 14:5; *2 Baruch* 48:3; 81:4; the DSS [1QS 3:23; 4:18; 9:18; 11:3, 5, 19; 1QH 1:21; 2:13; 4:27–28; 7:27; 11:10; 12:13; etc.). One finds in these passages and others that "mystery" refers to an end-time event now broken into this age or at least the revelation of an aspect of the age to come disclosed in this present age and to a divinely appointed seer.

We will now look at the occurrences of "mystery" in Paul's writings. We shall show two themes that the apostle attaches to mystery. First, a mystery is the revelation to Paul and/or in history of an aspect of the age to come that awaited the end of history. Second, Paul always sees in the revelation of the divine mystery a reversal, or an irony, that confounds the unbelieving eye. As far as I know, this second aspect of

---

6. For documentation of this point see C. Marvin Pate, *The End of the Age Has Come: Theology of Paul* (Grand Rapids: Zondervan, 1995), 27–28.

Paul's understanding of God's mystery has not been noticed by other interpreters of Paul. The following self-explanatory chart demonstrates these two points.

Pauline passage	End-time revelation and/or event now in history	Divine reversal or irony
1 Corinthians 2:7	The glory of the age to come was revealed in this age at the cross.	God is hidden under the opposite: The mere mortal cannot fathom the meaning of the cross; to them Jesus's death was failure and defeat but only those enlightened by the Holy Spirit perceive that the cross is the power of God for salvation (cf. Rom. 1:16).
1 Corinthians 13:2	The end-time gift of the Spirit has given the church spiritual gifts like tongues, prophecy, knowledge, and mysteries (in the sense that the spiritual gifts are themselves evidence of the presence of the end-time Spirit).	But even these eschatological gifts of the Spirit will pass away (most likely at the parousia) but love is eternal. This reality would have shocked the Corinthian church, which thought the preceding named gifts were the best and would last forever.
1 Corinthians 15:51–52	God revealed to Paul in this present age two end-time truths about the destiny of Christians: Those who are dead at the return of Christ will be resurrected from the grave, and those who are alive at the return of Christ will be translated (have their resurrection bodies placed over their human bodies); either way Christians will need immortal bodies because flesh and blood cannot enter heaven.	This truth that only the immortal body can enter heaven would have been the opposite of what many in the Corinthian church were saying, namely, only their immortal souls would go to heaven because the body is evil (a famous notion of Plato, under whom the Corinthian Christians were apparently spellbound).

Pauline passage	End-time revelation and/or event now in history	Divine reversal or irony
Romans 11:25–27; 16:25–27	The end-time prophecy of Gentile conversion is now coming to pass.	But the fulfillment of this prophecy reverses the OT order: from—first the restoration of Israel, then the conversion of the Gentiles—to—first the conversion of the Gentiles, then the restoration of Israel (see again our discussion regarding Rom. 11:25–27).
2 Thessalonians 2:6–7	The coming of the end-time man of lawlessness has already broken into this age in spirit.	The irony of this mystery centers in *pax Romana*, that is the peace and law the Roman Empire instilled will ironically be undone by its own rulers.[7]
1 Timothy 3:16	The end-time godliness that Jews believed would accompany the arrival of the age to come would do so because of Israel's renewed obedience to the Torah.	Quite to the contrary, however, Paul announces that end-time godliness has already entered this age through Jesus Christ and only those who believe in him, not try to keep the Torah, will be saved (cf. 1 Tim. 1:3–11; etc.).
Colossians 1:26–27; 2:2; 4:3	The end-time OT prophecy of the conversion of the Gentiles is occurring now in Jesus Christ.	Nevertheless, this is the reversal of the end-time expectation that first comes the restoration of Israel and then the conversion of the Gentiles, as we observed with regard to Romans 11:25–27/ 16:25–27.

---

7. For the dominant presence of the imperial cult in Thessalonica, especially its emperor worship, see C. Marvin Pate, *Apostle of the Last Days*, 86–90. The Roman politicians pushed the idea of *pax romana*, so to label Roman emperors as "lawless" would have been an oxymoron in the minds of Romans.

Pauline passage	End–time revelation and/or event now in history:	Divine reversal or irony:
Ephesians 1:9–10; 3:3–6, 9; 6:19	The union of Jew and Gentile in Christ is the beginning of the end-time expectation of the reconciliation of the cosmos; the former is an object lesson to the latter.	But the reconciliation of Jew and Gentile in Christ and indeed the future reconciliation of the cosmos is by faith in Christ alone not by the works of the Torah (see. Eph. 2).
Ephesians 5:32; cf. 5:21–6:9	The union of husband and wife reflects the mystery of the union of Christ and the church. But more than that, the haustelfn (house hold codes of conduct in the ancient world) anticipate in the present the end-time harmony of the universe (cf. again Eph. 1:9–10).	But the ancient household codes emphasized the dominance of the husband over his wife, the abject control of the father over his child (*pater familias*), and the control of the master over his slave. Paul, however, introduces a reciprocal dimension to the household codes that reflects Ephesians 5:21 (submitting to one another in Christ): Husbands, love your wives; fathers, nurture your children; and masters, treat your slaves the way God will treat you. Thus this reciprocal dimension in Christ takes the household code in a completely different direction that ancient Jewish and Greco-Roman society could have envisioned.

Moreover, as I have already mentioned, Paul understands this divine mystery revealed to him as reversing the Old Testament order of the twofold prophecy from the restoration of Israel and the conversion of the Gentiles (see for example, Isa. 45:15; 60:15–17; Mic. 4:13; Tobit 3:11; *1 QM* 12:13–15; cf. Rom. 11:25–27 especially with Rom. 16:25–27) to, first, the conversion of the Gentiles and, then, the restoration of Israel. Indeed, Paul could hope that his collection from the Gentile churches for the purpose of carrying that offering to Jerusalem would spark the end-time restoration of Israel (see Rom. 15:25–29; 1 Cor. 16:1–4; 2 Corinthians 8–9).

The warning attached to the mystery (v. 25a) is a caveat Paul adds to the revelation of the divine mystery: Gentile Christians should not become puffed up in their minds as if they are God's gift to the church. To the contrary, the only reason the Gentiles now enjoy a place in salvation history is because Israel has been temporarily set aside in the plan of God to allow Gentiles to become part of the people of God owing to their faith in Jesus Messiah. Such a caveat was the basic point made by Paul in Romans 11:11–24 and emphasized here in verse 25. The spiritual relationship between Gentile Christians and Israel is spelled out in verses 25–27.

The components of the mystery (vv. 25b–27) include the partial hardening of Israel (v. 25b), the fullness of the Gentiles (v. 25c), and the salvation of all Israel (v. 26–27). We must now discuss the details of these verses in some detail.

(1) The Partial Hardening of Israel (v. 25b)

The adverbial prepositional phrase, ἀπὸ μέρους, refers to πώρωσις rather than τῷ Ἰσραὴλ. Thus it is a hardening in part (partial hardening or blindness) rather that a part of Israel. This reading closes the door on replacement theology that thinks that believing Gentiles and believing Jews now are apart from Israel constituting a new entity, the church. Instead, Paul still thinks of Israel as a unity, but one that consists of Christian Jews and non-Christian Jews. To put it another way, the remnant that Paul discusses back in verses 1–10 is nevertheless a part of Israel. This important clue sheds light on how it is that "all Israel will be saved" (v. 26a), which we discussed above.

(2) The Fullness of the Gentiles (v. 25c)

Luke 21:24 gives a negative nuance to Jesus's words, "until the times of the Gentiles are fulfilled" (i.e., Jerusalem will be trampled upon by the nations until the Gentile dominance has run its course). Paul, however, provides a positive rendering of ἄχρι οὗ τὸ πλήρωμα τῶν ἐθνῶν εἰσέλθῃ to the effect that Israel will not accept its Messiah until the full number of Gentiles first receives Jesus as Christ. The two nuances are not contradictory. As we have seen in the Old Testament and in Second Temple Judaism, the Jewish expectation was that the Gentiles would trample over Israel until the divine time for the restoration of Israel. At that time God, or his appointed Messiah, will defeat the Gentiles and many of those Gentiles will repent of their hostility to Israel and her God and stream into Jerusalem to bring gifts of homage to Jews and their God.

The full number of the Gentiles coming to belief in the Messiah finds its counterpart in the idea in Second Temple Judaism that end-time events are following God's predetermined schedule, especially the conviction that the number of the elect as divinely planned was waiting its numerical completion (see *2 Apoc. Bar.* 23:4; 30:2; 75:6; *4 Ezra* 4:36–37; *Apoc. Abr.* 29:17; cf. Rev. 6:11; 7:4; 14:1; *1 Clem.* 2.4; 59.2; etc.).

Εἰσέλθη draws upon the Jesus tradition regarding his talk of entering the kingdom of God or into life (see Matt. 5:20; 7:21; 19:17; Mark 9:43, 45, 47/par.; 10:15; 23–25; John 3:5). Since Paul rarely speaks of the kingdom of God, it is most likely the case that Paul inherited εἰσέλθη from Jesus. Indeed, it can be said that all three phrases in our clause come from Jesus: the fullness of the times of the Gentiles (cf. Luke 21:24), the idea of an elect (cf. Matt. 24:22, 31; Mark 13:20, 27), and entrance into the kingdom of God (recall the references above).

(3) The Salvation of all Israel (v. 26–27) has been discussed in part above. Recall that we assigned the meaning "and thus" or "and so" to καὶ οὕτως. Also recall that we interpreted "Israel" to be ethnic Israel. "All Israel" means that for the first time in Israel's history all Israel (believing and unbelieving) will become one in that unbelieving Jews will become believing Jews in receiving Christ as their Messiah in and around the events of the Parousia. The Old Testament that comprises verses 25c–27 expands this latter idea.

Paul's quotation of Isaiah 59:20–21 generates three comments. First, Paul alters the LXX from ἕνεκεν Σιών (for the sake of Zion) to ἐκ Σιών (out of Zion) so as not to make Israel the object of national primacy in the last days. Second, the deliverer coming out of Zion surely refers to Jesus's Second Coming from the heavenly Jerusalem (see Gal. 4:26; cf. Heb. 12:22; Rev. 3:12; 21:2), not to his incarnation (cf. 1 Thess. 1:10). Third, Paul explicitly mentions the covenant in v. 27, which is the new covenant when God will cleanse Israel of her sin and give her a heart that is obedient to God (Jer. 31:33; Ezek. 36:27). Moreover, it will be Jesus, ὁ ῥυόμενος, who inaugurates the new covenant; indeed, who already inaugurated it through his death (see 1 Cor. 11:23–26). This point is important because it refutes the theory that there is a special way of salvation for Israel; that is, that there are two covenants: the covenant of the works of the law for Israel and the covenant of faith in Jesus Christ for Gentiles. To the contrary, for Paul Israel will be saved as he was saved, namely, through faith in Jesus Christ apart from the works of the law (see Rom. 3:21–26).

In light of our discussion regarding this section we may now state the central concern of Romans 11:25–27: the divine mystery revealed to Paul is that the conversion of the Gentiles to Christ will precede and even precipitate the restoration of Israel, a seeming reversal of the order of Old Testament prophecy.

Shared Need

What need of the original readers of Romans 11:25–27 is addressed? The passage spoke to a twofold need. First, the Gentile Christians who comprised the majority in the churches at Rome needed to know that

God has not finished with Israel. Neither the Gentiles' salvation nor Israel's failure to believe thus far should in any way produce an anti-Semitic or anti-Jewish mentality among the Gentile believers. Second, there is only one way to divine salvation, and it is through faith in Jesus Christ apart from the law. Is there a comparable twofold need that our text pinpoints that corresponds to today's audience? Yes, there is. Among today's Christian audiences, there are two extremes that our text addresses. On the one hand, Romans 11:25–27 reminds contemporary believers that God has not finished with Israel, and one of the concerns that flows from this conviction should be a zero tolerance for anti-Semitism. On the other hand, our passage does not treat Israel as an exception when it comes to the means of salvation; there is no biblical basis for a two-covenant way to God. Rather, Jews must come to God the way Gentiles must come to God—through faith in Jesus Christ alone.

Appropriation

Identifying the need of the contemporary audience that shares with the original audience begins the process of moving the passage's message from "then" to "now." The twenty-first-century appropriation of the message answers three questions: (1) How does the passage *connect* with today's audience? (2) What contemporary attitudes and actions does the passage *correct*? (3) What ways of thinking and/or acting does the passage *commend* to today's audience?

Contemporary listeners should *connect* with Paul's message in Romans 11:25–27 regarding their attitudes toward Israel. The two mindsets we identified above fit this application category. On the one hand, Paul's warning against anti-Semitism on the part of the Gentiles has an uneasy sound to it these days, particularly as the Western world appears to be turning against Israel thus joining the longstanding prejudice of the Middle East against Jews in their rightful land. Those of us who love Israel (and Palestinians too) are afraid that the Holocaust seems so distant now that it no longer alarm nations as to the atrocities once committed against over six million Jews, and that such genocide can happen again. Yet, on the other hand, a growing number of biblical scholars are joining famous pastors in arguing that the New Testament presents two covenants: one for Gentiles and one for Jews. Such a compromise is also disconcerting to those of us who are committed to the gospel of Jesus Christ which announces that both Gentile and Jew must come to God by way of Jesus alone. Perhaps the latter extreme is a kneejerk reaction to the former extreme.

Romans 11:25–27 can help to *correct* the preceding two extremes. On the one hand, it warns Gentile Christians, and by implication all the nations, not to harbor any hint of prejudice against Jews in general and Israel in particular. Such anti-Semitism can only do more harm than good. On the other hand, Christians have no authority to compromise the gospel because of the past atrocities done to Israel. We can have it both ways—love Jews and their homeland and share the gospel with them.

Romans 11:25–27 thus *commends* both love and integrity in relating to Jews in general and Israel in particular. Our passage correctly commends loving Jews, the Old Testament people of God, today. In a tangible way, loving Jews means that this is no time for the Western world to abandon its only democratic ally in the Middle East, whether in preventing Iran from obtaining a nuclear weapon or helping to eliminate terrorist movements like Hesbollah and Hamas, whose only goal is to destroy both Jews and Palestinians alike. On the other hand, Paul also would challenge the church to not negotiate away the gospel in showing its love for Israel. What is needed on the part of Gentile Christians is integrity in concert with its mission of fulfilling the Great Commission. An integral part of that mission is to love all people groups in the world, including both Jews and Palestinians. In other words, should the day come when terrorists groups are no more in Israel, then Jews will have the responsibility of treating Palestinians as their brothers beginning even now. If that solution should mean two separate states, then so be it. Unfortunately, the attitudes of love and integrity concerning Jews and Israel that are conveyed by Romans 11:25–27 will not allow for the separation of politics and religion in seeking peace so desperately needed in that region.

Homiletical Packaging

To me, the structure of Romans 11:25–27 identified above easily provides an outline for a sermon on this passage. The key concept that governs Romans 11:25–27 is "mystery" (v. 25), which is presented in three points.

The Mystery Revealed to Paul

A. The Meaning of the Mystery (v. 25)
B. The Warning Attached to the Mystery (v. 25a)
C. The Components of the Mystery (vv. 25b–27)
　　1. The hardening in part on Israel (v. 25b)
　　2. The fullness of the Gentiles (v. 25c)
　　3. The salvation of all Israel (v. 26a–27):
　　　　a. The meaning of καὶ οὕτως (v. 26a)
　　　　b. The meaning of "all Israel will be saved" (v. 26b)
　　　　c. The Old Testament basis of the salvation of Israel
　　　　　 (vv. 26c–27)

One might begin the exposition of Romans 11:25–27 with the following introduction: "At its heart, Romans 11:25–27 draws on the end-time secret that God revealed to Paul in history, namely, that the divine plan has always been to save both Jew and Gentile. Even Israel's present status of unbelief is being used by God as a window of opportunity for Gentiles to come to Jesus Messiah. And, in a reciprocal way, God is using the Gentiles' conversion to make Israel jealous so that she will claim her long-awaited Messiah. Let us now see the three points Paul makes about this divine mystery."

2 THESSALONIANS 2:6–7

6 καὶ νῦν τὸ κατέχον οἴδατε εἰς τὸ ἀποκαλυφθῆναι αὐτὸν ἐν τῷ ἑαυτοῦ καιρῷ. **7** τὸ γὰρ μυστήριον ἤδη ἐνεργεῖται τῆς ἀνομίας· μόνον ὁ κατέχων ἄρτι ἕως ἐκ μέσου γένηται.[8]

Textual Criticism and Translation

There is only one variant reading in 2 Thessalonians 2:6–7 and the translation of the two verses is straightforward. Such simplicity, however, is more than made up for by the longstanding debate over the identification of the restrainer, which we will discuss later.

The variant reading in our passage centers on the choice in verse 6 between ἑαυτοῦ and αὐτοῦ. The NASB and the NRSV opt for the latter word, "in his time" while the NIV chooses the former word, "at the proper time." The evidence for αὐτοῦ includes ℵ A I K P 33, 81 while the evidence for ἑαυτοῦ includes ℵ B D F G 0278, 1739.

Extrinsic Probabilities

In terms of the geographical distribution of the two readings, αὐτοῦ has two: Alexandrian (ℵ) and Byzantine (A I K P 33, 81), while ἑαυτοῦ has three: Alexandrian (ℵ, B), Western (D), and Byzantine (F G 0278, 1739). Regarding the dating of the two readings, both have Alexandrian support, but ἑαυτοῦ has two Alexandrian texts in its favor (ℵ, B) contrasted to the one Alexandrian text supporting αὐτοῦ (ℵ). Thus far ἑαυτοῦ seems to be preferred over αὐτοῦ because it is supported by all three geographical locations and it has two Alexandrian manuscripts in its favor, not just one.

Transcriptional Probabilities

The four questions that pertain to this perspective regarding these two readings unfold in the following way. The first two questions re-

---

8.   Aland, Aland, Martini, Metzger, *Novum Testamentum Graece.*

lated to the shortest and oldest readings pretty much balance out. They
are both one-word variants, and both have Alexandrian support, except
ἑαυτοῦ which has two manuscripts in its favor contrasted to αὐτοῦ. In
answer to the third question regarding the most difficult reading, ἑαυτοῦ seems to be more difficult than αὐτοῦ. The difficulty of this reading
is that the former is ambiguous as to the antecedent of καιρῷ while the
latter specifies that it is the time of the lawless one= αὐτοῦ καιρῷ. Such a
nuance, then, answers the question of which most likely caused the rise
of the other reading: αὐτοῦ was added by a later scribe to clarify ἑαυτοῦ
as the antecedent of καιρῷ.

Intrinsic Probabilities

It seems to me that verses 6–8 emphasize the sovereignty of Christ
over the lawless one. Note the following points: (1) the restrainer at
Christ's command holds back the lawless one (2) until he is revealed
(ἀποκαλυφθῆναι αὐτὸν) is a divine passive; (3) even though the spirit of
the lawless one is at work he is contained by the restrainer; (4) when
the lawless one is revealed (ἀποκαλυφθήσεται) is another divine passive;
(5) he will be destroyed by Christ at his parousia. This emphasis on
the sovereignty of Christ works better with ἑαυτοῦ than αὐτοῦ because
the latter allows some decision-making on the part of the lawless one,
his time, whereas the former disallows any initiation on the part of the
lawless one.

Conclusion

The combination of extrinsic, transcriptional, and intrinsic probabilities strongly favor ἑαυτοῦ over αὐτοῦ as the original reading.

Translation

I believe the best translation of 2 Thessalonians 2:6–7 is:

> And now you know what is restraining him back, so
> that he may be revealed at the proper time. For the
> mystery of lawlessness is already at work; only the one
> who is restraining him [will continue to do so] until he
> is taken out of the way.

Historical Analysis

Here we must deal with four important topics: (1) Paul's missionary
work at Thessalonica, (2) a Jewish eschatological reading of 1 Thessalonians
2:15–16, (3) a Deuteronomic reading of 1 Thessalonians 2:15–16, and (4)
the messianic woes as the culmination of the Deuteronomic curses on
Israel.

Paul's Missionary Work at Thessalonica

First and 2 Thessalonians are often labeled as "eschatological let-ters of Paul," because eschatology dominates those correspondences. Every chapter of 1 Thessalonians ends with a reference to the second coming of Christ (1:9–10; 2:19–20; 3:13; 4:13–18; 5:23–24), while 2 Thessalonians 2 is patently apocalyptic in its presentation of the signs of the times of Christ's return.

During Paul's second missionary journey, he and Silas traveled to the city of Thessalonica. There, they preached in the synagogue to both Jews and God-fearing Gentiles (once pagan Gentiles, who embraced the God of Israel) meeting with the same results as they did in Galatia: some Jews and many God-fearers accepted the gospel while the major-ity of Jews rejected it. The latter group stirred up the town to oppose Paul and Silas. Things got so bad that the two missionaries had to leave Thessalonica for Berea under the cover of darkness (Acts 17:1–9). Even though the Bereans were more positive in response to Paul's gospel, the Jews from Thessalonica traveled to Berea and incited the towns-people there to turn against Paul and Silas. Silas and Timothy stayed in Berea but Paul was escorted to Athens for his safety (Acts 17:10–15). From there Paul traveled to nearby Corinth and wrote 1 Thessalonians sometime in A.D. 51.[9] The primary purpose of 1 Thessalonians was to strengthen the faith of the Thessalonian Christians in the face of perse-cution. Such persecution Paul seems to have understood to be the mes-sianic woes/great tribulation (cf. 1 Thess. 5:3 with 2 Thess. 2:3–12).[10]

From 1 Thessalonians 2:15–16 we will see that Paul's opposition at Thessalonica was largely from non-Christian Judaism. By the time Paul wrote 2 Thessalonians in A.D. 54 some six months later, the plot had thickened in Thessalonica.[11] In both letters, Paul's inaugurated escha-tology contrasted sharply with the consistent eschatology of Judaism.[12]

A Jewish Eschatological Reading of 1 Thessalonians 2:15–16

Based on 1 Thessalonians 2:15–16 and Acts 17:1–9, we are able to reconstruct the eschatology of the non-Christian Jews at

---

9. The point of departure for establishing the chronology of Paul's writings and linking it to Acts is the Gallio inscription discovered in Delphi, Greece. It dates Gallio's proconsulate in Corinth, Achaia to A.D. 52 (cf. Acts 18:12).

10. For documentation of this claim I refer the reader to my, *The Glory of Adam and the Afflictions of the Righteous: Pauline Suffering in Context* (Lewiston, NY: Edwin Mellen Press, 1993), 291–312.

11. For documentation that Paul was indeed the author of 2 Thessalonians, see Ibid. 291–2.

12. By Jewish "consistent eschatology," I refer to those Jews in Paul's day who did not believe the Messiah had come and therefore that the age to come had not arrived. The following is indebted to Pate, *Apostle of the Last Days*, 78–85.

Thessalonica.[13] We begin with a Jewish eschatological reading of 1 Thessalonians 2:15–16.

The two clauses in 2:16, "always fill up the measure of their sins" and "wrath has come upon them to the utmost" have occasioned much debate relative to the identity of the historical allusion behind the verse. Suggestions include Claudius's expulsion of the Jews from Rome (A.D. 49; Acts 18:2) shortly before the writing of 1 Thessalonians; the death of Agrippa (A.D. 44), Acts 12:20–23); the insurrection of Theudas (A.D. 49; Acts 5:36); and the fall of Jerusalem (A.D. 70). None of these possibilities is fully convincing. The last one suffers from the problem of dating. The others do not seem to have been well enough known to fit Paul's casual reference here, which presupposes a widely held view. The best alternative, therefore, is that Paul is alluding to the commonly known apocalyptic tradition that the messianic woes were expected to overtake the people of God in the end-times. After some introductory remarks on "wrath" in Romans 1:18, Ernest Best turns his attention to 1 Thessalonians 2:16, compiling the evidence for interpreting it eschatologically, particularly the words "the wrath of God has come upon them at last."

> The final clause of the verse has been taken in a number of different ways because its component parts are subject to varying interpretations. *The anger* can be taken either as an anger which will be disclosed at the End (cf. 1.10) or as an anger working itself out in the present to punish men (Rom. 1:18); it is doubtful if 1 Thess. 2:16 can be wholly cleared of eschatological qualification yet because (*a*) 1.10 does not precede it, (*b*) the definite article picks out a known phrase, (*c*) the whole tone of the letter is eschatological, and (*d*) v. 16b suggests the fulfillment of a measure, a limit, we are compelled to take it in the former sense.[14]

The resulting meaning of 2:6 for Best is as follows:

> The clause . . . represents a complete reversal of values in Paul: the sufferings of Israel, the so-called Messianic Woes, were the herald of the End and God's anger

---

13. See Ben Witherington III's data regarding the strong presence of a Jewish population in Thessalonica, *1 and 2 Thessalonians: A Socio-Rhetorical Commentary* (Grand Rapids: Eerdmans, 2006), 7–9.

14. Ernest Best, *The First and Second Epistles to the Thessalonians*, Harper's New Testament Commentaries (New York: Harper & Row, 1972), 119.

would fall on their oppressors; now the Jews are not persecuted but the persecutors, not those expecting God's wrath to fall on others, but its recipients; the very people who were the object of God's grace (Rom. 9.4f.) are now the objects of his anger.[15]

We suggest that three more reasons should be added to Best's four: (1) 1 Thessalonians 2:15 highlights the death of Jesus which, as we contended elsewhere, signifies for Paul in general and 1 Thessalonians in specific Jesus's endurance of the messianic woes.[16] (2) 1 Thessalonians 2:15 draws on the eschatological notion emerging from the Old Testament that in the end times Gentiles would turn to God (Isa. 45:14–17, 20–25; 59:19–20; Micah 4:1–8). (3) 1 Thessalonians 2:15–16 and its condemnation of those Jews who rejected Jesus is to be understood as the actualization of the prophecy of end-time apostasy.

Jewish apocalypticism expected that the end of history would witness a large-scale turning away from the faith by the people of God (*Jub.* 23:14–23; 1 *Enoch* 91:3–10; *4 Ezra* 5:1–13; etc.). This expectation was included in Christian apocalypticism as well (Matt. 24:10–13// Mark 13:20–23//Luke 21:19, 34–36). In fact, there are a number of New Testament texts indicating that the eschatological apostasy began with Israel's rejection of Jesus (e.g., Gal. 1:6–7; 2 Thess. 2:3–12; John 6:7; 13:2, 27; 14:30; 17:12 [with reference to Judas]; Rev. 13:15–18). It seems that Paul draws upon this notion in 1 Thessalonians 2:15–16.

A Deuteronomic Reading of 1 Thessalonians 2:15–16

Since the work of Odil H. Steck,[17] it has become customary to view 1 Thessalonians 2:15–16 as influenced by the Deuteronomistic tradition. That motif can be reduced to four components we have discussed previously: (1) Israel had been rebellious to God throughout its history; (2) God repeatedly sent his prophets to call the nation to repentance; (3) Israel consistently rejected these divine spokesmen; (4) God judged Israel by sending her into exile in 722 B.C. and again in 586 B.C.—a condition that persisted in Paul's day, despite Israel's apparent regathering to her land.

These four components of the Deuteronomistic tradition admirably explain 1 Thessalonians 2:15–16. (1) Paul accuses the Jews of his day

---

15. Ibid., 121.

16. See Pate, *The Glory of Adam and the Afflictions of the Righteous*, 31–32.

17. Odil H. Steck, *Israel und das gewaltsame Geschick der Propheten: Untersuchungen zur Überlieferung des deuteronomistischen Geschichtsbildes im Alten Testament, Spätjudentum und Urchristentum, Wissenschaftliche Monographien zum Alten und Neun Testament* 23 (Neukirchen-Vluyn, Germany: Neukirchener, 1967).

of disobeying God in that they both reject Paul's gospel and attempt to prevent others from accepting the Christian faith. (2) Even though God sent His prophets to Israel, (3) that nation repeatedly rejected them. In doing so they reject Jesus, the culmination of God's prophets, including Paul. (4) God's judgment, the Deuteronomic curses, continue to abide on Israel. As James M. Scott has carefully shown, Paul most probably has in mind here the stark reality that the exile continued to impinge on Israel's existence, the most recent expression of which was Roman occupation.[18] Best earlier approximated a Deuteronomistic reading of 1 Thessalonians 2:15–16, especially the phrase, "wrath has come upon them to the utmost."

> [T]he whole phrase "while logically progressive, is re-garded by the aorist collectively, a series of *anaplērōsa* being taken as one." Paul is using words drawn from Gen. 15.16 (cf. Dan. 8.23; 2 Macc. 6.14) where they refer to the sins of the Amorites against Abraham the father of the Jews; he turns them against the Jews them-selves. It suggests a definite measure of sins which when completed will be followed by God's judgment (v. 16a); cf. Col. 1.24 and the filling up of a measure of suffer-ings. It is the implication of vv. 15f that this measure is nearly filled up—Jesus and the prophets have been killed, Paul and his fellow Christian missionaries have been persecuted, and the preaching to the Gentiles is being hindered. There has been a terrifying consistency about the conduct of the Jews throughout their history; now it has reached its climax.[19]

The Messianic Woes as the Culmination of the Deuteronomic Curses on Israel

The preceding two views of 1 Thessalonians 2:15–16 need not be contradictory. In actuality, they complement each other nicely in that Paul draws therein on the idea that the messianic woes were perceived to be the culmination of the Deuteronomic curses.[20] We have repeat-edly touched upon this combination in our research thus far. On this reading, the messianic woes that have fallen on Israel are completing the full measure of the Deuteronomic curses, because that nation has done the unthinkable: They have rejected their Messiah.

---

18. James M. Scott, "Paul's Use of Deuteronomic Tradition(s)." *Journal of Biblical Literature* 112 (1993): 645–65.

19. Best, *The Epistles of First and Second Thessalonians,* 118–19.

20. See Pate and Kennard, *Deliverance Now and Not Yet,* 29–115.

There are two more points to the Deuteronomist tradition: (5) Israel still has time to repent, and (6) if Israel repents, God will restore her to himself. Romans 11:25–27 attests to these last two points, as the first half of this chapter documented.

General Context of 2 Thessalonians 2:6–7

The general context of 2 Thessalonians 2:6–7 focuses on chapter 2 and the signs of the end times. In 2 Thessalonians 2:1–17, the apostle instructs his readers concerning the signs of the times and the parousia. It seems that someone or a group of members of the Thessalonian church had disseminated the misinformation that the parousia of Jesus occurred with the coming of the Spirit in ecstatic experience. In 2 Thessalonians 2, Paul corrects such realized eschatology with an explanation of his inaugurated eschatology—namely the parousia will not come until certain signs of the times occur, three in particular: apostasy (v. 3a), the removal of the restrainer, and the appearance of the man of lawlessness (2:3–11).

The fallout from this erroneous realized eschatological teaching on the believers in the church at Thessalonica was that they feared their departed Christian loved ones had missed the parousia and the resurrection because they had died before those events will occur. Consequently, both their bodies and their souls lay trapped forever in the grave. Paul had corrected that error in 1 Thessalonians 4:13–18 by writing that departed believers would be the *first* to be raised from the dead as they accompany Christ at his return. Therefore, those Christians had in no way missed out on the resurrection of the body.

End-time apostasy was pervasive in Jewish apocalyptic literature (e.g., *Jubilees*; *4 Ezra* 5:1–12; *1 Enoch* 91:7; 93:9; DSS.) and in the New Testament (cf. Matt. 24:12; Acts 21:21 to 2 Tim. 3:1–9; Heb. 3:12). This activity is regularly associated with the rise of false prophets or teachers in the latter days (Mark 13:22; 1 Tim. 4:1–3; 2 Tim. 4:3–4), as it appears to be here. Yet Paul makes it clear that such apostasy still lies in the future (2:3–4). The next section covers the other two end-time signs that have yet to occur, according to Paul.

Specific Context of 2 Thessalonians 2:6–7

The lawless one (2 Thess. 2:3b–5, 8–11) is a rival savior to Christ who was predicted to appear at the end of history (cf. 1 John 2:18; Rev. 6–19). Although Paul does not explicitly label this individual the "antichrist," that is probably who he has in mind here. This lawless one will exalt himself in the temple in an attempt to usurp the throne of God. Jewish readers would have immediately recalled three events: (1) Antiochus Epiphanes' sacrilege of the Jerusalem temple (Dan. 11:36), (2) the Roman general Pompey's campaign in Judea in 63 B.C. which precipitated Jewish apostasy (Ps. 17:11–22) and, (3) Emperor Caligula's more recent decree in A.D. 39 that a statue of himself be placed in the Jerusalem temple (see Philo, *Embassy to Gaius*, 203–346).

During the time when Paul wrote 1 and 2 Thessalonians, Claudius had a bronze coin issued in Philippi that equated himself with divinity. Later Caesar Nero abandoned all reserve and demanded to be worshipped as a god (see Rev. 13), and Emperor Domitian follow suit. The last two rulers targeted Christians because they would not bow before them. These infamous persons, along with the anti-imperial cult stance by Paul, combine to suggest that the apostle, like the book of Revelation, feared that the Antichrist was about to dawn in the form of the Roman emperor.[21]

The identification of the one who restrains the lawless man from appearing until God's appointed time is hotly debated. Suggestions include (1) the Holy Spirit at the rapture of the church, (2) the Roman government, (3) the parting of the ways between Judaism and Jewish Christianity (4) Paul himself, or (5) a holy angel like Michael. Michael, the angel of God, seems to be the best option, especially considering his role of deliverance on behalf of the people of God as spelled out in Daniel 12:1–2 and Revelation 12:7–9.[22] With Michael out of the way (at God's command) the lawless one will appear and through the power of Satan will dazzle many with his miracles and false teaching (2 Thess. 2:9–11).

In the meantime, the Thessalonians are to remain faithful to Paul's teaching and the true gospel of Christ (vv. 13–17). Paul's readers need to understand that the parousia has not yet occurred. Certain signs of the times still need to be fulfilled before Christ will return.

Literary Analysis of 2 Thessalonians 2:6–7

Our literary analysis of 2 Thessalonians 2:6–7 consists of examining its structure, syntax, semantics, and style.

Structure
Our passage consists of two sentences: verse 6 and verse 7. The careful reader will notice that these two sentences form a chiasm. Thus:

---

21. Many dispensationalists argue that Paul in 2 Thessalonians 2:4 is predicting that the Jerusalem temple destroyed by the Romans in A.D. 70 will be rebuilt in the end times and there the Antichrist will be enthroned as a god. This interpretation, however, is debatable. In my opinion, Paul more likely had in mind the ancient Jerusalem temple and the ancient Roman imperial cult, perhaps when Caligula decreed that a statue of him should be placed in that temple.

22. See Pate, *The Glory of Adam*, 297–99.

A   v. 6a   the restrainer who holds back the lawless one
B   v. 6b   the lawless one will come
B' v. 7a   the mystery of lawlessness is already at work
A' v. 7b   the restrainer who holds back the lawless one

The significance of this chiastic structure will be discussed below under the central point Paul is making.

Syntax and Semantics

We will now deal with both of these areas as we examine the identification of the removed restrainer in our passage. In this section we are particularly interested in the restrainer who, or what, is holding back the arrival of the antichrist. The last-mentioned sign of the time is fascinating and highly debated, as we noted above. Whoever or whatever the restrainer is, it must be something or someone that is *both* neuter (genderless), verse 6, and masculine, verse 7. We believe the confusion of these two genders accounts for the view that Michael the archangel is who Paul has in mind.

Seeing Michael the archangel as the one to whom Paul is referring in verses 6 and 7 nicely explains the change from the neuter (verse 6), to the masculine (verse 7). The switch in gender reflects Paul's ambiguity in knowing how to categorize angelic beings, a confusion that occurs elsewhere in the New Testament. In some passages, angels are referred to as neuter beings, neither masculine nor feminine (Matt. 22:30; Mark 12:25). In other passages, angels are referred to as males (Rev. 4:7; 10:1). Revelation 12:7 is enlightening on this last point, because it refers to Michael in the masculine gender.

Style

'Here we may be brief. 1 and 2 Thessalonians are the only place where one finds classic apocalyptic style in Paul's writings. The chart in chapter 6, comparing 1 and 2 Thessalonians with the Olivet Discourse, supports this conclusion.

Theological Analysis

Here we attempt to identify the central point of 2 Thessalonians 2:6–7, after which we pinpoint the shared need of the text which bridges Paul's day with our own. We then move to the step of appropriation. These three tasks prepare the way for the homilectical packaging of our text.

Central Point

The main point that one can derive from 2 Thessalonians 2:6–7 is that the already/not-yet hermeneutic governs Paul's understanding of the signs of the end-times. We see this eschatological tension specifically in the aforementioned chiastic structure that forms 2 Thessalonians 2:6–7:

A   the restrainer holds back the lawless one (v. 6a)
B   the lawless one will come (v. 6b)
B'   the mystery of lawlessness is already at work (v. 7a)
A'   the restrainer holds back the lawless one (v. 7b)

It becomes clear from this structure that Paul believed the mystery of lawlessness had already begun, but it was not yet complete, awaiting the arrival on earth of the person of lawlessness (elsewhere called the Antichrist). This idea reminds us of 1 John 2:18 where John states that the antichrist is coming (the not-yet aspect) but even now antichrists are here (the already aspect). These two passages join numerous other New Testament texts that we previously examined which show that the last days began with the first coming of Christ (the already aspect) and will increase in intensity until the return of Christ (the not-yet aspect). For our purposes, let us examine the signs of the end times Paul delineates in 2 Thessalonians 2:1–12 through the lens of the already/not yet eschatological tension. We will necessarily cast our net further than 2 Thessalonians covering 1 Thessalonians, 2 Corinthians 10–13 and 2 Timothy. A self-explanatory chart now follows in that regard:

"Already" Aspect of the Signs of the Times for Paul	"Not Yet" Aspect of the Signs of the Times for Paul
1. First Coming of the Messiah	1. Second Coming of Jesus Messiah/ Day of the Lord/Christ has not yet happened (cf. 1 Thess. 4–5; 2 Thess. 2:1–2 with 1 Thess. 5:19, the last reference suggesting that some in the church at Thessalonica were teaching that ecstatic experience with the Holy Spirit equaled the parousia)[23]
2. The mystery of lawlessness is already at work (2 Thess. 2:7)	2. The man of lawlessness will not arrive on earth until Michael the restrainer allows him to appear (2 Thess. 2:3, 6–8)

---

23. See Pate, *Apostle of the Last Days*, 90–93

"Already" Aspect of the Signs of the Times for Paul	"Not Yet" Aspect of the Signs of the Times for Paul
3. Caligula's failed attempt to place an image of himself in the Jerusalem Temple was a precursor of the end-time abomination of desolation of the temple (2 Thess. 2:4–5; cf. Dan. 9:24–27; 1 Macc. 1 with Antiochus Epiphanes' desolation of the Jerusalem temple)	3. The man of lawlessness (the antichrist) will desecrate the Jerusalem temple at the end of time by demanding that he be worshipped (cf. 2 Thess. 2:4–5)
4. Paul exposes the false apostles with their signs and wonders as empowered by Satan, who can turn himself into an angel of light (see 2 Cor. 10–13)	4. The man of lawlessness will be empowered by Satan to work miraculous signs and wonders (2 Thess. 2:9–10)
5. Paul's opponents are those who have been deluded into apostasy (2 Tim. 3:5–9) as expressed in their false teaching in the last days (2 Tim. 3:6; 4:3; cf. 1 Tim. 4:1–5)	5. Those Satanic signs and wonders will delude many into following the man of lawlessness and his false teachings (2 Thess. 2:11–12)
6. Israel is experiencing the messianic woes/signs of the times/great tribulation (all the same) as the culmination of the covenant curses (1 Thess. 2:15–16)	6. At the parousia, Israel will repent and receive Jesus as Messiah thereby finally experiencing the blessings of the new covenant/restoration of Israel (Rom. 11:25–27)

Shared Need

What need in the church at Thessalonica did Paul's already/not-yet construct of the signs of the times meet? Such an eschatological dynamic addressed at least two needs of the Thessalonian Christians. First, they needed to realize that they were in the midst of both the kingdom of God (technically the temporary messianic kingdom) and the messianic woes. This truth should steel the believers' faith and patience as they lived between the two ages. Second, more specifically, because the not-yet aspect of the age to come is still in place, those Christians who had died would in no way miss out on the parousia and the hope of the resurrection body (in addition to 1 Thess. 4:13–18, see also 1 Cor. 15:50–55; 2 Cor. 5:1–10; cf. Phil 1:23 with Phil. 3:20–21).

Appropriation

Here we meet the three questions characterizing this section on how the biblical text can be appropriated by the twenty-first-century audience: (1) How does this passage *connect* with today's audience? (2) What contemporary attitudes and actions does the passage *correct*? (3) What ways of thinking and/or acting does the passage *commend* to today's audience?

Contemporary listeners can *connect* with the idea that we are living in the midst of the signs of the times and that they will sooner or later culminate in the return of Christ. At that time, he will destroy the man of lawlessness and the one who energizes him—Satan. Accompanying the return of Christ will be the resurrection of the believer's body.

Paul's already/not-yet construct can *correct* two beliefs that have far-ranging effects. First, Paul would say to those who predict the date of the return of Christ or even claim that we are living in the last generation to chill out, because we have been living in the last days for almost two thousand years! Therefore, the culmination of the end times may be near or far away. Since we do not know which of the two is the case, it behooves Christians to live for the Lord every day, whether the parousia will happen sooner or later. Second, when one looks at the Pauline passages we noted and others, there is no room for the belief in soul-sleep. Rather, when Christians die, they go immediately into the presence of the Lord as bodiless souls (see again 1 Thess. 4:13–18; 1 Cor. 15:50–55; 2 Cor. 5:1–10; and Phil. 1:23). And at the parousia, the dead in Christ will receive resurrection bodies just as those who are alive at the return of Christ will receive their resurrection bodies. This reality inspires great hope to believers as they walk with the Lord in this life.

The already/not-yet eschatological tension *commends* believers to be faithful to the gospel of Christ as they live simultaneously in both the kingdom and the tribulation, in the overlapping of the two ages. Moreover, Paul's teaching on the two ages assures believers whose loved ones in Christ have passed away that they in no way will be disadvantaged at the return of Christ. They, like their living loved ones in Christ, will also receive the resurrection of the body at that time.

Homiletical Packaging

It seems to me that the best way to preach the already/not-yet eschatological tension reflected in 2 Thessalonians 2:6–7 would be to use the chart above, showing how all of the signs of the times reflected in 2 Thessalonians 2:1–12 have begun and will intensify as the day of Christ's return draws near.

One possible introduction might be, "We all know that we are living in the last days. But did you know that the last days actually began with the first coming of Christ, as the following New Testament passages teach: Acts 2:16–17; 1 Timothy 4:1; 2 Timothy 3:1; Hebrews 1:2; and 1 John 2:18? Second Thessalonians 2:6–7 occurs in the midst of Paul's list of the signs of the times in 2 Thessalonians 2:1–12. Here and elsewhere, we learn of the overlapping of the two ages: this age and the age to come. If we compare 2 Thessalonians 2:1–12 with other passages by Paul, we can see that the end-time events or the age to come have already begun. And we as Christians live in between these two ages. The following chart demonstrates the overlapping of the two ages relative to Paul's delineation of the signs of the end times."

After explaining the details of the chart, a possible conclusion might be, "And so the already/not-yet eschatological tension *commends* believers to be faithful to the gospel of Christ as they live simultaneously in both the kingdom and the tribulation, in the overlapping of the two ages. Moreover, Paul's teaching on the two ages assures believers whose loved ones in Christ have passed away that they in no way will be disadvantaged at the return of Christ. They, like their living loved ones in Christ, will also receive the resurrection of the body at that time."

Chapter in Review

Interpreting a biblical passage, and then delivering it to today's audience, can be reduced to three steps.

- Establish the text (textual criticism) and provide a translation of the passage.

- Examine the message the first-century author communicated to his original audience (exegesis).

- Build a bridge to twenty-first-century listeners and package the message in a way that makes it both striking and practical (exposition).

This chapter applied the entire process to Romans 11:25–27 and 2 Thessalonians 2:6–7.

8

SELECTED SOURCES

The Chapter at a Glance

In this chapter we offer a variety of resources that help to facilitate the process of interpreting biblical prophetic-apocalyptic passages, including the genres of apocalypticism, prophecy, and merkabah, as well as subgenres like *ekphrasis*, the Roman Triumph, the story of Israel, and the relationship between Israel and the church.

THIS CHAPTER PROVIDES THE RESOURCES needed to study the Greek New Testament, including editions of the Greek New Testament, Greek grammar works, Greek language computer software, textual criticism, concordances, lexicons, and theological dictionaries for word studies. We also include Old Testament and New Testament background works and theologies. Moreover, numerous studies related to biblical prophetic-apocalyptic literature in the Old Testament and New Testament are listed, both commentaries and articles.

RESOURCES FOR INTERPRETING BIBLICAL
PROPHETIC-APOCALYPTIC LITERATURE

The following list essentially compiles those resources used in the first seven chapters:

Editions of the Greek New Testament

- B. Aland, et al., *The Greek New Testament*, 4th revised edition (New York: United Bible Societies, 1998).

- B. Aland, et al., *Greek-English New Testament*, eighth revised edition (Stuttgart: Deutsche Bibelgesellschaft, 1994).

- E. Nestle, et al., *Novum Testamentum Graecae*, 27th revised edition (Stuttgart: Bibelgesellschaft, 1999).

Greek Language Computer Software

- BibleWorks, BibleWorks LLC, Norfolk, VA, www.bibleworks.com

- Gramcord, Gramcord Institute, Vancouver, WA, www.gramcord.com

- Logos Bible Software, Bellingham, WA, www.logos.com

Resources for Textual Criticism

- Kurt and Barbara Aland, *The Text of the New Testament. An Introduction to the Critical Editions and Theory and Practice of Modern Textual Criticism.* Translated by Erroll F. Rhodes (Grand Rapids: Eerdmans, 1987).

- F. F. Bruce, *The New Testament Documents: Are They Reliable?,* 5th ed. (Downers Grove, IL: InterVarsity Press, 1960).

- Bart D. Ehrman, *The Orthodox Corruptions of Scripture: The Effect of Early Christological Controversies on the Text of the New Testament* (New York: Oxford University Press, 1993).

- _____, *Misquoting Jesus: The Story behind Who Changed the Bible and Why* (San Francisco: HarperSanFrancisco, 2005).

- Eldon J. Epp and Gordon D. Fee, eds., *New Testament Textual Criticism: Its Significance for Exegesis. Essays in Honour of Bruce M. Metzger* (Oxford: Clarendon, 1982).

- Eldon J. Epp, "Textual Criticism," *Anchor Bible Dictionary,* ed. David Noel Freedman (New York: Doubleday, 1992), 6.412–35; 429.

- _____, "New Testament Textual Criticism Past, Present, and

Future: Reflections on the Alands' *Text of the New Testament."* *Harvard Theological Review* 82, no. 2 (1989).

- Michael W. Holmes. "Textual Criticism," in *New Testament Criticism & Interpretation*, eds. David A. Black and David S. Dockery (Grand Rapids: Zondervan, 1991).

- Bruce M. Metzger, *The Text of the New Testament: Its Transmission, Corruption, and Restoration.* Third Edition (Oxford: Oxford University Press, 1992).

- _____, *A Textual Commentary on the Greek New Testament,* 2nd. (New York: American Bible Society, 2005).

- Stanley E. Porter, *How We Got the New Testament: Text, Transmission, Translation* (Grand Rapids: Baker, 2013).

- Paul D. Wegner, *A Student's Guide to Textual Criticism of the Bible* (Downers Grove, IL: InterVarsity Press), 2006.

Concordances

- J. R. Kohlenberger, E. W. Goodrick, and J. A. Swanson. *The Exhaustive Concordance to the Greek New Testament* (Grand Rapids: Zondervan, 1995).

- G. V. Wigram, *The Englishman's Greek Concordance of the New Testament* (Peabody, MA: Hendrickson, 1996).

Lexicons

- W. Bauer, W. F. Arndt, F. W. Gingrich, and F. W. Danker, *A Greek-English Lexicon of the New Testament and Other Early Christian Literature,* third edition (Chicago: University of Chicago Press, 2000).

- J. P. Louw and E. Nida, *A Greek-English Lexicon of the New Testament Based on Semantic Domains,* 2nd edition, 2 volumes (New York: United Bible Societies, 1989).

Theological Dictionaries

- C. Brown, ed., *The New International Dictionary of New Testament Theology,* 4 volumes (Grand Rapids: Zondervan, 1986).

- G. Kittel and G. Friedrich, eds., *Theological Dictionary of the New Testament,* 10 volumes (Grand Rapids: Eerdmans, 1964–73).

Intermediate Greek Grammars

- F. Blass, A. Debrunner, and R. W. Funk, *A Greek Grammar of the New Testament and Other Early Christian Literature* (Chicago: University of Chicago Press, 1961).

- D. B. Wallace, *Greek Grammar Beyond the Basics* (Grand Rapids: Zondervan, 1996).

Kregel Exegetical Handbooks

- Herbert W. Bateman IV, *Interpreting the General Letters: An Exegetical Handbook* (Grand Rapids: Kregel, 2013).

- John D. Harvey, *Interpreting the Pauline Letters: An Exegetical Handbook* (Grand Rapids: Kregel, 2012).

Old Testament Introductions and Related Material

- Andrew E. Hill and John H. Walton, *A Survey of the Old Testament* (Grand Rapids: Zondervan, 1991).

- Tremper Longman III and Daniel G. Reid, *God Is a Warrior* (Grand Rapids: Zondervan, 1995).

New Testament Introductions

- D. A. Carson and D. J. Moo, *An Introduction to the New Testament,* 2nd edition (Grand Rapids: Eerdmans, 2006).

- R. H. Gundry, *A Survey of the New Testament,* 4th edition (Grand Rapids: Eerdmans, 2003).

New Testament Theologies

- George E. Ladd, *A Theology of the New Testament*, revised edition by Donald Hagner (Grand Rapids: Eerdmans, 1993).

- Howard Marshall, *New Testament Theology: Many Witnesses, One Gospel* (Downers Grove, IL: InterVarsity Press, 2004).

The Genre of Apocalyticism and Related Topics

- Dale C. Allison, *the End of the Ages Has Come: An Early Interpretation of the Passion and Resurrection of Jesus* (Philadelphia: Fortress, 1985).

- Gleason L. Archer Jr., Paul D. Feinberg, Douglas J. Moo, and Richard R. Reiter, *The Rapture: Pre-, Mid-, or Post-Tribulational* (Grand Rapids: Zondervan, 1984).

- David E. Aune, *Revelation 1–5* (Dallas: Word, 1997).

- J. J. Collins, "Introduction: Toward the Morphology of a Genre," *Semeia* 14 [1979] 1–20.

- Stephen L. Cook, "Apocalyptic Prophecy," in *The Oxford Handbook of Apocalyptic Literature,* ed. John J. Collins (Oxford: Oxford University Press, 2014), 19–35.

- _____. *Prophecy and Apocalypticism: The Post-Exilic Social Setting* (Minneapolis: Fortress, 1995).

- Itamar Gruenwald, *Apocalyptic and Merkavah Mysticism,* Arbeiten zur Geschichte des antiken Judentums und des Urchristentums, 14 (Leiden: Brill, 1980).

- D. Hellholm, "The Problem of Apocalyptic Genre and the Apocalypse of John," *Semeia* 36 (1986), 13–64.

- Ernst Käsemann, "The Beginnings of Christian Theology," in Käsemann, *New Testament Questions of Today* (Philadelphia: Fortress, 1969), 82–107.

- Klaus Koch, *The Rediscovery of Apocalyptic, A Polemical Work on a Neglected Area of Biblical Studies and Its Damaging Effects on Theology and Philosophy,* Studies in Biblical Theology 22 (Naperville, IL: Allenson, 1972).

- R. M. Kuykendall, *The Literary Genre of the Book of Revelation (*Ann Arbor, MI: University Microfilms, 1986).

- Andrew T. Lincoln, *Paradise Now and Not Yet: Studies in the Role of the Heavenly Dimension in Paul's Thought with Special Reference to his Eschatology.* Society for New Testament Studies Monograph Series 43 (Cambridge: University Press, 1981).

- W. R. Millar, *Isaiah 24–27 and the Origin of Apocalyptic* (Missoula, MT: Scholars Press, 1976).

- C. Marvin Pate and Calvin B. Haines Jr., *Doomsday Delusions: What's Wrong with Predictions about the End of the World* (Downers Grove, IL: InterVarsity Press, 1995).

- C. Marvin Pate, *Apostle of the Last Days: The Life, Letters, and Theology of Paul* (Grand Rapids: Kregel, 2013).

- Gerhard von Rad, *Wisdom in Israel* (London: SCM, 1972).

- D. S. Russell, *Apocalyptic Ancient and Modern* (Philadelphia: Fortress, 1978).

- Albert Schweitzer, *The Quest of the Historical Jesus: A Critical Study of Its Progress from Reimarus to Wrede.* Trans. by W. Montgomery (New York: Macmillan, 1910).

- Robert H. Smith, "Darkness at Noon: Mark's Passion Narrative," *Concordia Theological Monthly* 49 (1973), 333.

- Edgar C. Whisenant, *88 Reasons Why the Rapture Will Be in 1988* (Nashville: World Bible Society, 1988).

Subgenres or Major Topics Related to the Book

Ekphrasis

- Shadi Bartsch, *Decoding the Ancient Novel: The Reader and the Role of Description in Heliodorus and Achilles Tatius* (Princeton, NJ: Princeton University Press, 1989).

- C. Marvin Pate and J. Daniel Hays, *Iraq: Babylon of the End-Times?* (Grand Rapids: Baker, 2003).

Roman Triumph

- Mary Beard, *The Roman Triumph* Cambridge: The Belknap Press of Harvard University Press, 2007).

- Scott Hafemann, *Suffering & Ministry in the Spirit: Paul's Defense of His Ministry in II Corinthians 2:14–3:3* (Grand Rapids: Eerdmans, 1990).

- Nigel Rodgers, *Roman Empire: A Complete History of the Rise and Fall of the Roman Empire, Chronicling the Story of the Most Important and Influential Civilization the World Has Ever Known* (New York: Metro Books, 2010).

- H. S. Versnel, *Triumphus: An Inquiry into the Origin, Development, and Meaning for the Roman Triumph* (Leiden: Brill, 1970).

The Story of Israel

- J. Scott Duvall, J. Daniel Hays, C. Marvin Pate, E. Randolph Richards, W. Dennis Tucker, and Preben Vang, *The Story of Israel: A Biblical Theology,* ed. C. Marvin Pate (Downers Grove, IL: Intervarsity Press, 2004).

- C. Marvin Pate, *The Reverse of the Curse: Paul, Wisdom, and the Law,* Wissenschaftliche Untersuchgen zum Neuen Testament 2. Reihe 114 (Tübingen: Mohr Siebeck, 2000).

- N. T. Wright, *The New Testament and the People of God* (Minneapolis: Press, 1992).

- _____, *Jesus and the Victory of God* (Minneapolis: Fortress, 1996).

- _____, *Paul and the Faithfulness of God,* 2 vols. (Minneapolis: Fortress, 2013).

- _____, "Adam in Pauline Christology," *Society of Biblical Literature Seminar Papers* (Chico, CA: Scholars Press, 1983).

Israel and the Church

- W. D. Davies, *The Gospel and the Land* (Berkeley/Los Angeles: University of California, 1974).

- Peter Richardson, *Israel in the Apostolic Church.* Society for the New Testament Society Monograph Series (Cambridge: University Press, 1969

- Charles C. Ryrie, *Dispensationalism Today* (Chicago: Moody, 1965).

- C. I. Scofield, *Rightly Dividing the Word of Truth* (New York: Loizeaux Brothers, 1896).

Biblical Prophetic-Apocalyptic Related Studies on the Old Testament

- John J. Collins, *Daniel,* Hermeneia (Minneapolis: Fortress, 1993).

- K. Grayson, *Babylonian Historical-Literary Texts* (Toronto: University of Toronto, 1975), 24–27.

- Gerhard F. Hasel, "The Four World Empires of Daniel 2 against Its Near Eastern Environment," *Journal for the Study of the Old Testament* 12 (1979), 17–30.

- W. Lee Humphreys, "A Life-Style for Diaspora: A Study of the Tales of Esther and Daniel," *Journal of Biblical Literature* 92 (1973) 211–23.

- R. Mason, *The Books of Haggai, Zechariah and Malachi.* Cambridge Commentaries on the New English Bible (Cambridge: University Press, 1977).

- B. C. Eric and Carol Meyers, *Zechariah 9–14,* Anchor Bible 25c (New York: Doubleday, 1993).

- C. Marvin Pate, "Genesis 1–3: Creation and Adam in Context," *Criswell Theological Journal* (2013), 3–26.

- W. Rudolph, *Haggai-Sacharja 1–8, Sacharja 9–14, Maleachi.* KAT XIII, 4 (Gütersloh: Gütershoher Verlagshaus Gerd/Mohr, 1976).

Biblical Prophetic Apocalyptic Related Studies on the New Testament

Gospel Studies

- J. Bradley Chance, *Jerusalem, the Temple and the New Age in Luke-Acts* (Macon, GA: Mercer University Press, 1988).

- Craig Keener, *The Historical Jesus of the Gospels* (Grand Rapids: Eerdmans, 2009).

- C. Marvin Pate, *Luke,* Moody Gospel Commentary (Chicago: Moody, 1995).

- _____, "Revelation 6: An Early Interpretation of the Olivet Discourse," *Criswell Theological Review* (2011), 45–56.

- _____, *40 Questions about the Historical Jesus* (Grand Rapids: Kregel, 2015).

- C. Marvin Pate and Douglas W. Kennard, *Deliverance Now and Not Yet: The New Testament and the Great Tribulation* (New York: Peter Lang, 2004).

Pauline Studies

- John D. Harvey, *Interpreting the Pauline Letters: An Exegetical Handbook* (Grand Rapids: Kregel, 2012).

- C. Marvin Pate, *Adam Christology as the Exegetical and Theological Substructure of 2 Corinthians 4:7–5:21* (Lanham, MD: University Press of America, 1991).

- _____, *The Glory of Adam and the Afflictions of the Righteous: Pauline Suffering in Context* (Lewiston, NY: Edwin Mellen Press, 1993).

- _____, *Teach the Text Series: Romans* (Grand Rapids: Baker, 2013).

Revelation

- David E. Aune, *Revelation 1–5*, Word Biblical Commentary, Vol. 52a (Dallas: Word, 1997).

- _____, *Revelation 6–16,* Word Biblical Commentary, Vol. 52b (Nashville: Nelson, 1998).

- _____, *Revelation 17–22,* Word Biblical Commentary, Vol. 52c (Nashville: Nelson, 1998).

- G. F. Beale, *The Book of Revelation: A Commentary on the Greek Text* (Grand Rapids: Paternoster, 1999.)

- Raymond Calkins, *The Social Message of the Book of Revelation* (New York: Woman's Press, 1920).

- R. H. Charles, *The Revelation of St. John*, 2 vols. (Edinburgh: T. & T. Clark, 1920).

- Yarbro Collins, "Dating the Apocalypse of John" *Biblical Research* 26 (1981), 33–45.

- Ken Gentry Jr., *Before Jerusalem Fell: Dating the Book of Revelation* (Tyler, TX: Institute for Christian Economics, 1989).

- Steve Gregg, *Revelation: Four Views, a Parallel Commentary* (Nashville: Nelson, 1997).

- Craig S. Keener, *Revelation,* The NIV Application Commentary (Grand Rapids: Zondervan, 2000).

- J. Hemer, *The Letters to the Seven Churches of Asia in Their Local Setting,* Journal for the Study of the New Testament Supplements 11 (Sheffield: JSOT, 1986).

- Grant R. Osborne, *Revelation. Baker Exegetical Commentary on the New Testament* (Grand Rapids: Baker, 2002).

- C. Marvin Pate, *The Writings of John: A Survey of the Gospel, Epistles, and Apocalypse* (Grand Rapids: Zondervan, 2011).

- _____, et al., *Four Views on the Book of Revelation* (Grand Rapids, MI.: Zondervan, 1998).

- S. R. Price, *Rituals and Power: The Roman Imperial Cult in Asia Minor* (Cambridge: Cambridge University, 1984).

- W. M. Ramsay, *The Letters to the Seven Churches* (London: Hodden & Stoughton, 1904).

- Merrill C. Tenney, *Interpreting Revelation* (Grand Rapids: Eerdmans, 1957).

- Mark Wilson, *Charts on Revelation* (Grand Rapids: Kregel, 2007).

NEW TESTAMENT COMMENTARY SERIES

The usual recommendation is to obtain one good set of commentaries on the entire New Testament (e. g., The Word Biblical Commentary Series). Then, it is usually most helpful to obtain separate volumes on individual books, adding them evenly across the New Testament (i.e., one major commentary on each book, then a second major commentary on each book, and so on). The following listing seeks to capture the basic character of several important commentary series.

Baker Exegetical Commentary on the New Testament (BECNT) Baker.
This Greek-based series seeks to combine scholarship for pastors with readability for inquiring lay readers. Each volume includes the original Greek text, a transliteration, and the author's own English translation.

Bible Speaks Today (BST). InterVarsity Press.
The stated threefold ideal of this popular-level series is "to expound the biblical text with accuracy, to relate it to contemporary life and to be readable."

Expositor's Bible Commentary (EBC), Volumes 1–12. Zondervan.
EBC is an advanced-level series of generally good quality. Several works are in the excellent category. Technical issues are addressed in notes following the discussion of each section of Scripture.

International Critical Commentaries (ICC). T & T Clark, Ltd.
This technical, Greek-based series is intended for the user with some formal training. It provides exhaustive discussion of virtually every issue in a given passage.

IVP New Testament Commentary (IVPNTC). InterVarsity Press.
With exposition and application in the text and exegesis in the footnotes, this series moves by preaching portions. It aims to combine middle-level exegesis with readability.

New American Commentary (NAC). Broadman.
This Southern Baptist series provides middle-level volumes designed to help in the practical work of preaching and teaching. According to the dust jacket, it "assumes inerrancy, focuses on the intrinsic theological and exegetical concerns of each biblical book, and engages the range of issues raised in contemporary biblical scholarship."

New International Commentaries on the New Testament (NICNT), Eerdmans.
NICNT is an advanced-level series and is good for in-depth study. Technical issues are handled in footnotes.

New International Greek Testament Commentaries (NIGTC). Eerdmans.
This technical, Greek-based series is intended for the user with some formal training. A limited number of volumes are presently available.

NIV Application Commentary (NIVAC). Zondervan.
> This middle-level series seeks to "bridge the gap between the gap between the world of the Bible and the world of today." It focuses on the contemporary application of the text's original meaning.

Pillar New Testament Commentary (PNTC). Eerdmans.
> PNTC is designed to give serious readers of the Bible access to important contemporary issues without becoming overwhelmed by technical details. It seeks to combine serious exegesis with scholarship and pastoral sensitivity.

Tyndale New Testament Commentaries (TNTC). Eerdmans.
> This reasonably priced, popular-level series is a good option for starting to build a library.

Word Biblical Commentaries (WBC). Word.
> This advanced-level series uses Greek extensively but is still accessible to the general user. It provides excellent bibliographical information.

Zondervan Exegetical Commentary on the New Testament (ZECNT). Zondervan.
> This new series is designed "especially for pastors and students who want some help with the Greek text." The discussion of each passage includes seven components: literary context, main idea, translation and graphical layout, structure, exegetical outline, explanation of the text, and theology in application.

GLOSSARY

abomination of desolation. The desecration of the Jerusalem temple in 167 B.C. by the Syrian king, Antiochus Epiphanes

Adam. The first created person who, along with Eve, is portrayed as the source of the fall of humanity into subsequent sin.

already/not-yet. A phrase indicating that the age to come dawned with the first coming of Christ but will not be complete until the Second Coming of Christ.

amillennialism. A view of Revelation 20 that takes the millennium to be a figurative description of the present kingdom of God manifested in the church.

Ancient of Days. A title of God in Daniel 7 that is applied to Jesus Christ in Revelation 1.

Antichrist. The arch-enemy of Christ to appear at the end of history, who may be prefigured in the Roman Caesar in the first century.

Antiochus Epiphanes. The ancient Syrian ruler who desecrated the Jerusalem temple in 167 B.C.

apocalypse. A genre of revelatory literature with a narrative framework, in which a revelation is mediated by an otherworldly being to a human recipient disclosing a transcendent reality that is envisages eschatological salvation and a supernatural world.

apocalyptic literature. Ancient Jewish and Christian literature that deals with end-time events.

apostasy. End-time turning away from God by some of the people of God.

Arch of Titus. A monument in Rome that commemorated General Titus' defeat of Jerusalem and the destruction of the temple.

Armageddon. The end-time battle to be fought between Christ and Antichrist.

Babylon the Great. A symbolic allusion to ancient Rome.

beast from the earth. The false prophet of the Antichrist described in Revelation.

beast from the sea. A depiction of the Antichrist in Revelation.

birth pangs of the Messiah. The messianic woes of the great tribulation.

bowl judgments. The final seven judgments poured out on earth in the end times as described in Revelation 15–18.

Caesar worship. A first-century cult in which the Roman emperor was worshipped as a god.

Christ/Messiah. The Greek and Hebrew words for God's anointed one, especially Jesus Christ.

classical dispensationalism. A theological system that separates Christ's return into a secret rapture of the church before the tribulation period on earth and a visible Second Coming after the tribulation period.

consistent eschatology. The view that Jesus preached a soon arrival of the kingdom of God that did not arrive during his lifetime.

Cyrus. The Persian king who defeated Babylonia in 539 B.C. and issued the decree in 536 B.C. that Jews could return to their homeland.

Davidic Messiah. The Jewish expectation that their Messiah would be a descendent of King David and would come at the end of history to deliver Israel from her enemies.

Dea Roma. A Roman coin minted in the late first century that depicts ancient Rome as situated on seven hills and as protected by the goddess Roma.

Dead Sea Scrolls. A collection of biblical and nonbiblical texts discovered in 1947 in the caves adjacent to the Dead Sea and nearby the excavations at Qumran.

deductive sermon. A sermon that leads the general idea of a passage through the major points of the text.

delay of the parousia. The growing realization in the first century that Jesus's Second Coming might be delayed for some time.

Deuteronomy/Covenant Structure. Six components of the covenant that constitute the outline of Deuteronomy and play a major role in prophetic-apocalyptic material: preamble, historical prologue, stipulations, blessings and curses, appeal to witnesses, and document clause.

devil. One of the terms for Satan used in the Johannine writings.

dispensationalism. The teaching that God designed eight periods in which the history of the world unfolds: innocence, conscience, civil government, law, grace, tribulation, millennial kingdom, eternal state.

Domitian. The Roman emperor (A.D. 81–96) who demanded to be worshipped, and who persecuted Christians who did not do so.

Egyptian plagues. Ten divine plagues upon ancient Egypt that are the backdrop for the trumpet and bowl judgments in Revelation.

ekphrasis. A rhetorical description of a work of art that constitutes a subgenre within prophetic-apocalyptic literature.

eschatology. A term designating the end times that is similar to apocalypticism and deals with the signs of the times to be fulfilled before the return of Christ.

exegesis. The analytical work of interpreting the first-century message of a passage.

exposition. The synthetic work of moving the first-century message of a passage into the world of the contemporary listeners.

false prophet. The associate of the Beast/Antichrist in the book of Revelation.

four horsemen of the Apocalypse. The first four seal judgments of Revelation 6.

four kingdoms. A topos that describes history as consisting of four kingdoms, either Babylonia, Media, Persia, and Greece or Babylonia, Medo-Persia, Greece, and Rome.

four living creatures. Heavenly creatures who worship God continually in Revelation 4–5.

gamatria. Ancient cryptic readings of names based on their numerical value.

genre. A class or type of literature.

genre of apocalypticism. A special type of literature that consists of three components (form, content, and function) and rests on the substructure of Israel's story.

gnosticism. A later aberration of the Gospel that disparaged the body and taught that special knowledge would deliver from evil those who possessed it.

Gog and Magog. A title for the enemies of God to be defeated at the end of the millennium.

gospel. Both the genre of the four Gospels and the good news of those Gospels proclaimed to followers of Jesus.

great harlot. The ancient Roman Empire, as depicted in Revelation 17.

heavenly Son of Man. A title first found in Daniel 7 that Jesus applies to himself in the Gospels.

hellenization. The adoption of Greek language, culture, customs, and ideas brought about as a result of the conquests of Alexander the Great.

homiletical complement. What a passage says about the homiletical subject.

homiletical subject. The narrow aspect of a topic that a passage addresses.

historic premillennialism. A view of Revelation teaching that the church will go through the tribulation period before Christ returns to establish his one-thousand-year reign on earth.

historicist. A view of Revelation popular among the Protestant Reformers that the fulfillment of the events of Revelation occur in history.

idealist. A view of Revelation that views the events of Revelation as symbolic of the battle between God and evil throughout history.

incarnation. The truth that Jesus Christ is both God and human.

inductive sermon. A sermon that moves from specific evidence to the statement of a passage's central idea.

Jewish Revolt. The Jewish rebellion against Rome (A.D. 66–73).

Johannine Literature. Books in the Bible that are associated with the apostle John: The Fourth Gospel, the Letters of John, and Revelation.

Josephus. A first-century Jewish historian who defected to the Roman side of the war, was a witness of the fall of Jerusalem, and later became a court historian to Rome.

kingdom of God. The hope of the Old Testament, Second Temple Judaism, and the New Testament that God would descend from heaven in the end-time to deliver Israel from her enemies and establish his rule over the world.

lake of fire. The final abode of the Beast, False Prophet, Satan, and their followers.

Lion-Lamb. The imagery Revelation 5 uses to portray Jesus as both the Davidic Messiah and the Suffering Servant.

logos. The Greek word John uses to remind his Greek readers of the divine reason that permeates every person and his Jewish readers of God's spoken word that brought creation into being.

Maccabees. The Jewish freedom fighters, led by Judas, who resisted Antiochus Epiphanes in their efforts to liberate Israel.

mark of the beast. The number of the mark of the Beast in Revelation, perhaps referring to Caesar Nero.

Medo-Persians. The kingdom, led by Cyrus, who defeated the Babylonians in 539 B.C..

merkabah. The Hebrew name for the divine throne Jewish mystics longed to see.

messianic kingdom. The idea in apocalyptic works such as *1 Enoch, 4 Ezra, 2 Baruch,* and Revelation that the Messiah will establish a temporary kingdom on earth at Jerusalem for the purpose of exalting Jews and either destroying or converting the Gentiles.

Michael the Archangel. The angelic protector of Israel (Daniel 10–12; Revelation 12).

mid-tribulation rapture. The view of Revelation that Jesus will return halfway through the tribulation period to rapture his church to heaven.

mystery. A concept associated with Jewish apocalyptic works that reveals the end of time in the present via mystic ascent to the divine throne.

Nero. The first-century Roman Caesar who persecuted Christians, perhaps including Paul and Peter.

Nero Redivivus. The belief in the late first century that Nero would come back from the dead and lead a Parthian army to retaliate against Rome.

new covenant. The time longed for by the Old Testament prophets as the day when Israel would finally obey God from the heart.

new heaven and new earth. The restoration of the Garden of Eden following the return of Christ.

New Jerusalem. An image for the eternal state and the new heavens and new earth in Revelation 21–22.

Olivet Discourse. Jesus's most explicit teachings about the end times and his return, found in Matthew 24, Mark 13, and Luke 21.

overcome. A description in Revelation of Christians who are faithful to Christ in the face of persecution.

papyrus. A document written on material made from the papyrus plant.

parousia. A Greek term referring to Christ's Second Coming.

Parthians. The people group living east of the Euphrates and never conquered by Roman.

Pella. The TransJordan area to which Jewish Christians just before Jerusalem fell to the Romans in A.D. 70.

Philo. A Jewish philosopher-theologian in the first century who tried to harmonize the thinking of Judaism and Hellenism.

platonic dualism. The Greek philosophy (ca. 350 B.C.) that held to a sharp distinction between the soul and the body, the real world of the ideas and the shadowy world of the copies.

postmillennialism. The view of Revelation 20 that believes the Church will bring the kingdom of God/millennium to earth through the preaching of the gospel prior to Christ's Second Coming.

post-tribulation rapture. The view that the church will go through the tribulation.

premillennialism. The view of Revelation 20 that believes Christ will return to earth to establish a literal one-thousand-year reign after the tribulation period.

preterist. A view that understands that most, if not all, of the predicted events in the last book of the Bible were fulfilled in the first century.

pre-tribulation rapture. The view that the church will be secretly raptured to heaven before the beginning of the end-time tribulation.

prophetic-apocalyptic. A term that roots apocalypticism in Old Testament prophecy.

realized eschatology. The view that the Kingdom of God fully came at Christ's first coming.

Revelation of Jesus Christ. The English title and content of the last book of the Bible.

Roman triumphant processional. A parade in Rome that honored victorious generals while humiliating defeated armies.

Satan. The angelic being who led his followers to rebel against God and as a result was cast to earth where he tempted Adam and Eve to sin.

seal judgments. The first set of seven judgments poured out on the earth in Revelation 6.

Second Coming of Christ. The term describing Christ's return at the end of history to establish his kingdom on earth.

Second Temple prophetic–apocalyptic literature. The noncanonical books of *1 Enoch,* The Dead Sea Scrolls, *The Testament of Moses, 4 Ezra,* and *2 Baruch*, etc.

semantics. The meaning of words.

Septuagint. The Greek translation of the Hebrew Old Testament that was produced ca. 250 B.C.

seven–sealed scroll. The divine book Jesus opens to unleashes God's judgments on the earth Revelation 6–18.

signs of the times. The end-time events that precede the return of Christ, including apostasy, the rise of the Antichrist, cosmic disturbances, and unprecedented persecution of the people of God.

Son of Man. Jesus's favorite self-designation that draws on Daniel 7.

story of Israel. The Old Testament story of Israel's sin, exile, and restoration that is a key theme in Second Temple Judaism literature.

subgenre. A pervasive body of literature with a similar theme that is less pervasive than a genre.

Synoptic Gospels. The New Testament books of Matthew, Mark, and Luke.

syntax. The relationship between words.

temporary messianic kingdom. The idea that there would be a temporary kingdom established on earth by the Messiah that would afterward give way to the eternal kingdom of God.

text criticism. The science of collecting, comparing and contrasting ancient manuscripts of the Bible to determine the most likely original reading.

textual variants. Differences in wording found in ancient manuscripts.

topos. A self-contained unit that advocates a topic of proper thought or action.

trumpet judgments. The set of seven divine end-time judgments poured out upon the earth in Revelation 8–9.

Vespasian. The Roman general who attacked Israel in retaliation to the First Jewish Revolt in A.D. 66, began the siege of Jerusalem, and was selected to be the next emperor.

War Scroll. A document in the Dead Sea Scrolls that depicts the future end-time battle between God and his enemies in a similar way to that found in Revelation 19.

watchers. Angels described in *1 Enoch* who cohabitated with women as the cause of the appearance of sin into the world.

white horse. The color of the horse on which the Antichrist and Christ go forth to conquer.

Yahweh the Warrior. And Old Testament description of God that is adapted to Christ in Revelation 19 when he descends from heaven to fight God's enemies.

Zerubbabel's Temple. The Jewish Temple, rebuilt in 519 B.C., that began Second Temple Judaism.